Moving UpCountry

A YANKEE WAY OF KNOWLEDGE

Moving UpCountry

A YANKEE WAY OF KNOWLEDGE

by Don Mitchell

Illustrated by Roy Lewando

YANKEE BOOKS

a division of
Yankee Publishing Incorporated
Dublin, New Hampshire

First published in *Boston Magazine* under the
column head, "R.F.D."

First Edition
Copyright 1984, by Don Mitchell
Printed in the United States of America

Library of Congress Catalog Card No. 83-5111
ISBN: 0-89909-035-4 (hardcover)
ISBN: 0-89909-031-1 (softcover)

Designed by Jill Shaffer

To my parents

Other books by Don Mitchell

THUMB TRIPPING

FOUR-STROKE

THE SOULS OF LAMBS

Acknowledgements

The author gratefully acknowledges the encouragement, support, and thoughtful editing of this work by *Boston Magazine*, in whose pages it first appeared.

I also wish to thank my Vermont neighbors — men and women of wisdom, every one — for helping to set my feet on paths of knowledge.

Contents

CHAPTER ONE

The Homestead

*I*N 1972, MY WIFE AND I VISITED Vermont for a weekend and wound up purchasing a farm. This was a rash — if not downright crazy — act. But who has not entertained the fantasy of spurning modern life for a pastoral ideal? In the ethos of that era, fantasies required enactment.

We had come, both of us, from thoroughly suburban and hopelessly middle-class backgrounds. We had enjoyed fine and supremely impractical liberal arts educations; we had lived in San Francisco, Boston, L.A., Philadelphia; we had misspent several years dabbling in the politics and lifestyles and recreational intoxicants of the late Sixties. And, against all odds, we were on the road to mastering conventional adult lives in southeastern Pennsylvania — lives of career achievement, ample compensation for essentially cerebral work, and access to sophisticated cultural pleasures. Then — with scarcely any thought for the consequences — we lobbed what amounted to a time bomb into what had become our too normal, too predictable future. We bought one hundred and fifty acres of Vermont.

Maybe we simply thought we were acquiring a summer place

— a retreat, a getaway. I forget. We may not have realized we'd wind up living there. Possibly we saw our purchase as a species of investment, a shrewd hedge against inflation. Whatever, we must have been a real estate agent's dream: flatlanders who fall head over heels for — well, for a *landscape,* little more or less — and sign on the dotted line after twenty minutes' thought.

With a decade's hindsight, I ought to say we didn't buy a farm at all. The term "farm" should properly imply a reasonable economic unit of agricultural production, including the structures necessary for such production, such as a farmhouse, barns, sheds, grain bins, wells and ponds, and similar basic equipment. If one has bought a "farm," one should be able to *farm* it right away — not spend the next ten years gearing up.

What we acquired amounted to the pasture land and woodlot — but not the house, cropland, or farm structures — of a dairy farm the size of which became financially unviable roughly twenty years ago. Though sold as "bare land" — i.e., offered at a fixed price per acre — the land we agreed to buy did support one dilapidated hay barn and a partially collapsed sugar house. To a skilled eye, these buildings were so decrepit as to be more liability than asset, but lacking even one such eye between us, my wife and I considered these free buildings a real bargain.

We debated whether to tear down the sugar house for lumber to repair the barn, or vice versa. I proposed we try converting the old barn into a house for us to live in, estimating two years of owner/builder labor and a cash budget of five thousand dollars. In the process, I added, we'd learn the rudiments of carpentry. So that we could move on to other projects — barns for livestock, shops, machine sheds.

I won. We tore down the sugar house.

Looking back, a $5000 house sounds damned unlikely. Farfetched. One more pipe dream. We succeeded, though, with some thirty-seven bucks to spare. And stories that recall our halting, gradual adaptation to the rural lives we were not made for.

• Uphill. Up. Work.

When we first moved to Vermont, my background was so culturally deprived that I scarcely knew what barns were. Though

I could recognize them easily enough, I had precious little notion of what they were *used* for, what went on inside them. I suppose I saw them as picturesque hotels for cows. Chambermaids might plausibly come in to tidy up the stalls. Were there milking parlors? I imagined mightily overstuffed chairs. It certainly had never seemed likely that I'd ever need a barn myself.

But now I *owned* a barn, albeit one so rundown that the seller "threw it in" with the acreage we had purchased. And the depth of manure carpeting its thousand square feet of floor suggested that the chambermaids had long since given up on it. Puzzling for a while over what to do with the barn, we were dismayed to learn that just tearing it down could be expensive. So, instead, we proposed to right its walls, arrest its sag, and transform its vast interior into a house of sorts. All by ourselves — and carpenters we weren't.

These objectives, had we announced them publicly, would have caused an absolute sensation on our road. Our neighbors, like rural neighbors everywhere, were curious about the new folks. People were amused enough to hear the story we put out: how we meant to pour a concrete floor in the barn and stabilize it structurally and "bring in electric," to use the local phrase. We made these announcements standing confidently in our hay mow, surrounded by new electric saws and drills and sanders that we had not yet learned how to use, and could not even if we had. The nearest power outlet was a quarter mile away.

The tool we came to know best and soonest was more ancient. Prehistoric, even — as was our first task. We bought pitchforks and spent two full weeks shovelling manure. The local euphemism for this work is "cleaning out the barn." Our own euphemism, from our educated frame of reference, became "materials handling." We handled tons and tons of materials.

It measures what we were — and what a comfortable, advanced society had produced us — to say that we felt as though we stood on the frontier of human experience. As though no one else had ever savored honest toil, never tested strength and spirit against a broad, deep sea of dung. Here was archaeology — layered evidence that sheep and cows and pigs and horses had all occupied this building in the years and decades past. We encountered false floors — wooden planks slapped down on top of old manure by a hasty farmer to make a new pen or stall without shovelling down to bedrock. There was the clutch of eggs — how old? — that my wife uncovered, buried under several feet of bedding. And the calf's skull, perfectly preserved. Here was what, in college, we had idealized as real life — and we found it sweet and pungent, fertile and poetic, too.

We acquired a wheelbarrow to convey our mountain of riches out the barn door and up to the knoll we had chosen for our future garden. Very shortly we were committed to a *large* garden, for we'd buried several thousand square feet in manure. As I was chugging out the door one morning, urging the loaded wheelbarrow up a slippery path for the umpteenth time, one of my neighbors came into view hauling a huge machine behind his biggest tractor.

This neighbor was a man of wisdom, though I didn't know it yet. Little could I guess that, as a dairy farmer, he had spent a great deal of his life cleaning barns out, "handling materials." There was not a facet of this chore that he had not considered, and he'd made a very considerable investment in tools to make it easier.

The tractor bore down on me. I waved. He cut the diesel's throttle and climbed down from the glassed-in cab. "Morning," he said. "Thought I'd stop and visit."

"What's that thing you're pulling?"

"That? Manure spreader."

"It must hold a month's manure!"

"No, we fill it twice a day."

I set down my wheelbarrow, stunned. My heroics with the pitchfork took on miniscule dimensions. "But how do you *load* it?"

"Loader. On the John Deere."

"But what gets it off the barn floor?"

"Scraper. On the International."

Two more tractors, simply. So, I was an Old World craftsman at manure handling, painstaking and uncompromising in my methods. "Look at this stuff," I said knowledgeably, sifting a handful from the wheelbarrow through my blistered fingers. "Well rotted, perfect tilth — feel that? It's just like compost."

He had seen manure before. "Going to put a garden in?"

"Next year. Working too hard, this year. Haven't worked this hard in years."

"But," he said, "you're taking it uphill."

"So?"

"Uphill. *Up*."

He had a point. I could have sited the future garden downhill from the barn, and burned forty thousand fewer calories. But then I, the beneficiary of an advanced civilization's educational riches, would have missed out on my first lesson of Vermont Zen: uphill is up; up is work.

We *did* manage to make a house out of our barn, and though the garden is uphill, we carry vegetables *down* to the house. Sometimes we carry them down by the wheelbarrow load (I have washed the wheelbarrow carefully). Unfortunately, the kitchen is *up* a flight of stairs.

Long before the kitchen, though — long before the *stairs* — we had to replace the manure with more suitable flooring. Aggregates: pea stone by the cubic yard, shovelled and carefully tamped in place. Then a four-inch layer of concrete. Here again, our lack of understanding of *up* and *down* profoundly damaged the credibility we hoped to establish with our neighbors.

The high-water mark of my personal desperation with rural life came after only a few weeks' tenure in Vermont — the day a truckload of ready-mix concrete arrived for the new slab floor of our barn. Since that day, things have gotten better; they could not have got much worse.

I had studied up about concrete, to be sure. I had read manuals. I had watched construction workers pouring sidewalks and foundations, observed their use of long, straight boards to surface the concrete, seen how they worked the stuff with wooden floats and steel trowels. I acquired such tools for my wife and myself, and together we built concrete forms that seemed accurate and adequate for the important task before us. Once or twice, I might have wondered whether the job was more than two of us could handle, but I did not dwell on such concerns. I ordered my truck of concrete, and the great day came.

In rural Vermont, one can hear the whine of a concrete truck from miles away. All the neighbors hear it, too, and wonder who is pouring what. Concrete means new barns, new silos, weighty evidence that so-and-so's farm is on the upswing, or is here to stay. When I heard that droning truck and knew my old barn was its target, my heart raced like a kid's. Here was a major test, a chance to prove successful adaptation to a new, self-reliant life. Here was a way to show my neighbors I was worthy.

The big truck lumbered across a dewy pasture toward our sagging barn. I met it halfway, climbed on the running board, and explained to the driver that we hoped — we expected — he could disgorge his load into four separate quadrants created by our forms. Each could be reached by poking his dump chute through a different door or window of the structure.

"Sure," he said. He backed up to one door and dumped a couple of cubic yards. Our forms held tight; everything went just as planned. But then, maneuvering uphill to reach a knocked-out window, his wheels slipped. Uphill. Work. I still see them spinning madly, burning up the grass.

"Got my rear end rebuilt? But they haven't tied the transmission to only one differential yet."

"Meaning?"

"I don't have much traction."

Verily, he didn't. He struggled — he made his loaded truck crab sideways — but he could get nowhere near that window.

Or the other window.

Or the second door.

"What now?" I asked, appalled.

"Reckon I'd best put it all with that first pile."

"Wait a minute. How long do we have to spread this?"

"We?"

"My wife and I."

He looked at her — all ninety-six pounds. He smiled. "Three or four hours. No trouble. You'll make out."

"Dump it," I said. My own executioner.

Imagine our proposed floor, a slab twenty feet by thirty feet by four inches thick. Now picture a four-foot-high mountain of wet concrete occupying one-sixth of that area. As the truck groaned off, my wife and I grabbed shovels and began slinging the stuff across the barn as fast as we were able.

This worked up a sweat. But an hour later, we *still* had a mountain of concrete — and several smaller foothills spread across an unpaved expanse. In places we could see it setting. Along about now, a neighbor's boy stuck his head in to see what we were pouring. He was dumbstruck. He hurried off to spread the word that a catastrophe was well in progress.

Catastrophe crossed our minds, too. What if we collapsed into that slurry and just couldn't move? People would discover us, encased, and suspect a suicide pact. *Couldn't take Vermont life,* urban friends would say of us. *Killed 'em dead.* These dark thoughts were interrupted when one of my feet — each foot now weighed eighty pounds — came down on a four-inch spike poking out of a two-by-ten that had been a concrete form a couple of hours earlier. The nail went through my boot and my sock and quite a distance further, adding lockjaw to my scenarios for expiration. I yelped — but there was no time for dressing wounds. None whatsoever. Each passing minute made the sticky ooze less tractable.

More neighbors arrived to watch. Work, particularly hard, desperate work, is a great spectator sport in these parts. Some offered advice, some of it actually useful. We retired our shovels and sawed a long board back and forth to float the concrete off. By four o'clock we had commenced steel trowelling, where the concrete wasn't set so hard that trowelling had become absurd. By six o'clock we had something like a concrete floor, albeit one that can and does hold many gallons of water sometimes, in broad shallow puddles.

Water? Sad to say, the barn floor tends to flood each March, come spring thaw. We did pour a floor drain in the slab, to obviate this hazard. But in our haste we set the floor drain cunningly uphill.

Uphill. Up. Work.

• Alternative Concrete

The day after nearly being buried alive in ready-mix, I drove to town and bought a human-sized concrete mixer.

Few pleasures of rural life compare with owning — and using — the right tool for a demanding job. Chainsaws and hay balers come to mind, and come-alongs. But the best investment in a tool that I ever made was this little orange tiger, purchased brand new but without the electric motor usually supplied to run it. For we still had "no electric." I threw the mixer in the back of a pickup truck and drove it to an old machinist who came highly recommended. Fellow name of Martin Hickok. My neighbor alleged that this man even made his own *tools*.

I found him in a tiny, thoroughly cluttered shop, bent over a whirling metal lathe. "Making a tool?" I asked.

"Making a tool to make a tool. To make a tool that I can't buy anymore."

I was impressed. "Like to have you put a hand crank on a concrete mixer."

This surprised him. He turned off the lathe. "Where is it?"

"Right outside."

He came out and took a look. And shook his head. "Can't," he said.

"No?"

"Well, I guess I *could*. But you'd bust your back. She isn't geared right."

"Can you regear it?"

He shrugged. "Do anything. Expensive, though."

"I've got no electric. Yet."

"How about gasoline, then?"

He led me out behind his shop, where he had a pile of engines salvaged from junk lawnmowers and rototillers. "Need one with a governor, no throttle arm to fool with," he told me. And he found it. "Now, I'll fix this up for you if you'll make me one small promise."

"What's that?"

"Never, ever take this engine off and put it on a go-cart."

I promised.

"Go-carts have ruined more good little cast-iron engines —"

"Trust me," I said.

"Man likes to see things used the way they should."

I promised again.

"You come back this time tomorrow, I'll have her set to go."

And she was.

Now, a decade later, I would guesstimate that enough concrete has been mixed by that recycled engine to pave an acre handily. I can't be sure, because I rent the mixer out to friends, and I suspect most of them pour more stuff than they allege. But I rent it on a barter system, and the tool has repaid its cost many times over in such "fees" as old tractor chains, a beautiful woven shawl, a day's skilled labor raising trusses for my new machinery shed. I even get money sometimes. For myself, the half dozen sheds and barns and outbuildings I have managed to erect would have never gotten off the ground without the orange tiger.

The first great thing about pouring concrete with a little mixer is that one is forced to divide a big job into sections that can be accomplished in a pleasant afternoon's work with little risk of heart attack. If you want to stop and have a beer, you turn the mixer off. It can wait. Every time I do this, I feel very happy. Sometimes the mixer turns *itself* off. No cause for alarm. With a half-inch wrench I loosen the six bolts that hold the cylinder head to the engine block. Nothing to it. I pull off the head. With my fingernail or an old screwdriver, I scrape off dark, gummy products of internal combustion that have built up sufficiently to interfere with clean ignition. This minor overhaul requires ten minutes' time and costs nothing; then I'm back in business with what seems to be a new engine. What greater pleasures are there?

A second advantage is that the concrete from a small mixer can be tailored, load by load, to meet specific needs. Too dry? Too goopy? Too much gravel? One can change the recipe immediately. In the barn that has become our house, once we got beneath the manure we discovered daylight under five out of eight main bearing posts holding up the structure. Removal of the crumbly, rotted wood revealed still *more* daylight. Much more. The sort of concrete that we poured to shore up this alarming situation is not the sort of concrete that one uses in a slab. With ready-mix, this could have posed a problem, but not with our orange tiger.

But the clincher for owning a little concrete mixer is, it thrusts one squarely into the fascinating world of aggregates — of cold, hard stone — replete with the colorful and friendly men who spend their days in gravel pits. Here I have gained much wisdom.

According to orthodoxy, concrete is a mixture of cement, water, and fine and coarse aggregates — sand and gravel, that is — in specified proportions. One part cement, three sand, and five gravel make a typical concrete, but this is the nice language of engineers and building codes. In real life — up here, at least — the owner of a gravel pit looks for a vein of sandy gravel or gravelly sand in reasonable proportions, and this he sells as "bank run for concrete." Manifestly, every truckload must be somewhat different. I know that Henry Lefebvre's pit, which I like to patronize, has good bank run years and bad. Like wine, see?

1979 shaped up to be the best year I can remember for Lefebvre's bank run. I used just two truckloads, several weeks apart, but I could have poured a slab as smooth as silk with either one. Instead I used the stuff on footings, which is rather like cooking with Château Lafite. Less expensive, though: a seven-cubic-yard load of bank run costs just $28.84 delivered, including tax, and the price has not changed in the time I've lived here.

To order bank run, I call Mrs. Lefebvre at home on the telephone, and she calls Henry on the CB. Sometimes he arrives within an hour. He is always pleasant. Even on the day I got his truck mired in the runoff from an old dug well, he just cussed a bit about wet weather, killed a nest of snakes ("adders") trying to escape the scene, then spilled a portion of his load and drove across it to firm ground. That gravel dried a nagging mudhole we had long avoided draining.

I'm a small fish in the pool of Lefebvre's clients. One recent dairy barn, he told me, ran up a $10,000 tab for trucked-in aggregates.

"That," I reasoned out, "at $28.84 a load, is one hell of a lot of bank run."

"That was *fill*! They bought all their concrete in. Ready-mix."

"I don't like ready-mix," I told him, reminiscing.

"Course, they're not in business to make money, over there. Lawyers own it. Hope to make a tax loss."

"Sounds like they'll succeed."

"I guess so. Finest run of pea stone I've hit in seven years, they had me put it in a ditch. In a *ditch*, so help me!"

"Well," I said, "they paid. Right? I mean, what do you care if —"

He cut me off. He said: "Man likes to see stuff used the way it should."

"Yes," I nodded. "Yes, I've heard that."

In an age of scarcities, one can't keep from wondering whether a commodity as basic as coarse aggregates might go the way of lumber and petroleum and ground chuck. Such a turn of events would dislocate our way of life as surely as an end to gasoline. I expressed this fear to Henry Lefebvre recently, as his hard-worked truck dumped out another load on my premises.

"Hell, no," he assured me.

"You got plenty of that gravel left?"

"Listen. At the Town Meeting? Were you there? Last March?"

"Different town," I told him.

"Well, this fellow stood up. Flatlander, just moved up here. Said he thought we ought to asphalt-pave a few miles of roads each year? Till they're all paved? Easier to drive on, he said. Then this Selectman stood up. Said this here town owns a loader, owns a grader, owns a power shovel and two seven-yard dump trucks? And this here town owns one, two, three gravel pits? But he said this town don't own a single oil well. And asphalt's oil."

It is comforting to know my orange tiger will not lack for aggregates well into the murky, energy-starved future. But I'm saving up to get her regeared for that hand crank that I wanted in the first place. Then I'll have a fighting chance. I hope that Martin Hickok's still around to do the job for me — perhaps he would take, in partial payment for the work, a little cast-iron engine that has never seen a go-cart.

• The Dog Next Door

To peaceably relocate to a rural community, an urbanite ought to avoid swiping his neighbor's dog. Common sense. Nevertheless, my wife and I managed to do just that, effortlessly, when we transplanted ourselves to Vermont.

The dog in question was a rather large and mongrelized variation on a German Shepherd theme. Sold to his owners as a purebred puppy, his increasing lack of conformation to breed standards as he matured became a source of considerable chagrin for them. Floppy ears, jet-black coat, dour Labrador eyes — purebred Shepherd he was not. And he had a hidden personality problem: a guard dog by nature and by temperament, his life did not afford him enough that needed guarding.

My wife and I had taken possession of our farm by pitching a canvas tent in a tree-lined hollow that adjoined the sweeping pasture, where, by longstanding agreement with a neighbor dairy farmer, heifers roamed. Heifers are the teenaged girls, roughly, of the bovine world. Driven by nascent, awakening sexuality, subject to attacks of what amounts to the giggles, they explore any new phenomenon with galumphing curiosity. Our arrival on their turf must have been as interesting as anything that had ever happened to them. In retrospect, I cannot blame them for their actions.

Still, the first time we trudged back from an arduous day's work shovelling manure out of the old barn, only to find our campsite quite professionally trashed, I went into something of a state of shock. Heifers did not, at first, cross my mind; I feared such vandalism must be the work of local people, bitterly hostile toward flatlanders moving in and driving up the price of rural real estate. "Yankee, Go Home!" as it were — except that *they* were the Yankees, and we were only trying to join. I sunk my pitchfork in the earth. I sat down, head in hands. The feeling that one's neighbors in a pastoral country are out to drive one from the landscape is mightily disheartening.

My wife, though, running on ahead, found evidence of the true culprits. "Cows!" she shouted. "Cows have been here — there's manure on everything!"

Fresh manure. On everything.

When I had calmed down, I announced we'd have to figure out a way to fence the campsite. Fencing, though, was just one more arcane branch of human knowledge about which my former life had taught me nothing whatsoever. And I truly did not want a barbed wire atmosphere around our rustic tent and tarp; moving to Vermont was supposed to have been an expansive gesture, not migration to a mini-concentration camp. Anyway, I did not even know where people bought barbed wire, how they stretched it, how they fastened the stuff to posts, or where the posts came from. Too much to learn overnight. So I ran a couple of lengths of cotton clothesline from tree to tree and pulled it tight as best I could. I recall expecting that the heifers would take cognizance of its Gestalt and respect my flimsy fence as they did barbed wire.

Heifers — please take note — will *not* mistake a clothesline for barbed wire. Heifers will *eat* clothesline. And after that, they'll try to gobble Coleman lanterns, rucksacks, tent poles.

The second time we came back to a desecrated campsite, half a dozen of the delinquents were still lounging around, burping up wads of nylon and canvas. By miraculous good fortune, the neighbors' dog was with us — just paying a friendly visit. When I charged the heifers in a blind fury, brandishing my pitchfork and screaming out my lungs at them, the dog seized my mood and gamely joined in the attack. He was most effective. In fact, he chased them a good two hundred yards — long past the point where I became too winded to do much more than cheer him on. When the dog returned, I offered him my heartfelt thanks.

I feel certain that this episode was a turning point in the dog's formerly quiet, reasonably law-abiding life. Nobody had told me yet, but farm dogs are divided into two distinct types: those that guard and those that work. Working dogs — like Border Collies — are trained to drive or herd livestock. Guard dogs are not. And guard dogs are forbidden, absolutely, to chase cattle. Panicked cows, running from a dog, can hurt their precious teats. They're apt to abort, if pregnant. They can even founder and die of exhaustion. Dogs who chase cattle are liable to be shot, and not even the owner of such a dog would defend the canine's right to exist in a landscape filled with thousand-dollar dairy cows.

But I took a different view. I thought the dog was great — a real godsend to us — and the dog in turn was glad to meet a human who encouraged him to give free rein to his painfully repressed instincts. Freedom hall. The man from Philadelphia. It wasn't long before the dog volunteered to spend whole days crouched behind our little tent, waiting to ambush any heifers that might come around.

I never fed the dog. Every evening, he would excuse himself and dash home to wolf down his bowl of food; within ten minutes, he would be back on duty at the campsite. He slept with us — when he wasn't baying at the moon. More than once, while working in the barn, I would hear the neighbors' small children crying to him from across the street. To come home and play. Feeling bad for them, I would go try to shame the dog into taking some time off to honor family ties. Nothing doing, though; he had found his life's work in our service and would not be driven from it.

For several months, then, my wife and I enjoyed all the benefits of having a large, attentive dog, with none of the tedious and expensive drawbacks of ownership. When the dog's license expired, we did not have to go renew it. When he needed shots, or had to be dewormed, it was not our concern. He just *lived* with us. It got to be embarrassing, though, and finally the day came when our neighbors surprised us with an evening visit to the campsite.

We had acquired a picnic table by now, and the dog hung out beneath it. We had just finished supper; sensing intruders, the dog leaped from his hiding place and started barking wildly. Then he realized it was his family — his legal family, at any rate — and he made an effort to welcome them and show them around the place where he spent his days.

In his arms, the man of the household next door carried a half-empty sack of dog food. "We've solved the problem with this dog," he said.

"You have?"

"He's yours." The man set the bag down. "Here's some feed to get you started."

"Gee," I said. "Let me think. You know, I've never owned a dog before. I'm not sure I want to."

"That doesn't matter. All he does anymore is guard your place. It makes no sense for us to feed him."

I looked from my neighbor — who had not come to bargain — to the dog. I did not want the creature, but in truth he'd won my heart. "Okay," I agreed. "We'll take him."

"By the way," my neighbor told me, having closed the deal. "I hear he's been running heifers. You had better make him stop."

Make him stop! But the man's kids were telling their pet

good-bye, now, and I felt too much like a miserable dog-napper to pursue the issue. Soon enough, I heard from the heifers' owner — the renter of my pasture land. Did I own the dog now? Fine. If the dog hurt his heifers, he would hold me responsible.

Fortunately, our barn conversion project was far enough along that we were able to strike camp, now, and move into a portion of the building. The dog's guard duties became considerably easier, and subject to full-time supervision. But it placed a terrible strain on our relationship when I had to start punishing the dog for heifer-chasing — for the very behavior that I had rewarded at the beginning of our liaison. Such, however, are the perils of ownership.

Eventually, the heifers left, and we stocked the pasture with our own sheep instead. Our dog proved to be completely disinterested in these pint-sized, woolly ruminants. They offered him no challenge. Arguably, his presence on our premises does deter other — possibly more feral — dogs from attacking the sheep; unquestionably, he deters travelling salesmen and evangelicals just by sleeping in the driveway. On the whole, though, the dog's life today affords him no more to guard than did his life before we hove into it. Meanwhile, the dog's former owners have moved elsewhere.

Are there disadvantages to keeping a very large, very strong, very territorial dog on one's farm? Yes — though nearly everybody up here seems to have one. For me, the worst frustration is knowing that my dog is but a halfway house, an intermediate technology. Brilliant sheep guarding dogs are now available in New England — dogs that spend their whole lives protecting a shepherd's flock, killing all suspected predators on sight. Having such an enforcer would be a great relief; or, to go the working dog route, I might like to have a hyperactive, nervous little Border Collie to save me hours of labor trying to make sheep go where I want them to. The dog that I have will do neither of these things, and he loves his place here far too jealously to tolerate a rival on his chosen turf. In a contest between my large, slowly aging dog and some smart new pup, the pup would go the way of countless groundhogs, rabbits, and squirrels before him.

Someday, I do hope to own a dog of breeding and distinction and solid ability — but not before the present one is dead or lame with hip dysplasia. When I wish for something better, I remember that it was my dog who chose me, after all. Chose me in a time of dire need, and in full betrayal of a warm and caring home. Having made his choice, he stuck; he prowls the driveway even now in hope of routing heifers that don't come here anymore. Imperfect and unteachable, unshakable but independent, that dog of mine is something of a Yankee.

• Alternative Lumber

Vermont is the first place I have lived where there are two kinds of lumber: the smooth, dry, familiar type sold in sprawling lumber yards, and the rough, green stuff bought straight off a little sawmill. Rough lumber, because it has not been planed down to uniform dimensions, can present framing problems where precision is required. But for most farmstead construction projects, rough lumber works just dandy — and the savings are threefold. First, no middlemen to pay. Second, no transportation costs from Western sawmills to Eastern dealers. And thirdly, roughsawn two-by-fours presently contain thirty-five percent more wood, by volume, than the beautifully planed and kiln-dried studs that cost the earth at retail.

I took a shine to rough lumber instantly. Before long, one of my neighbors suggested an even greater economy. I owned a woodlot; I could fell some trees and engage a sawyer to saw them out for me. Thus I'd hire time at a mill, but not actually have to buy a stick of wood.

I liked this idea. I had already bought — though not acquired proficiency with — a fearsomely noisy, West German chainsaw. I took it to the woods and looked for trees that seemed worthy of becoming roughsawn studs and joists and rafters. There was quite a choice, but I knew very little about appropriate lumber species. Oak, though, I had often heard praised for one thing or another. I had many oaks, both red and white. Big. Thick. Heavy. Did I want my house to be a source of pride for years to come? I thought, oak's the wood for me.

Oak was my vanity, and a problem from the very start. Oak bent the hardened steel bar of my chainsaw; oak stalled the tractor skidding out my logs from the woodlot. It never occurred to me, though, that it might be hard to find a mill to saw oak. The hills seemed to be full of "little" sawmills doing custom work, mills run by a man or two and capable of sawing out a couple of thousand board feet of lumber in a working day. Surely one would take the worthy trees I offered? I learned too late that most sawyers much prefer to stick with pine and spruce and hemlock. They just hate to wade their old blades through a load of hardwood logs.

Still, winter brings slack times to the little sawmills of Vermont. You can get stuff sawn in January that would be turned away in June. Following a tip as to who might need some business, I paid a visit to the M&M Sawmill. Leon Manley and John Marcotte, sawyers, agreed to tackle my logs if I'd join them working in the mill.

"Doing what?"

"Grunt work. Hey — those suckers are *heavy*."

I agreed. I suppose I am a glutton for experiences of this sort.

"We'll start Monday," Manley said. "Here's our rule: if it's up to zero by eight in the morning, then we'll fire up the mill. Elsewise, wait until I call you."

"Zero, huh?" The M&M Sawmill stood in a cavernous, open-sided pole barn nestled in a windy hollow. "How about if it snows?"

He smiled wanly. "Generally, it warms up to snow."

Manley and Marcotte were an unlikely pair. Manley was thin and wiry; Marcotte was big and broad and thick. Both proved strong as oxen; I felt a pathetic weakling working in their midst. I wore mittens, for example, while the two of them were bare-handed. I got cold. I got tired. I ached all over.

Manley and Marcotte were talkative, and their talk was generally a free-wheeling argument about whatever came to mind. *I* was on their minds, mainly — me and my frozen hardwood. I picked up a marvelous industrial vocabulary and several new oaths. And I learned that, sawing custom logs, the customer is always wrong.

Monday morning I showed up, and they handed me a peavey bar. My job was to roll logs down a track and up onto the mill, then beat iron hooks into each log's frozen bark to hold it on the tracked carriage. In between times, they had me try to chop the ice and snow off upcoming logs with a hatchet. Rarely would I get a log cleaned up in time to mount it on the mill; this meant we sawed a lot of ice.

A circular sawmill is a very big machine, but a relatively

simple one. A blade turns; a carriage moves. What could be less complicated? However, the teeth are engineered to rip through wood and wood alone. Not snow and ice. Not dirt. And not — not ever — long forgotten fence staples buried out of sight under new sapwood. Such things eat up teeth, which can be individually replaced but cost forty cents apiece. They add up. The M&M Sawmill had a five-foot-diameter blade, with sixty-odd teeth spaced around its circumference. In four days, I saw most of them replaced.

Once, that first cold day, the blade started showering sparks like an arc welder. We were cutting sugar maple — I had made a mistake or two, harvesting my "oaks." "The hell?" Marcotte yanked back the carriage. We all looked to see what steel gift was buried in the tree.

"God damn *sap spile*!! Someone never took it out!"

I felt sympathetic — truly — but hardly culpable. That spout had been lurking in that tree since before I was born.

"Fifteen teeth buggered!" Manley howled.

"Look, it isn't my fault if —"

"Are these your trees?"

"They are."

"Then it's your fault."

"Only off a farm," explained Manley, "do we get this junk in trees. Buy from a logger up the mountain, and they're always clean. Because no one lives there."

Even up here, civilization exacts its price.

Teeth on a sawmill are expendable, replaceable. The body of the blade, though, is a thousand-dollar item. And something of an engineering feat: a huge, steel disc not a quarter inch in thickness that, at speed, travels in a perfectly flat plane. The teeth about its rim stick out the merest bit on either side, cutting a kerf just slightly wider than the blade itself. Nothing but the teeth should even graze logs passing through the mill.

On my second day of freezing at the M&M Sawmill, the body of the mill's blade began to rub and mark my logs. This creates some heat. "The hell?" Marcotte shut down the engine.

"Look at that — she's dishy!"

"Dishy?" I inquired.

"Out of true."

A saw five feet in diameter warped out of plane by a quarter of an inch hardly looks like a dish. Except to a sawyer. But, where it had rubbed red oak, the steel now was polished bright.

"Teeth dull?" Manley asked.

"No, not hardly." But Marcotte filed them again for good measure, while the blade cooled down. I measured the two-by-ten they had just sawn out. It was nine and seven-eighths inches at one end, but ten and three-eighths at the other. Poor.

"Ugly logs," Manley scowled. "Ugly, frozen hardwood."

"Maybe you've just got a softwood mill," I told him.

This remark had dramatic effect. "Start her, John," Manley hollered. "Start her up! Call this a softwood mill!"

We did finish that log, and the day's work. Next morning, though, the blade dished out again.

"The hell?"

Marcotte shut down the mill.

"Goosey!! Will you look at that?" Manley worked the hot blade back and forth, pushing its dishiness from one side to another.

"Call George Sadler. We'll have to take this to be hammered."

"Goosey?" I asked. "Hammered?"

Marcotte seized the biggest wrench I'd ever seen and proceeded to free the huge blade from its arbor. Manley got on the telephone. "What," I asked politely, "is hammering a saw?"

"Guy hits it with a hammer. Takes five minutes. Forty dollars."

"I could do that," I offered.

"So could I. But George knows where to hit it."

George Sadler, millwright, was a sixty-mile trip. There was no one closer, though, practicing his dying art. We strapped the saw blade to the roof of Manley's car, and I asked to come along — why not? Sure, he said. Marcotte stayed behind to putter around the mill.

Sadler was waiting for us. Saws of every size and shape cluttered his cold, dusty shop. The old man had the eyes of a shaman, a craftsman's hands, and the air of one long past regard for what men thought of him. His face looked worn and tired. But his thick arms took the blade that two of us had struggled with and rocked it up onto his anvil in a single, fluid motion.

He squinted at the blade, plainly seeing things I couldn't. "When's the last I hammered this?" he asked.

"Four months ago," Manley told him. "Suddenly, it's goosey."

"Doesn't need much. What's your governed r.p.m. supposed to be?"

"Eight hundred."

"What have you been cutting?"

"Hardwood. Hard, ugly, frozen oak."

"You bring me some sawdust?"

Manley produced a plastic baggie — a throat culture taken from his ailing saw. Sadler sifted the sawdust through his fingers. "Tell you right now," he said, "that's too fine." Without warning, he raised a hammer and struck the broad face of the saw blade. *Hard* — it rang out. And again. And again. I couldn't believe my eyes.

"That looks better," he said. It looked like a saw hit with a hammer. "No charge, this time. It shouldn't have needed that."

"What's our problem?" Manley asked.

"That fine sawdust's heating up your blade. Got to make it coarser, somehow. Tell you one old trick I know, for cutting frozen hardwood: take every other tooth out of the blade."

"You're kidding!"

"No, it works. Your log moves into the blade that much further between each tooth's bite. That coarsens up the sawdust. Just a little trick, see?"

Back at the mill, Marcotte yanked every other tooth out of the blade. "If this works," he promised me, "I'll even forgive you for that sap spile."

"Wonderful — gee, thanks!"

"Don't get excited. This won't work."

We mounted the blade and proceeded to cut frozen oak like butter.

"Like spruce in June," Manley raved. "Never cut so well."

I said, *"Now* you've got a hardwood mill."

"You shut up, you!"

Marcotte rubbed his full beard. "George Sadler, he knows. He *knows.*"

When my logs were sawn, I had two thousand board feet of oak; the bill was roughly two hundred dollars, cash money. Ten cents a board foot is a darn good price for oak lumber. Oak lumber, though, I soon found out, is mighty hard to work with. You can scarcely drive a nail in it without first drilling a hole. A twelve-foot two-by-ten is just about impossible for one man of average build to lift, much less to hold in place until it is fastened. Hand saws are next to worthless, and power saws emit the most painful noises ripping oak boards. And I found out, after all this trouble, that oak lumber really is no better — and in some applications, may be actually *worse* — than common softwoods used in basic residential framing.

Be that as it may, much of my barn conversion project was accomplished with roughsawn oak. Some months after my sawmill stint, but before the interior walls were sheathed, I invited Manley and Marcotte over to show them my construction project. They were, in a way, impressed.

"Nice lumber, guys," I told them.

"Crazy damn fool wants to frame his house in oak!"

"That's right," I said.

"You don't need that oak for — for studs?! You know what that's *worth*? You could have swapped that oak for hemlock, three board feet to one."

"But I want this barn to last another hundred years."

"Why? Why?"

"Why not?"

Neither one spoke. Silence. Was I, in the local phrase, not using stuff the way it should? Finally, Marcotte muttered: "That should last, by God."

I can't prove it, and I will never know, but I think the M&M Sawmill let me win that argument.

• A Barn-Dropping Party

When spring thaw drives the last traces of frost from Vermont's clay soils, old barns sometimes shift an inch or ten, groping for *terra firma*. This can be a disconcerting season for the barn's owner. In the barn that became our house, for example, sheetrock walls have cracked and door frames shifted; sheathing has been gently rippled by unforecast movements of the earth. I've become sanguine, though — and not just because I have framed walls with red oak. Habit holds this building up, and few forces are as mighty.

Habit doesn't always hold, though. These massive post-and-beam structures, erected in legendary barn-raising parties, were almost always built without benefit of concrete or masonry foundations. A terrible misfortune. A flat rock under each main bearing post, typically, is the only help provided; and some barns simply have no visible means of support. Sparing proper footings, the old-timers placed their bets on building frames sufficiently strong and rigid that they can heave around a fair amount without threatening to collapse.

A century later, many of these bets don't look so good.

Alex Kirkpatrick, an acquaintance in the next town, owned a barn a portion of which settled into a downright dangerous attitude. Alex is a chemical engineer turned farrier — he shoes horses — and though he keeps no animals, he needs his barn to store horseshoes and blacksmithing supplies and much essential junk that won't fit in his house. Then, too, he rents a portion of the barn to Jeffrey Sprague, a student of Asian languages turned freelance welder. As spring thaw progressed, the two of them became convinced that the leading bay of their barn was doomed. Worse, they feared that it might drag the whole structure down with it when it went. So they proposed to dismantle the listing section in a two-day endeavor they described as a barn-dropping party.

I was tapped to join this fun entirely by chance. The dump arm to my concrete mixer broke, so I stopped by Jeff Sprague's shop to see about getting it welded. I found him and Alex high atop a ruined silo that was drifting slowly northeast as the barn inched its way southwest. Such silos, built of concrete staves, are strapped together by thick steel rods — like barrel hoops — with their ends threaded so heavy lugs can cinch them tight. The two men were gingerly stripping these hoops off the silo and casting them down to earth near where I stood.

"What gives?" I asked.

"Time to brace the barn."

It was indeed high time. "How?" I asked.

"Bang these hoops out straight, then draw the sides together with them. Threaded ends, see?"

I saw. But I pointed to that leading bay — twenty feet by twelve feet by twelve feet high, it must have been. "Think you'll manage to pull *that* in?"

"That, we're going to liberate. Want to help?"

"No thanks."

"Hey. You'll learn some barn framing. Learn things taking an old barn apart that you'll never learn fixing one up to be your house."

"Maybe."

"Make it worth your while."

"How?"

"Give you all the roofing boards we liberate. Plus the steel roofing. Plus a beam or two, how's that?"

I had a weak spot, and he found it. Effortlessly. I needed building materials on the cheap. "When do you plan to do this?" I asked.

"Start tomorrow morning."

I showed up bright and early, with a variety of wrecking bars and nail pullers. Barry Gutman, a dancer turned roofing contractor, and Alice Cook, his partner, had arrived some time before me; they were busy high above me, prying lengths of steel roofing loose and sailing them earthward. "Mine," I told them. "Easy does it."

"Just like paper airplanes," said Alice. She was lithe and strong and seemed as comfortable as a cat up on that roof.

"What are you two working for?" I felt moved to ask. Somehow, I guessed it wasn't money; and, sure enough, Barry pointed to a 1939 Pontiac parked or abandoned near a mountain of manure. "He's giving you *that*?" I asked.

"It doesn't run," he told me. "Yet."

I wondered if I'd bartered my time away for too little. Alex arrived, then Jeffrey, and soon all five of us were crawling around on the steep-pitched roof, fighting for traction. Piece by piece, we dismantled whatever was supporting us. Fascinating work. Under the steel roofing were old hand-split cedar shakes. Beneath that — a weather seal? — were yellowed newspapers dated 1889. Beneath that were roughsawn roofing boards. Beneath that —

"Damn," I said. "This is getting shaky."

"Nervous?"

"Sure. There must be a point of no return."

With a hacksaw, Alex dropped a steel track that ran beneath the rafters, put there to guide a nifty nineteenth-century machine that trundled loose hay from carts or wagons up into the mow. The moment that track fell away, the web of rafters turned into a wobbly parallelogram. When Barry ordered all amateurs off the roof, I was happy to comply. From below, I watched him and Alice traverse carefully from one nexus of support to the next, dismantling each behind them.

Finally, Alice crawled out onto the leading pair of rafters and attached a rope to them. Seconds later she was slithering down it. Barry moved to the relative safety of a summer beam and directed our ground crew to heave on the rope, fighting a tug-of-war with the much weakened roof framing.

With a sudden clatter, our team won; there followed a relatively safe hour's labor clearing the debris away and stacking it outside. This done, Alex and Jeff took spirit levels and tape measures and squares and attempted to determine just how far the barn had moved, and why.

Out of six bearing posts spaced along the north sidewall, the second one in line had apparently heaved up nearly a foot. In doing so, it had splintered a good deal of the lumber it had been attached to. I had seen heaved posts before, but nothing on this order. "Must be some monster rock working in the soil," I said. "Underneath that post. Maybe we could dig it out?"

"*That* post hasn't moved," claimed Alex.

"No? The hell — just stand here and sight along the eave!"

He shook his head. "It's the other five posts. They've *sunk*."

"Go on. *Five* of them?"

"It gets awful swampy, sometimes. Under that north wall."

Jeff took my side, with the inscrutable wisdom of an Oriental scholar. "When you hear hoofbeats," he asked, "do you think it's zebras?"

Alex answered scrutably, with Yankee common sense: "Hell of a lot easier to cut a foot off of one post than to jack up five."

We bowed to this observation. The balance of the afternoon we spent tearing down the sidewalls of the leading bay with a care bordering on reverence, so that the mammoth beams could be used again someday. This attitude made the act of demolition somehow positive, a demonstration of respect. Hardly a person in Vermont, I imagine, has not helped to frame a building at one time or another; even a few days of such work create a lasting regard for honest carpentry. And near acquaintance with the handiwork of the early settlers, who hewed beams twenty feet long and a foot square by hand, and then joined them together as precisely as a chair or table, engenders something close to awe. Alex's promise had been kept. You learn things, taking down a barn.

Next day, we drilled holes through the posts and beams of the intact portion of the structure and threaded the steel rods from the silo into place. With his welding torch, Jeff manufactured massive washers right on the spot — like the steel discs one sees set in the sidewalls of old fieldstone buildings — and, bolting these to the silo rods, we torqued the barn's walls back into plumb with a socket wrench.

Finally, Alex took a building jack and lifted the offending post — the one that had either heaved a foot or else failed to sink — out of its mortise in the hemlock sill that ran along the earth. Barry Gutman zipped his chainsaw through it, cutting off the mysterious twelve inches. Then we tried to reproduce the tenon he had cut away, so that the post could be lowered firmly back into the rotting sill. One shapes a tenon with a chisel; but chisels with an eight-inch business end, for post-and-beam construction, have gone the way of butter churns and horse-drawn plows. The biggest chisel we had was a toy by comparison, and it served us poorly. Trouble.

"I could *make* a chisel, maybe," Jeff volunteered. He found some scraps of steel, sharpened one piece on his grinding wheel, and then welded a long handle to fit.

"What's *he* working for?" Barry asked.

"Working so the damn barn won't collapse and crush him."

"Or my tools!" Jeff hollered from his welding table.

"Nice to have incentive."

The chisel finished, Jeff aimed it at the stump of the post and gave a whack. It worked perfectly. Twenty minutes later we were lowering the post back into place on the sill. Result: a tolerably level, plumb, square building. Once again. Alex's cash costs: nine dollars, for beer.

We sat up in the hay mow, toasting our accomplishment and staring down on what we'd dropped. "To save the barn," said Barry, paraphrasing a Vietnam era slogan, "it became necessary to destroy it."

"Only *part* of it."

"So far. See what happens *next* spring."

"No — it's going nowhere now."

Barry scratched his chin. "I give it fifty more years."

"By then, it'll be a national historic site. The *government* will keep it standing."

As the sun set, I loaded my pickup truck to the gunwales with used building materials. "Fair enough?" asked Alex. "Any more, your springs are going to break!"

"More than fair," I said. I guess I got a little sentimental. I was thrilled to recycle debris from his barn into mine. I said, "How often can a person be a Liberator?"

• The Town Dowser

In our little Yankee town, the Zoning Administrator is also on the Board of Listers. This is a great advantage, because the instant a person applies to build something, the Listers know. Then they can quickly lift one's tax assessment to new heights.

Fernand Mayer — the citizen I speak of — wears a third hat, too. For an unelected, unappointed, but extremely valued post. He is the town's premier dowser, which means that people have him tell them where to drill for water.

We found ourselves in need of water, the parched August of our second summer here. Our growing farmstead was served by a dug well fed by two thousand feet of pipe from a dug pond fed by two pure and usually faithful springs — a complicated system, subject to unscheduled maintenance, but our water was both cheap and tasty. And abundant — except in a drought year.

I can still recall the patient, inexorable process of dessication. First the dug well's natural catchment finked out, meaning that the soil was bone dry down to eight feet. Then our springs — across a dry creek, up in a hardwood forest — ceased their steady trickle. We still had the pond to serve us, a reservoir adequate for three weeks. But pond water tastes, well, *pondy*, like decaying leaves; it got daily worse until even the dog disdained to drink it.

Then the pond dried, too.

Living without water — in a heat wave, in a house all too recently equipped with faucets, toilets, tubs, and showers — quickly evaporated the charm of the bucolic lifestyle, too. We found ourselves cursing bell-clear days and cloudless skies as we hauled water back from town in jugs, resenting every drop it took to keep our first two sheep alive; ourselves we limited to just enough water to cook with and brush our teeth. A big date, come Friday night, was driving twenty miles to a friend's house to take a shower.

We were not alone, of course. Newspapers were full of stories on the record lack of rainfall. Every inch lost, I read, would cost the county's farmers a cool million bucks in purchased feed for the coming winter. One could scarcely doubt it, seeing fields of corn as high as a spaniel's eye — and harvest coming soon. Vast tank trucks used by day to haul milk now hauled water by moonlight to thirsty dairy herds.

Finally, the only folks with water were those with deep wells. Deep wells, in these parts, are *deep* — four hundred feet would raise no eyebrows — and cost the earth. Even today, five thousand dollars buys a dandy chunk of rural Vermont, but it can cost twice that to make a toilet flush on the same piece of land.

Pocketbook be damned, in my thirsty frenzy such a price seemed reasonable. Necessary. I asked a neighbor to recommend somebody to drill a well.

"First off," he said, "you had better talk to Fernand Mayer."

This surprised me. "I need a Zoning Permit to drill a well?"

"Nope. But Fernand, he dowses."

"He does what?"

"He'll show you where there's water. No sense drilling blind."

I had heard of such a folk art, but I thought it must have surely died out long ago. "You mean he walks around with a forked stick, and —"

"Fernand, he don't use a forked stick. He uses bent coat hangers."

"Oh, come on!" I could imagine engaging a dowser for — well, for aesthetic reasons. I am a sucker for the rural picturesque. But the thought of hiring our jolly, round-faced Zoning Administrator to tramp around the yard with a bent coat hanger was not the pastoral scene I had in mind.

My neighbor didn't see it that way. "Got a good dowser lives right in town, you ought to use him."

"But it's so much voodoo."

"Nope. Fernand, he's scientific."

"Well," I said, "all right. I'll call him."

Sunday afternoon, right after church, Fernand's blue pickup

truck pulled into our driveway. He climbed out and — sure enough — in his hands were two bent coat hangers. Let me describe this carefully. He had bent each coat hanger out perfectly straight, then made a right-angle bend in each about six inches from the end.

"Awfully dry year, isn't it?" I asked, by way of conversation.

"One in seven, usually."

"How come you don't use a forked apple stick to dowse with?"

"Can't." He made a little shrug — it was just out of the question. "Applewood's too strong for me."

"Too *strong*?"

"Apple wants to find water just about anywhere. I can't hardly hang onto it." He looked around and sighted our old apple tree up on the hill. "*You* might try some apple, though. To start with."

"Oh, no. Listen, I can't do this."

I squatted on the ground, and he spread wide his arms with one coat hanger gripped in each hand just where he had bent it. Then he started on a series of walks across the lawn. He crisscrossed back and forth, nonchalant and casual and anything but a shaman — and I watched those coat hangers twist and droop and rise and rotate, finding water in the earth.

"Don't fool me — you're *doing* that!" I challenged.

He stopped, intent, the coat hangers twitching towards each other in positive attraction. Then he took his hat off and dropped it gently on the ground. Without a word, he crossed the yard and approached the hat from a different angle.

Finally, he said: "I always like to try to find where two or three streams *cross*."

"Streams?"

"Underground. Of course, they don't most likely cross at the same *depth*. No sir. But a driller's apt to hit one or another square."

I maintained my scepticism. "Must be water anywhere, I guess. If a man drills deep enough."

He set down his tools. He had had enough lip. He climbed to the apple tree up on the hill and cut a forked stick. Then he made me hold the thing torsioned in between my doubting wrists, and marched me across the lawn. Did it bend? Well, yes. It did — perceptibly. But not perceptibly enough to make me sure I hadn't caused it. Then I neared his hat.

That forked stick bent. Scout's honor, it bent for me.

Fernand Mayer took the apple stick, and, just like he'd promised, it became so lively in his hands that he couldn't even keep his grip. As a divining tool, plainly it provided him with more data than was useful. "I'm awful sensitive," he said, handing it back to me.

I could see that. And I saw his business was not fraudulent — not *simply* fraudulent, at least. He was dealing with essentially objective phenomena. Apple sticks would bend, coat hangers twitch — but I had to wonder, was this caused by water? "Okay," I said. "How deep is it?"

"Just coming to that part," replied Fernand, unfazed. He took one of the coat hangers and held it this time by the long end as he pushed the short end in the ground at the drill site. "*That* grounds the rod," he told me. I thought: absurdly metaphorical. Criminally vague. Then, pulling the coat hanger free, he commenced to let it bounce or bob gently in the air, counting each stroke as a foot of depth.

At twenty-nine bobs, it paused. "That's ledge," he told me, offhand. "Don't mean nothing." Then the wire bobbed again, and bobbed one hundred fifty times. When it stopped, he said: "*That's* water. Say one hundred and eighty feet down."

"Good thing for you your coat hanger's not metricized."

He smiled. No comment. But the wire bounced again, now, and it bounced a good, long time. When it stopped, Fernand whispered: "Four hundred and twenty feet."

"Awfully deep."

"You might get lucky, with that first stream at one hundred and eighty. Chances are, though, you'll have to drill the distance."

"At ten bucks a foot, right?"

"Plus the pipe. The pump. The wire. Make a mess of seven thousand dollars. But there's water there."

"One last question," I said. "Will this water taste good?"

He put away his coat hangers and surveyed the landscape. Slowly. Then I followed him over to a nearby protrusion of rocky subsoil. He picked at it for a couple minutes.

"Well?"

"Shale," he said. "Shale's bad. Apt to go quite deep. Water's apt to be quite sulphur."

"Meaning?"

"Apt to taste like rotten eggs." He broke a bit of shale in two."Why, I've seen sulphur so bad, *coffee* wouldn't hide the water. *Bad* coffee, even."

"Any way to filter sulphur?"

"I don't believe." He paused, scanning the parched fields, visibly weighing whether he should offer me some hard advice. Vermonters almost never offer hard advice. But I tried to look naive and eager. "Tell the truth," he finally drawled, "if I was you, I'd wait for rain."

We stood up together, and I asked him what he charged for dowsing.

"Charge? No charge — heck, son, I *like* to do this."

We never drilled for water. Rains came within a week — hard, soaking, drenching rains. Our springs began to run again, and they have not failed us in the many years since Fernand Mayer's visit. But I sank a brick in the ground where he had said to drill, in case I ever change my mind. I stub my toe on that half-buried marker once or twice a year, and think of untapped water in the earth below. *Are* there streams there, underground? I may never know. But I know that when the town's Listers see fit to increase my taxes, I think to myself: that man saved me a lot of money.

• *Pollenia rudis*

We strike a few odd bargains with nature, here in Vermont. An austere spring, devoid of bright flowering trees and shrubs, compensated by autumns of riotous and blinding color. Soils high in lime and potash, fundamentally fertile, but so clayey as to be almost untillable. A climate so severe that it spares us many insect pests; and yet, on a cold but sunny January day, visitors are startled to see houseflies flitting about a warm room.

Well, not exactly houseflies.

Vermont's lack of certain bugs was heady stuff, at first. I have never, for example, seen a cockroach in Vermont. They don't *like* it here — a fine state of affairs. Having kept house more or less energetically in and around Boston, San Francisco, Los Angeles, and Philadelphia, and having failed in all these places to keep cockroaches at bay, it took me some time to change a few compulsive habits. No more doing supper dishes after supper, for example. No more stealthy forays from bed late at night, no snapping on the kitchen lights to bust a hapless bug or two. But I've made a fine adjustment to living without the roach.

There are, in addition, no termites in Vermont — except for an isolated nest or two in Bennington. North of there, they will not venture. We do have carpenter ants, which turn a stud or two to sawdust; but carpenter ants live in your house and feed in the ground, whereas termites live in the ground and eat your house. I'll take the carpenters, any day.

Every five years or so a wet summer gets our dog to scratching with fleas, which he brings into the house. Every five years or so, we have to buy some flea powder.

That's about it for common insect pests, barring the odd mosquito. Paradise won? I thought so, till I met *Pollenia rudis*. The persistence of what looked like houseflies after cold weather set in was a mystery to me. Close inspection showed that these insects were a sort of fraternal twin to houseflies; their wings were slightly more deltoid — more windswept — and folded back neatly when not in use.

These peculiar flies might pace a *real* housefly in carefree flight across a room, but a person finds out which is which when one of them has a sort of *grand mal* seizure in midflight and drops like a stone onto the nearest horizontal surface, where it lies on its back trying to right itself by flitting its stylish wings. The fly will continue its remarkably noisy efforts until exhaustion, unless somebody gets annoyed enough to put the insect out of its misery.

These flies arrive in clusters. Hundreds, sometimes thousands, huddling together. We called them "cluster flies."

My cluster-fly problem was especially egregious in the large upstairs room which had at one time been a hay loft; we had panelled this room with authentic barn boards, for true rusticity. Rusticity with flies, as it turned out.

Old barn boards are not as easy to acquire as they once were. But eight years ago, a neighbor sent us up the road several miles to where an ancient barn on another dairy farmer's back forty had recently collapsed. We found the man unloading hay wagons, sending green bales up a long conveyor. "Like to buy some barn boards," I attempted to drawl.

He looked at me. For the longest time.

"Heard you had some," I pressed on, trying to seem local. "Heard you had a barn collapse."

"*Let* it collapse," he said. "Been trying to for years. How many board feet would you be looking for?"

I didn't speak board feet competently, yet. Good thing. I said, "Just enough to panel the walls in one room."

Now, old farmhouses here are typically a warren of nine-by-twelve-foot rooms. Many can be closed off in winter, for ease of heating, and it takes a lot of partitions to bear the heavy framing for a slate roof overhead. But I did not know these things yet. I was making a sort of Walking Purchase from a local Indian, for he was thinking nine-by-twelve while I was thinking twenty-one by twenty-four, with cathedral ceiling.

He scratched his chin. He fiddled with his suspenders. "I might sell you that," he nodded.

"How much?" As soon as I said this, the farmer winced. It was, I learned much later, entirely the wrong question. The right question would have been, "What will you take?" Or, better, "Would you take fifty dollars?"

"What will you *give*?" he countered, upset with my lack of bargaining manners.

"Fifty dollars?"

He nodded.

Three full days followed during which my wife and I tore barn boards off his heap of beams and pulled countless nails from them. This fallen barn was a good half mile from the farmer's house, and we never saw the man again — though if, eventually, he went to guesstimate how much wood we'd taken, he must have raised his eyebrows. Now that I speak board feet with utter fluency, I would say we took one thousand of them for our fifty dollars, which was quite a deal. If you want to have old barn boards in your living room.

Barn boards are roughsawn, so they never fit together particularly tightly. I was not concerned. We had placed fiber-glass insulation behind them in our living room, and the barn's exterior was finished in clapboards. Nonetheless, as that first winter bore down on us, north winds seemed to penetrate the living room as though the walls were made of lattice. Winds and, as it turned out, flies.

I thought I had discovered something new under the sun. But, along about Thanksgiving, I visited a neighbor who was busy efficiently vacuuming up a number of the same type flies — living and dead — from around the windows of her house. "What do you call those things?" I demanded.

"Well, some call them buckwheat flies. Watch —" she crushed a couple, and indeed, a faint odor of buckwheat honey could be whiffed. "But most just call them cluster flies."

"I've got quite a few of them. Clustering, like you say."

"They come inside the walls for winter," she said. "For warmth. Not food — they won't touch your food. Oh, you'll get used to them."

But I never did. And, though I do believe they were not out to *eat* my food, these flies nonetheless acquired an uncanny knack for timing their midflight epileptic seizures to occur when they were directly over dinner plates, or mugs of coffee, or morning scrambled eggs. Worse, they would spiral down into one's face and hair while one slept. I would rather have half a dozen hungry mosquitos singing in my drowsy ears than have a single cluster fly doing its clumsy death rattle tangled in my hair.

Discovering that most of my neighbors had cluster flies gave a certain peace of mind; as winter wore on, though, it became apparent that I had many more than they did. *Many* more. Where my neighbors might sweep up a dozen on a sunny morn, I would have a hundred or more crawling around the windows, blocking out the light. It behooved me to study their habits and their life cycle. I went to visit our county Agricultural Extension agent; sure enough, he had heard of cluster flies, too.

These insects, he taught me, lay their eggs in soil — particularly clay soils, particularly where manure is spread. That's around here, for sure. The larvae are parasites of earthworms, which they attack. Mature larvae pupate in the soil and emerge as flies. In contrast to houseflies, which can breed every fortnight, cluster flies have only three or four generations in an entire year.

In summer, adult cluster flies live outdoors and dine on fruit juice and flower nectar — hence their sweet odor. But when cold weather comes, all they want in the whole world is warmth. So they head for houses, squeezing through the teensiest holes and cracks in exterior walls to lay back for the winter. By December, those flies that feel the need for exercise go zipping around heated rooms by day and disappear behind the walls at night. They do this especially where interior walls are a cinch to disappear behind.

One of my neighbors stopped by to wish us a happy New Year and allowed as how our buckwheat flies were "desperate thick." He perfunctorily admired our barn-board panelling, and then asked if I'd looked behind a board or two.

"Looked for what?"

"You got a cat's paw nail-puller?"

I did indeed — well broken in, from prying nails out of all those antique boards. Moments later he was taking off a wide piece of my rustic interior, humming to himself. "Jesum *Crow*," he whispered when it came free. "Look at that!"

About a million cluster flies were huddling on the insulation. "Close it up!" I yelled, alarmed. "Holy — quick, nail that board back!"

"Listen, these old boards aren't much to hold back buckwheat flies. And neither are those rotten clapboards out there."

I had built the perfect cluster fly abode.

"What you want to do, just let the fire go out in here so the walls get cold. That'll make the flies get sleepy. Take off the boards, then. Vacuum up these flies."

"Good idea," I told him.

There is one thing he forgot to tell me, though: to empty and clean out the vacuum cleaner immediately. Truth be told, I didn't do this. Truth be told, the vacuum began to stink a few days later. Like fermenting buckwheat honey. Truth be told, that vacuum cleaner is no longer with us.

But I never pried off very many of those boards. They were fragile, and my heart just wasn't in it. Instead, we closed off the hayloft living room till spring, on the hunch the flies would freeze or starve in below-zero walls. This proved very largely right. We began using the room again along about Easter, and no plague of flies ensued. However, something else did: dark, broad-shouldered beetles wandering aimlessly around the house. Hungry-looking things.

I took one to my county Agricultural Extension agent. "Larder beetle," he pronounced. "They eat the cluster flies that died inside your walls, all winter."

"Damned nice of them."

"You ought to see quite a few of these, now."

This, I thought, is just as though a city apartment's roaches suddenly acquired *fleas*.

We weathered the larder beetle horde, in time, and found a fair solution to the whole situation by smearing a couple of cases of caulking compound, crack by crack, into our exterior walls. This impedes the entrance of the flies, somewhat. We still have them — everybody does, smack in the dead of winter — but they no longer control our quality of life. One flits even now above the typewriter, but I do not need to swat it. Any moment it may drop from the sky like a fighter plane hit by anti-aircraft rockets; my dog has taken, recently, to gobbling flies up as they fall. For a tired hound on a cold winter afternoon, that's a drop of buckwheat honey.

CHAPTER TWO

The Husbandry of Sheep

*I*N A DIMLY RECOLLECTED PAST life, I was not a shepherd. It must have been wonderful, though I can't imagine what I did with all the time that not-being-a-shepherd must have afforded me. Had I known, in those presumably misspent youthful days, that escaping to Vermont would bring awesome responsibilities for me to shoulder — playing God to a flock of helpless ruminants — I might have found some less pastoral landscape to relocate to.

As I have explained, when we moved here heifers roamed the land. The heifers were a nuisance, but not nearly so great a nuisance that a rational person would determine to replace them with livestock of his own. Nor was I convinced I could make money as a livestock farmer — although I did aim to beat the going heifer pasture rental of a mere $150 per year. I could well appreciate that Yankee farmers have a hard financial row to hoe, though, and I would not have tried to join their ranks out of the profit motive.

Fact is, I got into sheep because I came to feel that owning livestock might help to legitimate my somewhat puzzling presence in this rural community. We had, after all, purchased a farm in much the way that other couples buy a painting. Once we got to know our neighbors, we discovered they considered this to be, at least, wildly incomprehensible; at worst, they felt it morally reprehensible. Had we continued to live near Philadelphia and only paid sporadic visits to our country place, they would have understood us. Many flatlanders do the same. But to *live* on one's own farm with no intent of working it, shaping it, growing with it — mere connoisseurs of landscape — *that* made my wife and me radically suspicious characters.

Once I got to know my neighbors, I quickly went beyond understanding this perspective on the newcomers. I adopted it. I *was* suspicious. What effrontery, to acquire as an amenity what these honest, hard-working Yankees were toiling all their lives to nurture. How could I join? How could I even signal my respect? The more I pondered these questions, the more a single answer loomed forth: Raise livestock. Just like they did.

But what *kind* of livestock? Cows, frankly, scared me; the sheer size and power of the bovines chowing down our pastures could turn a casual morning walk into an alarming dash for cover in the woodlot. There were bulls to think of, too. And milking — I knew myself well enough to doubt that I would long endure a twice-daily milking chore. So cows were out. I thought of goats seriously enough to visit a local goat farm; for better or worse, a buck there picked my pocket. Professionally. I was on the point of buying something, and there was no wallet. By the time we found it, half-masticated and wholly ruined, I was no longer a prospective customer.

Then I learned that sheep could be relied upon to crop my land. Sheep were not too big; they were not nasty or aggressive. In fact, classically defined, sheep are small grazing animals whose only defense is flight. That sounded fine to me. I bought a couple of lambs, and then a dozen young ewes, and over several years I allowed the flock to grow until I had no room for heifers.

Sad to say, even now I cannot boast my neighbors treat me as an equal — a fellow Yankee farmer. This is dairy country, and I am not a dairyman. But I am no longer a suspicious character, and, as a shepherd, I share many of their deep concerns. The high cost of hay. The weather. The many novel, interesting ways in which farm livestock get sick or fail to produce or even sometimes die. The relative values of various pieces of machinery. The weather. The impossibility of ever making a dollar farming. Taxes. The weather. When conversation lags, one can always talk about the weather.

I won't claim I've come to belong. It *feels* that way sometimes, though. And, when anybody asks, I can tell them plenty more than they could ever wish to know about the husbandry of sheep. For me, it has come with the territory.

• *In Utero*

The first spring that my wife and I lambed out our flock of sheep, we managed to attend each birth but never pushed a hand Inside. We were squeamish — and maybe a bit disdainful of obstetrics. We were also lucky to be spared major lambing crises.

There was one night, though, when I smelled trouble. A largish ewe had had a lamb so small — five pounds — that I thought there ought to be a twin. While I watched, she *did* pass a garnet water bag such as might precede another lamb. An hour passed. Then two. The ewe contracted, fitfully, to rid her womb of afterbirth. Afterbirth? No, I told her. I wanted another lamb.

Finally I called a vet — at random, from the yellow pages. My sheep had stayed healthy; I had never called a vet before. It was roughly one A.M., on a Sunday night with a cold rain falling. "Hate to get you up," I told him.

"Are you *sure* it's twins?"

"I think so."

"Did you get a hand inside her?"

"No. I couldn't." Did I lie? I didn't tell him that I hadn't actually tried. The problem wasn't a tight cervix; it was a helpless shepherd.

"Sounds to me like she's all through. But — you want me to come out?"

I paused, trying to guess his fee. How much was that twin lamb worth? Not enough. But, I thought, this is the price of education. "*Please* come."

"Give me twenty minutes."

I gave him directions, then went out to check the ewe again. Like the symptom that disappears in the doctor's office, like the noisy engine that runs smoothly only at the garage, my ewe had now finished labor. Her dark red placenta lay bright upon the bedding straw, and she looked at ease while her lamb — her one lamb — nursed and bleated. I picked the placenta up and threw it out behind the barn so that the doctor, on his way now, wouldn't see it there and think I was a total idiot.

Soon enough, his truck pulled in. "Morning," I said. "Awful night."

He didn't yup, he didn't nope. "Where's that ewe?"

I led him to her. He bared a forearm and washed up with disinfectant. Then — in just a second — he was in her. Up to his elbow. The ewe struggled once, but the man pinned her with his knee against the wall of the pen. Without expression — with professional detachment — he probed the nooks and crannies of her womb. Then he slipped his arm out. He said: "She's all done."

"She is?"

"She's finished. No twin. Have to wait till next year."

"Gosh, I'm sorry. Making you leave bed."

He held his hand — now painted with the womb's bright colors — next to mine. His was bigger. Beefier. "Say you couldn't get inside her?"

"Mmmn."

"You'd better learn. Easier on both of us. Now, that's fifteen dollars."

Even in Vermont, I doubt a man could get a doctor out of bed for fifteen dollars. Let alone a lawyer. And this vet had made a thirty-mile round trip in his pickup. But that was his farm call fee, night or day, rain or shine, and I'd given him no cause — no surgery, no medication — to charge any more.

I paid. He went home to bed.

Shamed at having called a vet to do what a good shepherd should have, I bared *my* arm now and soaped it. Then — because the ewe was still dilated, and her womb was empty — I reached in and reconnoitered that dark cave. It was muscular and wet, and warm. Passages and cul-de-sacs seemed to run in deep, far from the central chamber. Not an unpleasant room, though no doubt it could get cramped. And — one has to say this — the thought of a lamb or lambs lying there, prepared for birth, seemed utterly preposterous.

As a reluctant midwife, I argued that "in nature" sheep survived quite nicely without humans helping them give birth. And perhaps some do — but I know now that *my* sheep wouldn't, nor most farm sheep that have been cunningly selected to encourage multiple births, heavy birth weights, rapid growth rates, superior muscling. Sheep "in nature" do not care much for these profitable traits. Sheep "in nature" are not well served by having twins; on our farm, though, we have come to aim for triplets.

Sometimes we do better. When a ewe delivers quads, though, midwivery is of the essence. And, with each passing year, I'm amazed at the variety of inauspicious positions in which lambs attempt to leave the womb. Gradually I have become a willing interventionist.

It was a year after my veterinary call before I reached into a ewe again, and this time her womb wasn't empty. Night was fading into dawn — the time when most sheep like to lamb — and, arriving at the barn, I saw a tail dangling from a ewe. Just a tail. The mother was in considerable discomfort.

I had read up on ovine obstetrics — what there is to read — and I knew that little tail signalled a frank breech birth. It meant the lamb's hind legs were aimed up toward the ewe's head, and the broad, muscled buttocks of the lamb were battering the cervix. This is a nearly impossible position; without assistance, the lamb nearly always dies. Sometimes the ewe, too. The books I had read were clear: someone had to get in there and push the lamb back where he'd come from and find those hind hoofs. Then, one at a time, the hoofs and legs had to be snaked out to lie beside the tail, and then the lamb had to be pulled out quickly, before it drowned in fluid.

I worked my hand in, making slow progress in between uterine contractions that had the rhythm and the force of breaking waves. Their pressure made my fingers ache. I could scarcely push the lamb back in though. There were two more lambs, I eventually learned, jockeying about to see who would be born next. Even a normal birth can be no picnic for the baby; for triplets, it must be a rough-and-tumble family brawl.

Having gained scant ground — but afraid the lamb was near expiring — I grabbed a hind hoof and bent it back so hard I feared I'd break the leg or tear the uterus, one or the other. Neither happened. I drew it out, little by little, and at length I realized that I was going to win. This is the midwife's secret knowledge: flesh can stretch. And give, more than one could dare expect. Living flesh is unlike any other substance on this earth. I got that leg out.

Then I plunged back in and found the other, flipped it, eased it out; then the ewe expelled her lamb.

I held it by the hind legs; it shook its head, and gobs of pale gel streamed from its nose and mouth. The womb is an ocean: one can drown. But now the mother turned and slapped her tongue across that face and licked it clean with sloppy kisses. The lamb drew a breath, and lived.

Since that first thrill of making a successful obstetric rescue, I no longer feel queasy at reaching inside the womb. I can still get fooled — and anxious, and distraught — but I've never had to rouse my vet from his sleep again. The womb is a finite space; the possibilities for lambs to occupy that space are finite. Shepherding affords no thrill, though, greater than that of delivering alive what could not otherwise have been born. For this, one does not count the hours waiting in a dark, cold barn.

My son is very young; I like to think his being raised so close to farmyard birth and death will spare him the confusing feelings I had to overcome before probing the mysteries of the womb. But I fear it won't. I showed him a ewe in labor, when he was some three years old. "See there?" I said, squatting with him on the bedded barn floor. "Where that sheep's all sucked in? That's her womb, and there's a baby lamb right inside there."

"There is not," he said.

"Really! It'll come out soon, and in the morning you can see it."

He looked at me. "No, I won't."

There was no arguing with him. Birth is hard to comprehend, as much for three-year-olds as for adults. We discussed wombs again a few weeks later when a friend was visiting. An extremely pregnant friend. "Just like our sheep," I explained to him. "And once, believe it or not, kid, *you* were in *Mommy's* womb."

He considered this, then ran to her and dove beneath her skirt. "I'm going right back there!" he shouted.

• Fleeced

When I first embarked on my career as a part-time shepherd, I held the common view that wool was something valuable. A specialty fiber, with unique properties of warmth and durability.

Natural, not like orlon, rayon, and other ersatz aspects of twentieth-century life. And woolen products cost the earth. To a shepherd, though, wool must be — well, simply *hair.* Hair that *grew,* with no encouragement whatever, out of millions of follicles on the back of every sheep. Couldn't stop it if you tried. All you had to do was shear the stuff off, once a year or so. Who would doubt that growing wool could handsomely reward a shepherd?

At the time such thoughts inspired me, I only owned two sheep. They were lambs, to tell the truth, and I was raising them as a species of self-propelled lawnmower. Autumn came; the lawn stopped growing, and the lambs had reached sufficient size to put into the freezer. But before dispatching them, I felt compelled to try to harvest the several pounds of precious wool from their backs. I thought I'd teach myself to shear.

Of course, I had no shears. But I obtained a catalog of supplies for sheepmen and discovered with dismay that electric shearing machines begin at $120 and run up to around $500. Even I suspected that my wool crop was not *that* valuable. Luckily, there was a listing for old-fashioned hand shears, too. Fine, tempered English steel. A mere $8.95. Here was appropriate technology, I reasoned, for the pair of lambs I wished to shear. "Ideal for tagging and crutching operations," the catalog copy read. This was Greek to me, though. Then, with equal obscurity, it noted: "Shears are shipped unrigged — rig to your own specifications."

I had no specifications, in point of fact. But the shears that I received in the mail some weeks later conformed nicely to my classical ideal: here was the sturdy tool shepherds had wielded for many centuries prior to rural electrification. Two broad, polished blades were joined by a bow of bright spring steel, thoughtfully smoothed and curved to fit the human hand. The cutting edges were all business, too — they were razor sharp. I now owned one hell of a scissors.

I learned soon enough that shears are not like scissors. When one snips with shears, the muscles in one's hand must overcome the tool's built-in spring. The springiness is needed to assist in *opening* the shears after each cutting stroke, when they are buried in a forest of wool. Assistance, though, is often not enough. My blades often needed to be *pried* back open — with two hands — in an awkward gesture that destroyed all forward progress. Nothing on my sheep shears corresponded to the simple thumb-and-finger holes on scissors, which allow one to open and close the blades easily.

Few things in life are as frustrating to me as failing to make a tool work. So I made my wife spend an exhausting couple of hours with me, wrestling an unhappy lamb to the ground and trying to immobilize it while I snipped away the odd square inch or two of wool. A specialty fiber, I explained to her, with unique properties of warmth and durability. Then I would wrestle, and she would snip — except her hands lacked strength enough to pry the shears apart after each cutting motion. The lamb, quite sensibly, kicked each time he had a chance; his kicking caused him several minor, inadvertent flesh wounds, and finally it caused *me* one. I threw the shears down angrily and sucked blood from my index finger.

"Maybe," my wife suggested, "you should shear them once they're dead."

"Very funny."

"No, I mean it. To get practice. They won't kick, then."

That was true enough. So, on the traumatic day when I offed my first lamb, I put down the sticking knife and reached for my English hand shears. This was unwise, I now understand, for a host of reasons not least of which is that a hot corpse should be transformed into a chilled carcass just as soon as possible. To prevent spoilage. One ought to be skinning and eviscerating a dead lamb, not fooling around trying to learn how to shear. Oblivious, though, to such principles of butchery, I spent another good hour harvesting some ten percent of the wool on my lamb's back. He did not kick, but I concluded that hand shearing called for men with wrists like steel. It was not for me. When I gave up, I could scarcely work my fingers.

"Maybe," my wife commented, "you should shear it once it's skinned."

I confess I tried that, too. I confess I could not shear sheep: could not shear them on the hoof, nor dead, nor even skinned. I supposed I was not man enough — painful to admit. But giving up on shearing did not sour me on sheep; next spring, I bought ten ewes and undertook to build a flock. And when, some months later, I determined it was time to shear them, I decided to engage professional services.

Shearers in New England are not listed in the Yellow Pages; one has to learn of them by word of mouth. They all work on a per-head-shorn basis, but the fee for small flocks can be several times that for large ones. Travel and set-up time for a high-capacity shearing rig are important costs; once the tool is set in place, its operator wants to shear a hundred sheep, not ten. So, although I turned up several names of potential shearers, I was not in much of a position to dicker.

What I did have, though, were grandiose expansion plans. Ten sheep this year, fifty next, and then — who knows? I aimed to tempt a shearer to get in on the ground floor of something big, and set his fees accordingly. Most were not drawn to this bait, but one was. He sheared large flocks, he told me on the phone, for $1.75 per head; he offered to shear mine for only twice that, which was a good deal less than other prices I had been quoted. A respectable deal. But I balked for a moment, as I'd learned to do in price negotiations, to see if he would go lower.

He said: "Or, no cash at all. I'll just take the wool."

Take the wool! I grinned, I almost laughed into the telephone. What did the man take me for? Wasn't wool a luxury — a premium fiber? If wool were not vastly more valuable than the labor cost of having it shorn, I ought to have my head examined. So I nailed down a shearing fee of $35 — or $3.50 per head — and set a date for him to come.

When the man arrived, I was mightily impressed with the beef in his back and arms. Like a Yankee Sumo wrestler. I was equally impressed with his shearing rig's size and power and complexity. A large electric motor was fastened to a beam of my little barn, and steel shafts with universal joints directed its substantial output to the shearer's handpiece. I supposed it would cut through steel wire just as well as wool.

His tool in place, he grunted and I walked the first sheep toward him. He flipped it, almost effortlessly, and began the quick, efficient harvest of my crop of wool. Rather than hold the sheep in one spot and move around it with the shearing tool, this man held the tool in roughly the same spot and moved the sheep around *it*. She did not kick or squirm, either; he knew a couple dozen holds or pressure points to immobilize a leg or neck or shoulder while he sheared it.

Well within an hour of starting to shear, he'd finished. My ten little ewes milled about, skinny and undressed — *fleeced* — and I packed their wool into a sack that weighed, when full, fifty-seven pounds. I paid the man his fee, and then a little extra.

"Thanks," he said.

"Hey, this was worth it. I've tried shearing. I just can't."

"What'd you use for shears?" he asked me.

So I found the tempered English tool — a tad rusty, now — and showed him. He tried them out. "Not bad," he said. "Nice action. Good for tagging out a few sheep, or for crutching them. Course, you've got to rig them."

"Whoa," I stopped him. "Could you just explain that?"

"What?"

"Tagging. Crutching. Rigging."

"Tags are wool that's got manure on it. Tagging cuts those off. Crutching, that's just clipping wool from off the udder. Before lambing. Helps your lambs to find the teats."

I was grateful, and a little dumbstruck. Only an idiot would have used my tool to try to shear a sheep; but the jargon of his occupation was not in my dictionary. I asked, "How about rigging?"

"You got a strap of leather?"

I searched till I found one, and minutes later he had rigged my shears — which is to say, he tied the strap so that my hand, when slipped between it and the shears, could work the blades in both directions. Just like scissors. "That," he said, "is rigging. It's damn hard to use these shears without it."

I told him I knew that.

Some months later, I took my wool to an annual pooled sale run by the Vermont Sheepbreeder's Association. There I got a big surprise. Wool is a commodity. Wool is grown throughout the world. Wool will keep in storage indefinitely — it needs no refrigeration, no special handling. There are several hundred million sheep in the world, and they all grow wool — some 3,500,000,000 pounds of it each year. Woolen goods may cost the earth, at retail, but to a shepherd wool off a sheep's back is worth about 60¢ per pound. Good years, it brings 80¢; in catastrophic years, such as 1982, it scarcely brings 40¢.

I sold my precious wool crop for a couple of dollars less than I'd paid to have my ten sheep shorn.

People often ask me if I'm raising sheep for meat — for lambs, that is — or for wool. I no longer ask myself that question, though.

It wouldn't bother me if sheep grew no wool whatsoever. Now that I have well over a hundred of the critters, I have bought electric clippers and have learned to shear, after a fashion. I seldom do, though. I'm too slow. What my professional shearer can knock off in a solid afternoon of work, takes me a couple of weeks. I haven't got that kind of time, so I continue to pay him the lion's share of the paltry price I get for wool.

I have read that in Australia — where sheep are big business — scientists are working to perfect an injectable depilatory. Hit up each sheep with a few cc's, and a couple days later all that wool virtually falls right off. Unique natural fiber that wool is, I would applaud the development of such an unnatural device for harvesting the stuff. In the meantime, I am resigned — as I suppose my sheep are — to annually getting fleeced.

• Easter Lambs

I started keeping sheep in flagrant disregard of my neighbors' advice: they swore there was no way to make sheep pay. Not in Vermont, they said. I wanted to show them, though — and, in fact, I knew a couple of things they didn't. Yet.

One thing I knew was that Boston — just four hours away — provides a strong Easter lamb market every spring. Easter lambs are sold at light weights — fifty pounds or less — but often they're so scarce and prized that a fifty-pound lamb at Easter can fetch more than a ninety-pound lamb in autumn. There's a lot less hay and grain in that fifty-pound lamb, too.

"Ayup," commented one of my dairy-farming neighbors, "but when do you have to get those Easter lambs on the ground?"

"On the ground?"

"*Born.*"

I guessed: "February first?"

"Price isn't high enough, then."

I skipped the Easter lamb market, that first year, and on February first I felt mighty glad I had. It was no weather for trudging to the barn at all hours of the night, trying to distinguish false labors from the real thing. And it was too cold for newborn lambs to have an even chance of surviving their critical first couple of days. No, we lambed the first of April, and by Easter our biggest lamb wouldn't have dressed six pounds. We sold them in September, at a price that raised no eyebrows.

The price of fresh American lamb varies seasonally, because the vast majority of sheep are kept on Western ranges where it makes no sense to tamper with nature's cycle of fall breeding, spring lambing, and feeding out the crop of lambs on summer pastures. That brings a glut of lamb to market every autumn, at what is predictably the lowest price of the year. My wife and I found April lambing pleasant — undeniably spring-like — but it seemed that aspiring Yankees ought to try to beat the system just a little bit — by lambing, say, early in March to sell fat lambs in midsummer. Fat lambs in summer, while not rare, do bring attractive prices.

So we turned the ram in sooner, that year. A fit ram is a remarkably libidinous creature who, penned apart from his ewes all summer, is so glad to finally see them that he scarcely pauses to eat until he's bred each one. This takes about two weeks, given the ovine estrus cycle and given a ratio of one ram to fifty ewes.

The lambs arrived on schedule, five months later. March, however, can still be winter in Vermont; we found ourselves wading through snowdrifts to the barn. Nights could get right down to zero. My neighbor dropped by to look the lamb crop over, and I told him: "Heck, if we've got to lamb in *this* weather, it might as well be February!"

"You still want those Easter lambs?"

"The price is going wild, this year. Dollar and twenty cents a pound. Liveweight."

"Live? Really?" This impressed him.

"It's kind of a special market — Greeks, Italians down in Boston. Easter is their Thanksgiving, see? The biggest feed of the year."

"Dollar and twenty liveweight," he repeated. "Look at that."

"They can't get enough of them."

"Good price. But not good enough, yet."

That year we sold fat lambs in July, except for some runty ones that didn't feed out till September. We took a beating on those. By now I was regularly engaging the services of Edward Lyman, a custom slaughterer, and Edward often brought Francis Corbett — an older shepherd from a nearby town — on lamb-killing days.

When I learned that Francis Corbett had kept sheep for forty years, I asked him what he thought of raising lambs for the Easter market.

"*Some* years, there's a dollar in it." Corbett chewed tobacco, and brown spittle dribbled down his cheek. "It mostly depends when's Easter."

"Oh?"

He spat at one of my dead lambs, even as he skinned it. "*Some* years, you get Easter way the hell back in March. Ever lambed in January?"

"No."

"Well, don't. Too damn cold. Everything can die. Still, when Easter comes too late, there's too many lambs around. Price drops."

I asked, "So you kind of have to aim for the middle?"

"Something else," he went on. "There's *two* Easters, know that? — regular and Greek. You can go after either one. Except they're both the same, some years."

"A moveable feast," I said.

"That's right. You've got it."

After talking with old Corbett, I went to the library and dug up Easter tables in a reference work. The old man had the picture: Easter is the first Sunday after the full moon on or after the vernal equinox, which means it can fall between March 22 and April 25. Greek Easter follows the exact same formula, but uses the Julian calendar rather than the Gregorian one. Both Easters *can* coincide; but they can also be as much as five weeks apart, with profound effect upon the supply and demand for Easter lambs.

The wily shepherds of New England start consulting calendars eight or nine months before Easter, to hit the brief but frenzied market with lambs of maximum profitability. Generally, feeders aiming at this market lose money on lambs weighing below forty pounds or much over fifty, and they feed these lambs for a market that disappears, without a trace, the day after Easter. It is a game of inches. There just is no more highly skilled branch of livestock production.

Some years, though — as Francis Corbett taught me — anyone can play. My third year at shepherding was such a year: Western Easter fell on April 16, and Greek Easter came a week later — late enough for lambs born the first of March to get into the action. But I recollected Corbett's warning: years when anyone can play, the price is apt to drop.

I formed a two-pronged strategy. I would turn the ram in on October first, lamb out the ewes the first of March, and feed their babies to beat hell. In a strong Easter market, I might unload the whole lamb crop; otherwise, they would certainly all fatten to conventional slaughter lamb weights by midsummer.

I marked all these dates on a calendar, thinking: "You sly Yankee, now you know the ropes." But one night — two weeks before October first — my ram demolished his pen of hardwood pallets, jumped two fences, and joined the sex-starved flock. I found him among them the next morning, delighting several ewes. "Stop that!" I commanded, but he wouldn't hear of it. Hours later, after an unequal struggle against nature, I hauled him back into the barn and slammed the door. I told my wife: "We may have some early lambs, next winter."

We had five of them — and they arrived in a record-breaking cold wave: ten straight days in which the mercury made it up to zero only once. I recorded nighttime lows: twenty-nine below, thirty-one below, thirty-four degrees below zero. Fahrenheit.

We expected lambs — and I comforted myself that, if they lived, it would prove we could raise Easter lambs in *any* year, oblivious to Julian calendars and moveable feasts. We expected lambs — but at, as my neighbor put it, "sixty-three degrees of frost," it's hard to drag oneself from bed to barn on speculation. One night I checked a quiet barn at midnight, but at dawn my wife found triplets: one frozen stiff, one with just a frozen leg, and one thriving in the sunshine of mother love.

"Mabel!" I scolded — Mabel was the ewe's name, not my wife's. "Mabel, how *could* you?"

Mabel could. She eyed me stubbornly, long past caring. She had lambed outside, incredibly, though all the sheep had access to the barn's dry shelter. Afterbirth lay frozen solid to the snow. I rushed the chilled lamb into the house, thawed its leg with a hair dryer and then returned it to Mabel. Her attitude was: "Listen, buddy, in this cold one lamb is plenty." But I taught the other one to grab a teat from time to time when Mabel wasn't paying attention, and we supplemented that with bottles every couple hours.

Lambs don't grow at thirty-one below; they just try to keep warm, and milk is all they have for fuel. Feeling bad about the lamb that froze, I checked the two survivors several times a night. And that is how, three nights later, I saw another ewe go into labor on the coldest night of winter. I would watch a few contractions, dash back to the house for warmth, and then go watch for a few more minutes. Five layers of clothing could not keep the cold out. The ewe passed a water bag — a sac of amniotic fluid; it broke on the straw and moments later my knees were frozen to the bedding. Finally, at dawn, she twinned.

From womb temperature — about one hundred degrees, in sheep — to thirty-four below is a thermal shock of the first order. The lambs' wet fleeces froze to their backs instantly. Ewes love to lick their lambs dry, building strong maternal bonds; this ewe, though, was not eager to lick two woolly popsicles. I apologized to her and raced the lambs into our kitchen, returning them dry and warm an hour later. Thank goodness, she recognized them. Both lived and thrived, and eventually made good as Easter feasts for unknown celebrants in Boston.

Unfortunately, though, the market did collapse. There *were* too many lambs around, as Francis Corbett had warned me. And there was an utterly unforeseeable market wrinkle: the near-nuclear disaster at Three Mile Island caused lamb feeders throughout Pennsylvania and nearby states to avoid the important Lancaster livestock auctions. They feared quarantine. So a flood of displaced lambs glutted the New England market, and prices fell from well over a dollar to as low as 80¢ a pound.

I tore up my calendar of moveable feasts. Having gone to all the trouble of producing Easter lambs, I wound up selling just ten out of sixty. Next time Corbett came to kill a few lambs, though, he was sanguine. "Too many players," he said. "Maybe next year — when's Greek Easter?"

"Don't ask me," I told him. "I'm out of that game." It was exactly as my neighbor had said: the price just can't get high enough to make it worth a person's while.

When we get a February blizzard, and a siege of cold, I sit in my rocking chair and read a book and watch the fire. And I think: Easter lambs are being born this very minute. Here in snowbound, picturesque Vermont. On someone *else's* farm. They will be delicious and expensive. And worth every penny.

• The Third Lamb

The shepherds of New England seem generally agreed, now, that the way to make sheep pay is to get more lambs per ewe per year. That is, to do whatever can be done to increase multiple births. Nationwide, about nine-tenths of a lamb is born each spring per ewe bred; but exotic breeds of sheep exist — particularly sheep from Finland — which reliably produce quadruplets.

Few sheepbreeders *want* quadruplets. Such lambs are apt to have low birth weights, look scrawny all their lives, and dress out poorly when they're slaughtered. Twins, though, are something else. Everyone wants twins. A simple way to get them is to cross-breed ordinary sheep with the prolific type — Finnsheep, we call them. I do this. It works. To average twins on a flockwide basis, though, a person has to deal with the odd set of triplets. This entails annual struggles with *maternity*, that grand and oceanic and mercurial instinct.

To point out the obvious, a ewe has two teats. *Only* two. That means just two baby lambs can nurse her at the same time. Where there is a third lamb, he will prosper only if he weighs about the same as his siblings and gets in there and fights. And only if his mother loves him.

I took motherlove for granted — what could be more natural, more purposeful, more *right*? — until the first time I saw a ewe fail, utterly, to accept one of her own lambs. This was several years ago. The lamb was a triplet, and its mother had a style, a demeanor, I would characterize as overly efficient and businesslike. Efficiently, businesslike, I found her beating this little product of her womb across the pen one morning with her thick, woolly, stubborn head, and bashing it against the barn wall.

I tend to anthropomorphize the behavior of my animals — a terrible weakness — so, after giving the lamb a slug of artificial milk, I sat right down and had a long chat with the ewe about maternal instinct. Soft tones, soothing strokes: "Stella," I cooed, *"that's your lamb!* You *made* that baby! Don't you just *love* it? Oh, you wouldn't want to *hurt* it! *Would* you?"

Bash! Thwack! Pow! I thought she'd break her little baby's ribs.

I was patient. I kept talking. And from time to time, I managed to sneak the lamb under the ewe's hindquarters for a hit of milk. Briefly, I'd keep mom distracted, but when ewes give suck they like to turn their heads and sniff the pretty *derrières* of who-ever's getting lunch. One whiff of this hapless, hated lamb's rear end, and the ewe's hind leg would lash out madly — bopping the lamb and neatly burying her teat in folds of flesh and wool.

After a good hour's effort at persuasion, I gave up. Life is too short, and time too dear in lambing season. Giving up on mother-love means having a lamb to bottle-feed for five weeks — a sweet but marginally profitable enterprise, at best. Every year we bottle-feed a few, for one cause or another; but it is demanding and ridiculously underpaid work. We no longer seek candidates.

MOTHER BASHES NEWBORN — this was headline stuff. It *bothered* me, as though it might have somehow been my fault. Some months later, thumbing through a livestock supply house catalog, I came upon a product in a spray can formulated to evoke motherlove. Aha! Other shepherds had encountered this same problem, and here was the answer to exasperated prayers. Spray this stuff onto a lamb, and mom goes wild. With *affection* — so the ad led me to think. Worked on lambs and calves and piglets, too. All-purpose.

That stuff must smell *good*, I thought. I sent right off to buy a can; when it came, I was surprised to find it hardly smelled at all. To me, at any rate. But I was willing to grant ewes, cows, and sows a more sophisticated nose than one mere human with a deviated septum.

Soon enough — next spring — I had another outright failure of maternal love. I smiled slyly at the recalcitrant ewe. "Wait till you just smell what *I've* got!" I promised her, going for the flashy spray can. *Fssst! Fssst!* I perfumed the unloved lamb, then present-ed her with it. For maybe one second, doubts flickered across her face. She eyed me suspiciously. Then she tossed her head and sent the still unaccepted lamb sprawling.

"Not only does this stuff not smell," I told my wife. "It doesn't *work*." She was unsurprised — this was not the first time I had bought the emperor's new clothes. Maybe, though, the spray had worked for others; maybe my sheep were more sensitive. Discri-minating. I could well believe that. I threw out that scentless perfume, but, in retrospect, I do not begrudge having purchased it. For it set my thinking in the right direction: urging love on a lamb-bashing ewe was not a matter of soft words, of offering her my reflections on maternal instinct. It was a matter of making the lamb smell right. The lamb smelled wrong; change that, and she might accept it. Mightn't she?

I sought the advice of another, more experienced breeder of prolific sheep. "Placenta," he advised me solemnly. "Listen: when you get triplets, wait for the placenta to come out. Just slather all three lambs with it — make 'em all red and gooey. That way, they should all smell alike."

Ewes *do* like their own placentas. Given opportunity, they'll usually try to *eat* them — notwithstanding that sheep are thoroughly herbivorous, while a placenta is a hunk of meat. Now, though, my wife and I started snitching ewes' placentas for our own purposes. Not only did they encourage maternal bonding at birth; we found that, even several days postpartum, a nice placental rubdown could alter a ewe's flagging acceptance of some little bugger.

Placentas can be handy; there's a problem with them, though. They typically are not expelled till several hours after birth — and that can be too late. For the unbonded lamb, and for the shepherd, too. Shepherds go home to bed. Shepherds need their sleep. By morning, though, a tardy placenta will have disappeared: eaten, or well-trampled into deep bedding. And the third lamb may be hungry.

Fretting over what else might be done, I had a stroke of genius. Lambs are born awash in amniotic fluid which the ewe presents in a membranous water bag. Rather than waste this hot liquor from the womb — rather than let it soak a patch of bedstraw — I began collecting each ewe's amniotic fluid in quart-sized freezer packs. I could number these to match each ewe's ear tag, then set them to one side. Any maternal difficulties later, and I had the heady goods to remind a mother of birth's splendor. Powerful persuasion. We lamb in March; an occasional freak thaw can render the "library" of catalogued placentas and uterine waters so much smelly goo. But when the weather runs our way — holding just around the freezing mark — the uterine fluids can be stored for days. With this tool at our disposal, mother-bonding problems here have been reduced to almost nil.

Advanced shepherding, however, expects a little more than getting mothers to love their own lambs. Experts can get ewes to love somebody *else's* lamb — a neat trick if there ever was one. Many times one wants to do this. A mother may die. Or contract mastitis and be unable to nurse. Or a ewe with twins may lose one. In the ideal lambing barn, such accidents are all adjusted by shunting lambs around: every mother winds up rearing two lambs, no more and no less.

In trying to foist lambs onto unnatural mothers, I found my high jinks with placentas and amniotic fluid were just about worthless. Even in tailor-made grafting situations. Once, I delivered triplets and a single lamb almost simultaneously; grafting off one triplet to create two sets of twins should not have been difficult. The lambs were perfect equals in size and in age, and I had fresh, still-warm uterine materials to work with. I swiped a triplet, swabbed it carefully with the membranes that had surrounded his intended sibling, and offered it to the ewe with my best poker face. "Congratulations, Emily!" I crowed. *"Twins!"*

Nothing doing. *Bash! Thwack!* Mothers know — they *know*. For several hours I persisted, fighting an ever-losing battle against child abuse. And then — when I gave up — the lamb's *real* mother wouldn't take him back. Know why? He didn't *smell* right — he smelled like the foster mom who wouldn't take him, either. Result: another bottle lamb.

After that debacle, I gave up trying to make ewes love somebody else's lamb and rested content with knowing I could make them love their own. But in the thick of a recent lambing season, a wise and seasoned shepherd — transplanted to Vermont from Australia — called me crack of dawn, one morning. "Got a mess of triplets?" he inquired.

"Too many, as usual."

"I've just had a bad night. Fine ewe gave me twins, and both died. They got tangled up inside."

"Bad luck," I sympathized.

"Never mind that. Lad, I thought I'd bring the ewe down to you — you can stick a couple of your triplets onto her. She's got *pots* of milk. If she's not nursed out, she'll get infected sure."

"Wait. You mean, you'd —" I thought he'd gone crazy. "This can't work," I told him. "Not with my lambs."

"What won't work?"

"This foster mother business. God knows I've tried it. Won't work with my *own* sheep, much less with some ewe you want to truck here, after —"

"It'll work, lad. I know how! Don't you worry, it'll work!"

I sighed. "All right. Bring her down here."

They arrived, shepherd and ewe, a good ten hours later. He'd been right: the ewe was fairly bursting with milk. She was wild-eyed, and no wonder, arriving here at a strange farm, with a strange flock, fresh from an obstetric nightmare. The ewe was strong, and strained angrily against the leash her owner had fashioned for her out of used baling twine.

We pulled her into the barn, pushed her in a pen, and then the Australian tied her head up snug. I could smell defeat already. "I suppose," I said, "you'd like a couple of newborns? So she'll maybe think they're her own lambs?"

"Newborns?" He laughed. "Who wants newborns, lad? Get me something *hungry!*"

So we toured the barn and found two triplets, each about three weeks of age. Twenty-pounders. We set them in the pen with his ewe, and she stamped and kicked and growled as though she'd kill them. "No!" the shepherd shouted, and he smacked her muscled shoulder. Hard. She calmed; seconds later, he deftly plugged one of the lambs onto a teat. She strained again, but then relief at being milked complicated her emotions. She turned to sniff the lamb but couldn't. Because her head was tied.

The shepherd plugged the other lamb onto a teat. Again, the ewe kicked blindly. "No!" he roared, and smacked her again. Soon both lambs were virtually purring, full of milk for the first time in their lives. The ewe seemed fairly cowed — for the time being, anyway.

"She's big and strong," her owner assured me. "She can stand a bit of beating."

"What — am *I* supposed to beat her?"

He loosened up her halter, just enough that she could stoop to eat hay and drink water from a pail. "Keep her tied like this for six days. Feed her well, too. For the first three days, every time you come into the barn make her nurse these lambs. *Make* her, understand? And then, on the fourth day, just stand at the barn door and scream at her. She ought to nurse them for you. After six days, untie her — by then, I'll wager you she loves her lambs."

I did as he told me — it was his ewe, after all, and I was helping her avoid mastitis. I hit her, yes, and screamed my lungs out at her as he'd taught me. And after six days, she loved them as a mother. For five months she nursed those foster lambs — never

let them leave her sight, in fact — and one of those lambs became my best-grown for the year.

Maternity is lovely, when it works. It is an awesome force. Maternal hatred, though, can be equally powerful. Whether mothers have a right to refuse maternal bonding — to bash lambs — I do not know. But having tried the full gamut of encouragements to maternal love, I know that nothing worked so well as when an expert licensed me to bash his ewe right back.

• Deadpan

Arriving at the barn one midsummer morning to perform my daily chores, I found my prize ram loitering about, dull-eyed and droopy-eared. Sick — or under the weather, at any rate. He had been turned out with the ewes, as usual when it was not breeding season, but the ewes were off grazing far away. Sheep do not hang out alone unless there's something vastly wrong.

What to do? I looked him over. No injuries, no lameness. No fever, no cough or runny nose. Nothing for a veterinarian to look at, really. So like any self-respecting keeper of livestock nowadays, I went to get the penicillin bottle and dispensed a shot. This is, arguably, terrible medicine — a paradigm of treatment in the absence of a diagnosis. But it scarcely costs a nickel, and sometimes a vet will charge a good fifteen dollars to do nothing more. By afternoon the ram was back on pasture, and I felt damn smart.

Next morning, though, he looked sick again. His stomach had bloated out. More penicillin brought negligible results; that afternoon, I confined him to a pen where he stood trembling and gasping for each breath. Now, finally, I was scared. A flock sire ram is a valuable animal, chosen to be half the gene pool for every single lamb. Mine was looking like a goner; it was time to call the doctor.

When a vet comes to my place, I try to get my money's worth from him in education. This is never easy, for the taciturn Vermonter rarely volunteers information. It has to be mined. So, while the good man took my ram's temperature and looked him over, I pumped him with questions. Why wasn't Mister Right eating? Why wasn't he chewing on his cud, or even passing dung? Why, if he was so sick, wouldn't he even lie down? Was his nose perhaps too hot? Too cold? Finally, the vet grabbed his stethoscope and plugged it in his ears, as much to shut me off as to listen to the animal's heaving chest.

"Acts quite poisoned," he pronounced. "Must have eaten something."

"Such as?"

He gestured toward the pasture. "Any wild laurel out there? Lamb kill? Chokecherry?"

"No. None."

"Well, his digestive system's shut right down. That's no joke, with four stomachs."

I said, "I've got lactating ewes out there, and growing lambs — sheep that are *working. Hard.* And this guy's the only freeloader in the bunch. He's got it easy. So why him?"

"Don't know."

"Any treatment?"

"Treat the symptoms, I guess. That's all I can do."

His symptomatic treatment was a half cup of medication poured down a vein in the animal's neck. A mildly bloody procedure. "What's that stuff?" I asked him. "What are you giving him?"

"Calcium gluconate. With dextrose, and electrolytes."

I wrote this down for future reference; he watched me, amused. Then he dosed the ram's stomach with a sort of veterinary Pepto-Bismol. "Well?" I asked. "You think he may recover?"

"He's awful far gone."

"Sorry. I should have called you sooner."

"Well, you might have. Anyway — by morning, he'll be much improved or dead. If he's living — if your ram's still living, call me back."

I watched him pack his things and climb back in his pickup truck.

For a would-be Yankee, I used to take such reverses in the farming business pretty hard. I stood patting the ram's nose and making helpless apologies to him; I had not yet adopted the true, flinty ethos up here which dictates that one show no sentiment at such times. One might cuss, or spit at the barn wall, or lapse into bitterly sarcastic thoughts. Rather than commiserate with the sick creature, though, one simply tries to make it as comfortable as possible. One does not cry; one tries to do something useful.

I tried to think how my neighbors would respond to such a tragedy. If my ram, say, were their bull. I did recall seeing a cow milk blood in a dairy barn, a couple years earlier. The herdsman milking the cow did not break down and bawl. "Strawberry shake!" he muttered. Then he threw the milk away, disinfected all the milking tools, and led the cow off to a makeshift sick pen.

A few days later, I happened to be back there when a vet came to see the cow. By now, each one of her teats resembled a fevered, cankered, warty fist. The vet looked them over, nonchalant, and asked the farmer's herdsman how the cow was milking.

"Fifteen thousand."

"Fifteen thousand *what*?" I inquired.

"Pounds of milk. A year."

"Good calves?" asked the vet.

"Real good."

The vet knelt by her udder and took what appeared to be a pane of dark glass from his satchel. Then he gently stripped milk from each teat onto it, for examination. From the first teat came a dribble of pus. The second ran red blood. The third, with firm coaxing, squirted a thick green whipping cream. The fourth — but by this time I had clutched my stomach and half-shut my eyes — gave out a stringy brown goo.

Impassive, the vet carried over the samples to show us. I was appalled; the hired man showed absolutely no emotion. Then he asked, deadpan: "Is that where they get yo-gurt from?"

The vet kept his lips shut tight, but his eyes crinkled. He enjoyed a joke, plainly. "Let me get her temperature." While he rummaged for his rectal thermometer, they discussed the pros and cons of medication. Penicillin, like most veterinary antibiotics, carries a thirty-day withdrawal time before slaughter. If the cow were medicated but died anyway, the carcass would be condemned. If she were *not* medicated, and slaughtered promptly, part of the farmer's loss could be recouped in meat.

I was fascinated. "You mean," I asked, "if you medicate her, she had better live?"

"Else we get a new vet," the hired man said.

The vet chuckled. "Running quite a fever," he announced. "All right, I'm going to give her a bottle. Pull her head up nice and snug, will you?"

We did. The vet took a quart of something from his kit, and fitted its mouth with a rubber hose. Then he poked a needle in the cow's neck — she squirmed violently — and pushed the hose onto it to drain medicine into the cow.

"What's that stuff?" the hired man asked — but not the way I'd posed the same question. Not for knowledge.

"Swamp water after the rain. You like a sip?"

The hired man's eyes laughed exactly as the doctor's had, but his lips stayed pressed together. When the bottle had drained out, the vet withdrew his apparatus. We untied the cow. Immediately she went down upon her knees, then on her side. Then she lay motionless, as though down for the count.

"God*damn*, doc. I *said* we ought to take her to the butcher. No one listens to me. Should have tied her up right by the barn door — who do you think's going to have to drag her out of here?"

"Take her out in pieces," the vet suggested.

"And get my chainsaw all bloody?"

"Honest, I believe she'll make it." The cow moaned now, faintly. "Anyway, I've got my truck all tuned up for a getaway." He packed his bag, promised to return next day, and started for the door.

The cow lay groaning regularly now, on the damp barn floor. The herdsman set off to get clean bedding for her, and fresh hay.

That cow recovered — I would wager she is milking still — in spite of having been the butt of dry Yankee wit, of appalling gallows humor. Calcium gluconate caused her to survive, perhaps, but calling it swamp water was a way of survival, too — for her keepers, who, day in and day out, have learned to care and keep caring somehow or other.

Visiting my ailing ram at nervous intervals to see if he were alive or dead, I realized the sanity of my neighbors' attitudes — and realized how ineffectual were my emotional wallowings. I stopped having little heart-to-heart talks with my sick animal and concentrated instead on making him comfortable. Clean water. Salt. The most attractive hay I had to offer. Evening came, then dark; his condition changed not one bit, but I smiled grimly, spread new bedding, and went to sleep.

In the morning, he was still alive. I called the vet right up. "Hey, he hasn't died!" I shouted in the phone, exuberant.

"No?"

"He's breathing better. And the bloat's gone, too."

"Is he eating?"

"No."

"Any droppings?"

"No. But —"

"Okay. I'll be out to see him."

By the time the vet arrived, my newly prized animal was nibbling hay. And producing dung again — never have I greeted manure so happily. The doctor wrestled another dose of antacid down the ram's throat, and poked him with a parting shot of penicillin. Just for luck.

"When's he got to breed something?" asked the vet.

"A couple months yet."

"Shouldn't have much trouble."

"Well, my hat's off — you sure saved his life."

"Only by gosh and gum." He shrugged. "Take two aspirin, call me in the morning."

"If you wake, that is," I added, deadpan.

"That's right." He smiled at me, eyes only. Deadpan.

• Love Without Fear

Nothing makes a hobby farmer feel more professional than being called to help out some *worse* hobby farmer in a pinch. Then, for once, one is an expert. Toward someone else's situation, one can exhibit cool savvy and hard commercial attitudes that are, strangely, never applied to one's own operation. Hobby farmers long to have their efforts taken seriously by real, profit-oriented tillers of the soil; still, the respect of fellow hobby farmers often has to do.

So I always hurry to the aid of a distant neighbor on a mountain several miles away. He lives with some fifteen sheep, a dozen chickens, three goats, two peacocks, and a llama. That's right, a llama — one of those overlooked ruminants that he feels deserves a place in North American agriculture. I don't know from llamas, but this fellow only calls me when some sheep requires intensive care. I get a drink or two, an hour's pleasant conversation, and then I drive home to *my* hobby farm feeling like a real farmer.

One cold February morn, a couple years ago, he called me in a breathless frenzy. "Julie is in labor!" he said nervously. "She's trying to lamb!"

"That's a problem?"

"Julie's *stitched!*"

"She's what?"

"My vet came out to stitch her up, a couple weeks ago. Otherwise, she's apt to prolapse when she goes in labor."

Now, I was no stranger to the cruel phenomenon called prolapse. Out of every thousand ewes, one or two will fail to keep their reproductive tracts from turning inside out and spilling all across the barn floor when their hour of deliverance is come. This makes a memorable mess, but a hastily summoned vet can wash the several organs off and tuck them back where they belong; the ewe then gets to raise her lamb and, once she has weaned it, prepares to be rendered mutton. Few shepherds anywhere would risk keeping a ewe who prolapsed — she would be all too likely to repeat the experience.

So I asked my colleague: "What makes you think she'll prolapse?"

"Because she did last year. Year before, she *almost* did — but I had her C-sectioned."

"Really??" Now, the cost of C-sectioning a ewe has to dwarf any conceivable value that her lambs might have. "Julie," I observed, "seems to be more trouble than she's worth."

"I *like* Julie."

"Okay. Have you called the vet back?"

"Tried to — but he's busy. Some emergency. A cow."

"Don't know how much I can do," I said. "But I'll be right over."

Julie was not, in my expert opinion, in labor. Or perhaps one look at my unsympathetic face squelched her effort at contractions. She turned me a baleful eye, then sauntered off; sure enough, her female parts had been sutured shut with what looked like a length of old shoelace. She would have exploded before lambing past *that*.

"I could check her cervix," I suggested. "To see if she's ready. But I'd have to cut those stitches."

"She may spill out on the spot!"

"Well — what did your vet expect?"

"He said to call him when she goes in labor. He'll come get her, then, and take her into town for another C-section."

"What's he charge for that?" I wondered out loud.

"Hundred thirty-five."

I would like to place this figure in perspective. A *good* ewe — one who, for example, never prolapsed — *might* be worth $135. In a good year, she might produce that much in the gross income from twin lambs. The *net* on that gross, though, would be closer to thirty bucks. Sectioning a single ewe could wipe out all potential profits from keeping five *good* ones for an entire year.

"Sheep like this must cost you plenty," I said.

"I *like* my sheep." Julie turned to bat her eyes at him, gratefully, and I thought: Hell, no use fighting over keeping sheep as pets. I felt great — *I* was the real farmer, for a change. He was to me as I am to my neighbor dairymen. Pet sheep, pet llama — *I* was a *commercial sheepman*. So I could be big about this.

I said: "Fine. I understand. I like sheep, too."

Just then, a veterinary pickup truck roared up the driveway. The vet had been summoned here next by two-way radio. I helped him tote his cases over to the barn and watched him size up Julie.

"Wouldn't say she's working very hard, yet," he drawled. "But I might as well take her in. Lamb inside there should be close to term."

Julie's owner nodded, visibly relieved. And then he had a brainstorm. "Doctor? I've been sort of thinking. While you've got her cut open this time, could you also do a hysterectomy?"

I slapped a hand across my mouth to keep from grinning foolishly. Because, as nearly everybody knows, the value of a farm animal is quite closely related to efficient reproductive function. No room for barren females. But the vet — who knew his client — deadpanned masterfully. He scratched his head. "Gee," he said, "I don't think I've ever seen a ewe hysterectomized."

"You *haven't*?" The owner's voice was mildly enraged at this admission of inexperience.

"Don't see why I couldn't try it, though."

So we loaded Julie onto his truck and saw her off on her annual surgical trip into town. "How's *that* for professional incompetence?" the owner snorted once the vet was down the road. "Guy calls himself a large-animal doctor, says he's been trained to work on sheep — but he's never even seen a hysterectomy!"

"Most folks," I gently suggested, "wouldn't *want* a ewe who couldn't breed."

"No? What would they do?"

"They'd *eat* her."

"People are so goddamn heartless," he said. "I *like* Julie."

Julie had been carrying twins — twin ewes, even — but they died of prematurity. Not her fault, of course. And then, after years of dubious production, Julie became the only hysterectomized ewe in my acquaintance.

Some months later, quite by chance, I learned about a hot new strategy for synchronizing conception in a flock of sheep. Getting ewes to breed all at once — in a single heat cycle — can shorten a shepherd's typical lambing season from six weeks to three, with consequent savings in exhaustive obstetric labor. Well worth the effort. And the trick to pulling off this feat, experimental work had shown, was making timely use of a vasectomized ram.

Vasectomized. Surgically.

I had to laugh, at first, thinking this was just some new, expensive version of castration. Male lambs raised for meat are very often castrated — by a simple, non-surgical procedure involving a variety of essentially blunt instruments. And *castrati*, not surprisingly, tend to have reduced libidos — not a trait of obvious value in a breeding program. My initial impression was mistaken, however; vasectomy really was a sophisticated tool. Vasectomized rams apparently retained normal sex drive and function; they simply could not "settle" ewes.

The system works like this: an aggressive shepherd finds a particularly horny and well-grown ram lamb, and whisks him off to the vet. For $135, more or less, the vet removes a section of each *vas deferens* from the animal's testicles. Now, two weeks before the shepherd wants to breed his ewes, he sends this harmless fellow into their midst to get them all hot and bothered. Then, on day fifteen, out comes the sterile ram and in goes Mister Right. The happy ewes line up to greet him.

I don't have a big conception problem with the sheep I raise, but I know someone who did. Julie's proud owner has been known to lamb his fifteen ewes out over a ten-week stretch — a numbing season of midnight barn checks in sub-zero cold. So I told him, when I heard this nifty idea, that he needed a vasectomized ram for his flock.

He thought I was making fun of him. "Vasectomized. You mean, a ram to go along with Julie?"

"No. A ram to get all your *other* ewes steamed up. Every one ovulating at the same time." And, as I explained this to him, he began to nod his head. Seemed to be a good idea. I urged him on until, plainly interested, he picked up the telephone and called his veterinarian. Could he make a date to bring a ram in for vasectomy?

I could just imagine the doctor on the other end, fighting to preserve composure. "I don't think," the vet said carefully, "I've ever *seen* a ram vasectomized."

"You haven't?!" The man raised his voice. "But this is the latest thing!"

"Don't see why I couldn't try, though."

So my fellow hobby farmer now owns a pair of sheep who can love without fear. And do. They seem to recognize that they are — well, not exactly *made* for each other. *Altered* for each other, I suppose. As for the other ewes, they drop their lambs now right on schedule. All at once. A nice, tight group.

That's the week when I leave town.

• Advanced Lambing Facilities

Lambing out one's entire flock of ewes in a single, tight group in the middle of winter does make good sense. Parasites and pathogens are relatively dormant, and the shepherd has few other chores competing for his time. Deep-winter lambing, though, requires a depth of masochism that this shepherd, anyway, has difficulty summoning forth from his peaceable psyche. This shepherd, for example, just hates being cold. Hates to be perpetually drowsy for three weeks straight. Hates to have to wear clothes caked with freeze-dried amniotic fluid — a potent starch — for days on end. Over time, such conditions can dampen anyone's enthusiasm for the miracle of birth.

A couple of years ago, with lambing season imminent, I had a minor stroke of genius. I designed and built a portable, heatable, perinatal suite out in the barn. Four feet by five, it boasted nearly full headroom and a roof that could pop out to spill postpartum humidity. Insulated walls. Wired for bright lights, hair dryer, and FM radio. Shelves for obstetric tools, lubricants, and towels.

This facility made winter lambing almost tolerable. When a ewe was well advanced in labor, I would usher her into the suite and manage the delivery in high-tech comfort — punk rock blaring day and night over the anxious grunts and cries of parturition. And, when no births were expected for a few hours, the shepherd himself could sprawl in that warm booth and take a snooze.

Problem was, those snoozes could be difficult to rouse myself from. With the door shut tight, I could not hear or see what the expectant ewes outside were up to. Finding out was something of an effort — it meant getting up, and it meant getting cold. I *hate* that. And so, more than once, I slept right through births where a shepherd's care might have prevented outcomes less than happy. With the shepherd crashed out in it, this new obstetric facility sometimes proved more liability than asset.

So, last February, facing fully a hundred ewes to lamb out in a three-week frenzy, I got another brainstorm. The portable birthing room would now be exactly that; I would build an additional, permanent office for human comfort elsewhere in the barn. With observation windows. To save space — and to isolate this civilized improvement from manure and muck and mud — I decided to suspend it from the rafters of the barn. Six feet off the floor, with ladder access: high and dry.

It took a solid week of cold-weather carpentry, but I completed this suspended office before the first ewe dropped her lambs. This overhead compartment — "cocoon," I called it — measured only six feet by ten, and its severe roof pitch limited head room in most of that modest space. Nonetheless, it felt marvellously spacious, on account of its one glass wall perched over two thousand square feet of pregnant, ruminating sheep. If a shepherd could but keep his eyes propped open, labor on the barn floor below would not escape his notice.

I furnished my cocoon with a real bed, easy chair, desk, and coffeemaker, too. And a hotplate. Typewriter. Stereo, bookshelves, clothes hooks. And — of course — I had a heater competent to warm that tiny room in any weather. In fact, the cocoon had everything except a wet bar. And except a door that could be latched and unlatched from both inside and out.

This last point proved significant. On each side of the office door, I mounted barrel bolt-type locks to hold it tight against its frame, preventing heat loss. I *hate* heat loss. But I had not quite foreseen how having the cocoon would change our lambing habits, which now heavily involve my wife and my wife's mother as well as me. Both of these intrepid women manage four-hour shifts at lambing; each can handle routine births, and each wakes me for what is *not* routine. Waking me used to mean a mad dash to the house, but thanks to the new cocoon I now can sleep at arm's length from the obstetric action. A distinct improvement.

At first, entering the office to snatch forty winks, I would lock myself in; but then no one else could enter to relax and warm up without disturbing me to unlock the door. This made for troubled sleep. Soon enough, I learned to let my wife or her mother lock *me* in — from the *out*side — so that they could come and go at will. If they encountered problems downstairs in the birthing room, they would climb to the cocoon, unlock the door and rouse me.

Ten days into lambing, though, the sleep I get is mighty

sound. I can be quite hard to rouse. My wife's mother claims she burst into the office late one night — at midnight, say — and shook me. "Help!" she cried. "I've got a head! No legs!"

"I love you," she reports that I replied. From Dreamland. "I love your legs. I love your dark eyes, your lips —"

"Head!! No legs!! Come help me!!"

"And I love your tiny feet —"

She threw something at me in the cocoon. "Wake up!"

I stumbled down the ladder, pushed that lamb's head back into the womb and found its legs and snaked the thing out without even waking up. Can't recall ever stirring from my bed of bliss.

Twenty minutes later — my wife's mother alleges — she was back. Excited. "Twins! Sorry to bother you again, but — this one's just a tail."

This time I was not plighting my affection to some succubus or other. I stirred and murmured: "Push the butt in, find the hind feet. Pull the lamb out quick."

"You can't sleep through this!"

"Look," I said. "It's only life and death. I'm awfully tired. Give it your best shot."

"Get up! Get that lamb out!"

Again, I can't recall a thing. But I am told I made another descent to the chamber of obstetric horrors. I am told I pulled the breeched lamb in something like five seconds, dropped it by its twin and climbed back into bed. I never woke.

Sometime later, though, I did wake. Shrieks were coming from below. "Triplets!! Hurry — oh, my God!! There's two feet and then — just a neck!"

I left bed, irate, and got as far as the door to the cocoon. It was locked, of course. From the outside.

"Hurry, please!! Get down here!"

"Not so fast," I hollered back. "I'm locked in. Remember?"

There was a pregnant pause. I saw the door to the obstetric suite shake in its frame, and then I saw something else. My wife's mother wailed: "*I'm* locked in, too!"

It was true. The door to the obstetric suite has a simple latch that can be lifted from both sides. But ewes pacing around the barn had managed to knock a hardwood construction pallet — used as a partition — against the door. It was wedged quite cunningly in place, and that was that. She was stuck, and I was stuck,

The Husbandry of Sheep **77**

and she became hysterical. Nobody would miss us until breakfast, either.

"Help!! Help!!" She rattled the walls. "What do I do?"

"May as well try to get that lamb out."

"How?"

"Find some baling twine," I said. "Up on the shelf. Tie a length of it around each foot. Then push the whole thing *way* back in — that head's bent down beneath the chest, most likely. Haul it up, okay? Then trace that twine back to find the front legs again. It should come right out."

"I can't do that!"

"May as well try. To pass the time, you know? You need any more advice, I'll just be up here snoozing."

"Don't you dare!"

I smiled. "Night-night." But she couldn't hear me.

Some time later, shouts awakened me again. "Eeeek!! It's — it's quadruplets!!"

I pressed my face against the glass. "Get that last one out?" I shouted down.

"Yes, I did. He's fine."

"Good. I'm proud of you."

"This one's — oh, no. Oh, no."

"Tell me what you feel."

"No head. No legs. No tail. Just a — just a back, I think. A backbone."

"Damn," I said. "Now *that's* a tough one."

"Any bright ideas?"

"You're not going to get that out," I told her. "Too bad. We can't win 'em all."

"Maybe you should smash that glass up there. Break out and help me."

"Wait a minute! Wait! The roof!"

"You can't —"

"*Your* roof!" I told her. "I built it so it pops right out — to spill humidity. Can you push it up?"

"I — yes!"

"Climb up on those shelves, then." From my perch, I saw the roof lift off the birthing room and slide to one side. I saw my mother-in-law clamber out. Minutes later I was soaped up, executing deft maneuvers in a womb as deep as my arm is long.

The fourth lamb tumbled out. Alive.

"Good night's work," I told my shaken assistant. "Pretty exciting, huh?"

She looked at me. "That office door," she said, "had better get a proper latch."

Advanced lambing facilities have — beyond my wildest hopes — brought a measure of comfort and efficiency to our annual lambing chore. And, for one who hates the cold, they have made mid-winter lambing actually tolerable. But I never guessed what *else* they would afford this jaded midwife: the primordial, indescribable sensation of being holed up — trapped — *stuck* within the womb.

CHAPTER THREE

The Wrong Crops

W HEN I UNDERTOOK TO TRY TO PASS
for a Vermont farmer, I knew next to
nothing about the financial dynamics
of farm enterprises. Like many in this happy state of bliss, I used to
publicly mourn the loss of an idealized diversified family farm in
favor of highly focused, highly efficient, single-product agricultural businesses. Milk producers, corn producers, pork producers,
wheat producers, egg producers, broiler producers, soybean producers — what a tragedy, I would maintain, that single, family-
based agricultural units no longer tried to amalgamate many of
these elements as they had in days of yore. Why this obsessive and
stultifying specialization?

As I watched my neighbor farmers go about their busy lives, I
found abundant evidence that this disease of monoculture had
plainly undercut the fabled quality of rural life. Why, I knew dairy
farmers who no longer planted gardens! There was just no time to
waste on so inefficient and labor-intensive a chore as growing
one's own vegetables. Dropping by at dinnertime, I was as apt to
see these men and women of the soil sit down to a frozen pizza or
canned spaghetti as to a table groaning with farm-fresh, home-

grown victuals. Their children would snack on cheese doodles and Kool-Aid. Should the supermarkets fold, should the truckers go on strike, these farmers were not much more likely to survive than the hordes of urban parasites who produce not one scrap of the food they consume each day. True, the dairy farmer would have milk. And bargain hamburg, too. But the cornucopia of real, honest nourishment that would have graced the table of my mythopoetic Yankee farmer is rarely found today, and getting rarer all the time.

Even as I focused my own efforts toward building a sheep enterprise of sound, commercial scale, I vowed to fight the tide. Chickens and ducks would poke around *my* barnyard, and I would grow the grain that fed them. There would be a pig, too, turning sundry garbage into bacon and pink hams. Honey and maple syrup would sweeten our fare; we could even plant some buckwheat to produce pancakes without patronizing Aunt Jemima. I would resurrect an agricultural past: as a farmer, when it came to food, I deserved to have it all.

Nowadays, however, I grow sheep. And very little else.

Looking back, I feel I did make conscientious efforts to grow quite a diversified array of farm products. Heroic efforts, on occasion. And I've come to feel that if a person truly wants to grow, say, eggplants — even in Vermont! — it's possible to find a way. But what is resoundingly, stunningly impossible is finding any way of making eggplant production — or a host of other interesting crops — worth a Vermonter's while.

Agriculture is a high-volume, low-margin business. It's damn hard to turn a profit even when one has the advantages of specialization and economic scale; without these advantages, one is doomed to red ink. A reasonably well-heeled and thoughtful devotee of farming might still choose this course: might raise, as I did, pork and eggs and many other staples at substantially greater cost than they could be obtained for at the Grand Union. But in my case, at any rate, these ventures proved incompatible with my larger project of trying to make credible my new agrarian *persona*. Even to myself, as though the neighbors didn't matter. Eggs that cost me 80¢ each to produce created, in this context, a terrible psychic burden.

Out of the universe of edible substances, relatively few have found a stable niche in human diets. Out of the universe of foods that humans choose to eat, few indeed can be wisely recommended for Vermont farmers to produce. And out of that *small* universe, fewer still proved appropriate for *me* to try producing.

But before I learned these hard facts, I squandered much time and effort — money, too — fooling with what must be characterized as The Wrong Crops.

I. ANIMAL

• Chickens

It was my wife who really hankered to keep some ducks, once we had established ourselves as aspiring Yankees. But every Vermonter she discussed the idea with asked her if she had kept chickens. "No," she said, "should I?" Though people up here hate to *tell* another what to do, she got the clear impression that chickens were a sort of beginner's duck. A starting place for novices at the game of Fowl.

There are many kinds of chickens, and we soon learned that they all possess a characteristic bug-eyed, hyperactive stare. I think this must be because, more than other creatures, chickens have borne the brunt of genetic engineering by wily humans bent on getting more for less. In today's world, the poultry farmer needs to know *exactly* how many grams of feed will yield a jumbo egg or a pound of flesh. And today's breeders can deliver.

In fact, as erstwhile farmsteaders, the more we learned about modern chickens, the more we found these superbirds repugnant. Why, they didn't even have *names*, unless one considers something like SX-274 a name. I consider Barred Rock a name. Or White Leghorn. But "Mini ®"? These birds were nothing more than units of production — only incidentally living creatures — in vast, inhuman egg factories where everything could be quantified to the *nth* degree.

The more we learned, the more we yearned to acquire some nice, old-fashioned birds and help them to become even more old-fashioned. Something big and hardy — feed conversion be damned — something independent and well enough adapted to go foraging around the barnyard, supplementing grain feed with ordinary scratch. And furthermore, as against the laboratory breeds that must be engineered specifically for egg production or for meat, we wanted to find birds that could go both ways, so to speak. Dual-purpose birds.

Eventually, we latched onto a mail order source for "day-old" Rhode Island Red chicks, which seemed to meet our main desiderata nicely. They were even a brown-egg breed, which suits eccentric local taste. There are many other ways to start a modest flock of chickens; one can purchase fertile eggs, at one extreme, or somebody else's over-the-hill layers at the other. We thought it sensible to purchase day-old chicks. Fifty of them. Someone else had done the tricky job of incubation; we would undertake the work and risk of actually raising the birds.

Chickens of acknowledged dual-purpose breeds afford a certain price advantage, since demand exists for males and females alike. In contrast, males of the superlayer breeds are offed as day-old chicks, because they are not apt to feed out into broilers profitably. Superlayer chicks, then, are relatively dearer — since only half the incubated eggs produce a marketable product.

How are day-old chicks sexed? — i.e., how can one tell the difference? In the "sex-linked" breeds, it is quite easy: males are one color, females another. But many breeds, including Rhode Island Reds, are not sex-linked. Enter the chicken sexer, a highly skilled professional who spreads a day-old chick's cloaca and sees there what no one else can. After three days, even *he* can't see it, and differentiation is impossible until secondary sex characteristics manifest themselves. At six to ten weeks, say.

Six to ten weeks is six to ten weeks too long to feed males of the superlayer breeds. The poultryman would take a bath. So the chicken-sexer chucks all cockerels into a trash bin, and at day's end they are ground up for hog feed. However, with dual-purpose breeds such as Rhode Island Reds, cockerels can be sold. For less than baby hens. Much less. It turned out we could order day-old chicks three ways: unsexed, i.e. "as hatched"; guaranteed females; or guaranteed males. Here are prices we were quoted on a lot of fifty chicks:

> As-hatched: $36.   (72¢ each)
> All pullets (♀):$51.   ($1.02 each)
> All cockerels (♂):$25.   (50¢ each)

"What is that — a sucker bet?" my wife asked.

"No, wait a minute." I pulled out a calculator. Something about dealing with chickens, I learned early on, just *demands* quantification on the part of humans; I was eager to apply shrewd Yankee parsimony to this new agricultural venture. "Look," I showed her. "If we buy fifty chicks as-hatched and get an even break on sexes, we come out two dollars ahead over buying the same birds sexed."

She was, rightly, skeptical. "What if you draw thirty cockerels and only twenty pullets?"

I punched the figures in. "We'd lose only sixty cents. But if the division breaks the *other* way —" I hit the buttons, salivating. "Then we gain four dollars and sixty cents."

"What's the *mu*?" she asked. "What's the *sigma*?" My wife is smart.

"The hell?"

"Never took Statistics?"

"The hell with your abstractions," I said. "I'm talking cash, here. Net."

Needless to say, I talked her into unsexed chicks. "As-hatched." On the day they came, I spread a few cloacae and felt confident we'd done okay. Beaten the system. But the weeks went by — six weeks, ten weeks — and things began to get much noisier around the barnyard, come the crack of dawn. Lots of big combs, big wattles. Lots of fancy strutting. Finally, we tallied up: forty-one cocks, nine hens.

"That's some *mu*," commented my wife. "Some *sigma*."

"Obviously," I complained, "someone sexed those chicks. And screwed us."

But I could prove nothing, and for all I knew some luckier tightwad garnered forty-one hens and just nine cocks for the same money. At any rate, I said, it now behooved us to get accomplished at throwing chicken dinners.

I have read that Frank Perdue owns a slaughtering facility which birds enter, shackled, at one end, on conveyor belts, to emerge at the other end killed, scalded, plucked, and dressed with packaged giblets tucked inside — all untouched by human hands. If true, that is a nifty trick. The first cockerel *we* offed required four and one-half hours to get from roost to oven, and that's a major diseconomy for hungry people. Plus the process made the kitchen stink so badly that we had to dine *alfresco*. Long after dark.

With practice, though, we got our time down to something reasonable. We commenced inviting hapless friends to supper on the homestead, and after a couple of drinks we'd stroll out to the chicken coop to choose the entrée. This forged, no doubt, some lasting impressions; but in those days we were proud — political, in fact — about the life-choices that had brought us to a place where we could raise our own meat.

In the farmstead folklore I was reared on, one kills a chicken by laying its head down on a broad oak stump and chopping through the neck with a sharpened hatchet. *Thunk!* One chop. Early in our run of forty-one chicken dinners, however, I learned that this chopping was not easy. Our cocks seemed to understand quite well what I had in mind when I aimed an ax at them; they would twist and squirm and crane their necks wildly. I didn't, after all, want to miss their heads and lop my hand off, but I came close enough one night to give me cause for fright.

By now, I had lived upcountry long enough to know that when a person has this kind of problem, someone else has had it, too. And no doubt knows some good solution. So I went to ask a neighbor: "How do you hold a chicken still to chop its head off?"

"Wring its neck," he said. Of course.

"How?"

He made a little wrenching gesture with his hands, but then he told me of another, easier way. For youthful birds, like mine. "Just grab the whole thing by the throat and swing it once around. Over your head. In a big circle." He demonstrated this with an ary bird: like a single revolution of an airplane propeller. "You do that, and you'll just *feel* the neck stretch," he assured me. "Stuns it real good."

I'm always amazed at how much knowledge in the fundamental arts of rural living is available merely for the asking. I went home, and swung a chicken round, and lopped its head off smartly. People were impressed.

Trouble is, you can't eat forty-one cockerels in a week or two. It takes months, with any sort of dietary vision, and in those months the birds kept growing bigger. Tougher. Feistier. The evening came when a cock, swung once around my head, would have a perfectly intact neck. Very well — I'd take a second whirl and let the G's build up. Next week, though, it took *three* whirls.

Finally, inevitably, the evening came when three revolutions had not wrung a bird's neck. Dear friends from Boston were our dinner guests, and after a survey of the barnyard — drinks in hand — they looked upon me as a sort of Mister Natural. A man accomplished at things rural. Very well; I sent a bird ascending on its fourth revolution. Suddenly, its fattened body separated altogether from its head, and described a high, wide parabolic arc as it sailed into the pasture sixty feet away. In my hand I held the now

somewhat irrelevant head; but I dropped that in a hurry when the chicken's body took off running — fast, so help me — in the opposite direction.

Well, we caught the bird — it couldn't run forever, that way — but then not one of us could bear the thought of eating it. And my guests said rather bluntly that this was not what they had in mind when I had offered to throw a chicken dinner. So we threw the poor bird on the compost heap and drove off to a restaurant. Steak house, as I recall. "The less you tell me how this got onto my plate," my friend commented, carving up his meat, "the better."

Throwing an entire dead bird onto the compost heap was a big mistake, because it offered sundry varmints far and wide a taste of fresh, raw chicken. One raccoon, in particular, decided this repast was worth repeating soon; a few mornings later, my wife went to the henhouse and found the first casualty. We were down to only five more cocks, at that point, plus the nine hens that had not quite yet reached the age of laying. Oops — eight hens. Oops — seven.

We tried to defend our chickens. We lavished rolls of chicken wire on their digs until it resembled a concentration camp for birds. But our nemesis proved good at yanking out heavy wire staples with his claws. We hired in a trapper; five days later, he allowed as our coon was too smart to make it worth his time. His traps would serve him better elsewhere. Two more pullets bit the dust.

Finally — again, on a neighbor's tip — we turned the handful of remaining chickens loose. So that they wouldn't be sitting ducks, so to speak. We tossed them feed each morning, some of which they actually found. And, toward the very end, we actually began to get a homegrown egg or two. Fresh. Organic. Natural.

But just as egg production became solidly established, my wife managed to meet a woman anxious to be rid of half a dozen ducks.

"*I'd* like ducks," my wife informed her.

"Have you ever raised chickens?"

"As a matter of fact —"

• Ducks

The upshot was, my wife proposed that we should trade our rag-tag flock of fowl for the other woman's. An even swap. Ducks, my wife assured me, were a better bird in every way.

"Don't ducks need a pond?" I asked her.

"Ponds are nice for ducks, but not essential." she said. She had several back-to-the-land-type books spread on the rug before her. She had done her research.

"You think ducks aren't *water*fowl? Ducks don't have webbed feet? Ducks weren't *made* for swimming?"

"Listen, these are —"

"Ducks are going to like it just waddling around the barnyard?"

"These are *laying* ducks." She pointed to a picture of them in one of her books. Tan little beady-eyed things. "They're called Khaki Campbells. Some can lay an egg a day — like chickens."

"What's to keep the same raccoon that killed the hens from killing these?"

"These can fly. These forage better, too — they can live outdoors, and it won't take grain to keep them."

"Free lunch, huh?"

She shrugged. "Free omelette."

I was still suspicious, though. "Okay, so they just run loose. What if they disturb the sheep?"

"Oh, they won't — "

"The sheep come first. Remember?"

She went to find her well-thumbed copy of *One Man's Meat*, by E. B. White, and read to me a lovely passage — a moving passage, even — about lambs lying gently on a clutch of goose eggs, keeping them from freezing till the bird was prepared to nest. "Things work out," declared White firmly, "if you leave them alone."

I hadn't yet identified the ideal referred to here, but now I see it as a particularly brazen presentation of the mythopoetic barnyard — the barnyard as peaceable kingdom. Pigs and sheep, cows and chickens, horses and goats and geese all bedding down together as though farm life were a Christmas crèche. Or the Children's Barnyard at some urban zoo. Little could I guess what considerable havoc this notion of harmony among God's creatures was destined to wreak on my farming efforts.

Fact is, I have seen some barnyards that approach the high ideal. I have seen geese herding a band of old ewes about, and piglets suckling on a calm cow's swollen teats. But I have learned — painfully — that such miracles do not occur on my own premises. Here, disparate species do not choose to get along; their living habits place them perpetually at odds. Here, each attempt at diversified farming has led me further down the road to monoculture.

Nonetheless, in those early years I had a weakness for the idea of a mythopoetic barnyard. "All right," I conceded. "Ducks."

The swap was not difficult to consummate. Chickens had not worked out for us, my wife told her duck lady, but she could assure her that these five hens were true survivors. Every last one.

The ducks arrived — five unassuming Khaki Campbell layers and one large, doting Rouen drake — in a plastic feed bag on a cold November morning. As soon as the duck lady drove off with our chickens, I realized we had been bested in this little deal: our hens were laying at the time, albeit sporadically, but these ducks were not scheduled to drop an egg till springtime.

"An egg a day?" I recollected.

"Well — only in season. What did you expect?"

I expected little, really, but I couldn't help remarking that the true Vermonter not only refuses to feed unproductive animals, but even manages to exchange them for others with no such drawback. Hobbyists, we were. And, like all hobby farmers, I just hate to be characterized as such. Or to prove it by behaving less than shrewdly in the marts of trade.

A second problem was that, without disparaging the ducks' will or ability to forage for their grub, their pickings got damn slim once snow blanketed the earth. Our birds would huddle in the barn — cold — and pick apart the sheep's manure, which struck me as rather an extreme approach to poultry nutrition. So I broke down and purchased the proverbial sack of grain, and built the ducks a varmint-and-sheep-proof space in which they could enjoy it.

Trouble is, when you feed grain to a single creature in a barnyard, every other animal immediately demands his share. Sheep, in particular, develop a sort of social contract with their keeper and will not tolerate what they perceive to be injustice. Mine responded to the graining of the ducks by wasting hay wantonly, pulling great mouthfuls out of the racks and trampling them with abandon. This seemed, at first, like shooting oneself in the foot, but soon enough their message came through loud and clear. I hate to see hay wasted — and I hate having to clear it off the barn floor later.

So I had to feed the sheep a little grain — no small expense — in order to be allowed to feed the ducks. An outright bribe. *Baksheesh.* Apart from that, we all wintered reasonably well. Then, making my lambing rounds late on the night of the twenty-first of March, I came across two duck eggs in a corner of the barn. It was vernal equinox: equal light and equal dark. Time for ducks to lay. I whooped with glee and lavished feed on everything in sight. I was immensely proud of those ducks, for the first and perhaps the only time.

I ran to the house and roused my wife. "Look at this!" I crowed, holding up the eggs. "First day of spring! What rhythm! What an internal calendar! Those birds understand the music of the spheres!"

"Now you'll get your omelette," she promised, getting out of bed. She cracked the eggs — still warm — into a bowl. I stared at them. Same size, same basic shape as hen's eggs. But the color! These yolks were Day-Glo orange.

"What's wrong with those eggs?" I asked.

"Huh?"

"That's a funny color. Isn't it?"

"These are goddamn homegrown fresh organic eggs. Laid in the last hour. You couldn't buy better — "

"*Duck* eggs."

"Of course they're duck eggs. What did you expect?"

I wasn't sure. A hen's egg, I reflected, is a civilized sort of egg. Austere. Domesticated. These things looked wild. The yolks sat right up, fat and sassy, and the whites had a brooding, gelatinous quality. They were much too physical, those duck eggs.

"Too real," I said. "Too *ducky*."

" 'Ducky' is not a pejorative."

"*You* can eat them," I said.

To be perfectly fair, in time I learned to eat these eggs in baked goods — chocolate cake, say — without any distaste. And we could serve them easy-over or scrambled to unsuspecting guests; but I personally never learned to sit down one-on-one with a duck egg at breakfast. It was just a different product.

Spring weather arrived, and we turned the ducks outside to forage for their keep. Big day. They waddled all around the place, searching for the pond. "Where's the damn pond?" the drake kept inquiring of me with his shifty eyes. I offered him a secondhand baby bathtub — I even made a show of sinking it in April mud — but he scorned the thing. Soon his entire harem learned to give me his reproachful stare.

"What did you expect?" I asked. But I knew that they expected something grander than a plastic birdbath.

My wife had not lied: ducks running loose on new grass required no grain feeding. Unlike chickens, though, the ducks did not return daily to their coop to sit and lay an egg. Instead, each found a little private place off by herself — or several places, for variety's sake — and we had to hold a daily Egg Hunt. In between two bales of straw, under piled cedar fenceposts, on the ewes' hay feeder — fun. Until the day I cracked the first truly rotten egg.

"The hell?" I asked.

"It must be old."

"But we gather these eggs every day."

"That doesn't mean — look, you find an egg out in the barn-yard, you have no idea what day it got laid. Right?"

My mental alarm clock rang. "Fresh eggs, huh? Fresh eggs?!"

"You don't like it, put the ducks back in the coop."

"And feed them grain!"

She shrugged her shoulders pleasantly. "Well, there's no free — "

I slammed the door. Lunch. There is no free lunch.

We didn't confine the ducks, but instead moved on to stage two: ducklings. This was where the ducks would truly prove their value over chickens. The modern chicken, it must be understood, will not sit on a clutch of eggs and incubate a batch of chicks. People have bred the *broodiness* out of hens, in order to get more eggs from them. *People* now take charge of the incubating end of things. Ducks, however, have been spared the best efforts of our aggressive genetic engineers. So by not collecting eggs, and by encouraging our strapping Rouen drake to fertilize his women, we expected to be roasting ducklings by midsummer.

At about this time, my sheep flock reached a number for which I decided I could no longer carry water twice a day. I invested in an automatic, self-filling, self-heating watering device of marvelous design and labored for three days to install it in the barnyard. The gadget only holds about a quart of water at a time, but the moment that an animal sucks up a drop, a drop flows in. Counterweighted valve, on a buried pressure line running back to the house. Rolls Royce — it set me back a couple of hundred dollars. I threw my pails away and lived for several days in heaven. No more water chores.

Until the ducks mistook the watering device for their long-lost pond.

Lactating ewes, of which I then owned thirty-seven, need to drink several gallons of water per head per day to keep their udders full with milk. Lots of water. But they won't drink at all, I discovered, from an automatic waterer where half a dozen ducks have recently had a beach party. One can clean the waterer, but I would have had to clean it many times a day to keep it suitable for thirsty sheep. Ducks like water, bless them. Ducks turn water very quickly filthy.

"Ducks have got to go," I told my wife. "Ducks and sheep don't mix."

"But one of them's already nesting!"

"Where?"

"In the hayfield. Came across her just this morning. Ten big eggs, she's got."

"So she can stay," I offered in a spirit of compromise. "But ditch the rest. Quick."

Laying ducks in June are somewhat easier to give away than non-producing ducks in winter; within a couple of days, another eager, back-to-the-land couple came to see our ducks and left with them, starry-eyed. "No more fowl!" I decreed the moment those birds had left the place. But, of course, we still had one fowl nesting in the hayfield, crazed by the glaring sun and wondering, as usual, which way was the pool. The grass grew tall, her incubative efforts stretched on interminably, and one morning I announced that haying weather was upon us.

I would not have mown the duck. I am not heartless. But I had machine trouble that summer — trouble with the weather, too — and wound up asking a neighbor to finish off some acres while I sought repairs to my aging sickle-bar mower. No problem. Neighbors can be called on here when someone gets into a jam. Now my neighbor's mower is a very wide and indelicate machine run behind an eighty-five horsepower tractor. The fresh mown grass goes flying through huge rollers — like clothes through a wringer washer — to speed drying time; the whole rig must weigh several tons. And I forgot — I *forgot*, I swear — to place my neighbor on the lookout for a nesting duck.

I suppose I raked her up and baled her, eggs and all, a couple of days later. Pity. I confessed, though.

"You did *what*?" my wife shrieked.

"Well, come on. Nesting in a hayfield — what did you expect?"

"No roast duck for you!" she sniffed.

No roast duck. I took it in stride though; after all, I had duck under grass.

• Pigs

Spring in Vermont is brief: a mere two weeks, sometimes. All the rash actions that can, in more temperate climes, be spread out over several months, need to be accomplished with a breathtaking compression here. So it was that, one May morning several years ago, I set out to acquire some pigs. By day's end the deed was done.

"Why?" my wife asked, several hours too late.

I had a host of reasons. Chief among them was the then ballyhooed suspicion of the Federal Food and Drug folks that meats cured with sodium nitrite might be particularly carcinogenic. Bacon, for example. I like bacon. And pork sausage, too. Homegrown and custom-processed, these meats could be obtained *without* nitrite cures; this, I thought, would be a smart dietary goal.

One of several "custom cutters" in this broad valley is the establishment of Edward Lyman. It was Lyman who had told me, some two years before, that I ought to raise some pigs. That *everybody* should, in fact. The first time I met him, he was cutting a pale, lean, twenty-pound pork belly into lovely strips of bacon. "Try to find meat like *that* at the supermarket," he challenged.

I shrugged. "Couldn't."

Then he handed me the packet of spiced preservatives he would use to cure this premium product. "See? None of that sodium nitrite you hear about."

I was impressed. I asked, "Is it hard to raise a pig?"

"Hell, no. Nothing to it. Spring piglets feed out cheap, too."

Naturally, I thought about it. But an aspiring farmer can't do everything at once; I had too many other acts to get together, primarily involving sheep. Shish kebabs bumped pork chops off our menu of homegrown treats. Still — the pig thought lingered.

It lingered because Edward Lyman became *my* custom slaughterer and processor — transforming twenty-five or so of my lambs each summer from on-the-hoof to in-the-freezer for a local clientele. Custom slaughterers do not buy livestock or sell meat; they work on a cash basis for whoever owns an animal he wants to eat. Homegrown pigs, a tradition on Vermont farms large and small, comprise a big part of their business.

Lyman runs no *abattoir*; he drives an old pickup truck all over the county to kill livestock on their owners' premises. He skins and guts them right there, then transports the fresh carcasses back to his cooler and cutting room. For the animals, at least, this is distinctly humane: one moment a creature is chowing down happily in familiar quarters; next moment, the proverbial ax falls. There's no time for terror, which is probably the Endgame state of live-stock who get shipped one hundred or one thousand miles to get offed on clean, efficient kill floors by commercial butchers.

On-premise slaughtering, however, has one disadvantage for the owner of the premises: Lyman leaves a pile of guts behind him everywhere he goes. The hundred-pound live lamb in which I've come to specialize yields forty pounds of guts — this is what it means to possess four stomachs. After a busy morning watching Lyman ply his trade, I sometimes have four or five such piles in the broad barn doorway.

Guts attract — and breed — flies just about as fast as Ed Lyman spills them. They need to be buried quickly. And buried *deep*, where dogs can't find them. Dogs eating sheep guts are one stage in the life cycle of a tapeworm known as *Echinococcus granu-losus*, which can also use humans as intermediate hosts. A hidden liability of shepherding for those shepherds who will not make time to bury guts. Vermont's clay soils in midsummer get about as hard as concrete, though, so — short of a backhoe — how does one get rid of offal?

I learned, in time. One buries the stuff in the garden, where a shovel makes a dent because the soil has some tilth to it.

Guts make, no doubt, for an excellent organic soil amend-ment. But a garden with two dozen shallow graves of rotting innards is a garden one needs a roadmap to walk in safely. Sooner or later, the inevitable happened — to a visiting medical student, no less. On an unguided garden tour, this unlucky person found himself knee-deep in slime and maggots. This while strolling through the sweet corn.

"What on earth is this?" he bellowed.

I brought him the garden hose. I said he wouldn't want to know.

I made the acquaintance of an older, wiser shepherd in a nearby town who did a bit of custom slaughtering himself. "What," I implored him, "do you do with the guts of lambs?"

"Feed them to my hogs, of course."

This rang a bell. Aha: pig feed. The very stuff of nitrite-free bacon and sausage. Only later would I learn that *hog feed* is not *pig feed*, necessarily. (Hogs, weighing a thousand pounds and more, can chow down the most revolting stuff with splendid equanimity. Pigs, though, even hundred-pound pigs, are little babies by comparison. With baby-like digestive tracts.) At the time, I just saw garbage in, pork chops out: an exquisite recycling, a marvelous convergence of farmsteading goals.

That misapprehension — that piglets could be reared on lamb guts — pushed me over the brink. I sallied forth and returned with a pair of piglets purchased from an old Vermont couple who were trying to quit the pig business. Too much feed. Too tiring. Their dozen sows looked tired, too. But we struck a bargain that seemed fair until I got the piglets home and placed them on a scale; *caveat emptor*, as usual. I washed the little darlings, wormed them, set them up in fabulous digs recently vacated by our flock of ducks. And, since I had no lambs that had yet reached slaughter weights, I purchased for them fancy pig mash from the local grain store.

By the time I first had Ed Lyman out to slaughter lambs, the pigs were up to sixty pounds each. Pigs grow mighty fast. Naturally, I took Lyman to see them.

"Well-started pigs," he commented.

"I bought them to eat up all those lamb guts you leave behind."

"Say what?"

"A little experiment in recycling."

Lyman whetted his sticking knife. Thoughtfully. "Wouldn't feed those little piglets guts, if I were you."

My heart sank.

"Not unless you cook them first."

"*Cook* them?"

"For twenty minutes. Just below a boil."

"Holy — that's an awful bother."

"Look, you've got some money in those pigs. What'd you have to pay?"

"Thirty dollars each."

"And you've put a couple hundred pounds of grain in them, right?"

"Three hundred, so far."

"Well, then. Don't go and make them sick just to get your guts cleaned up."

Cooking one hundred odd pounds of lamb guts on the kitchen stove creates an odor that can drive a man's wife right out of the house. For days on end — my wife pitched a tent, in fact. I confess I stepped outdoors, myself, during one such recycling spree. To breathe fresh air. I came back to find a large pot of innards boiling *over*. Down the counter goo cascaded, trickling off at low points to drip onto the kitchen carpet, which wicked it up nicely.

"Septic trouble?" visitors would ask, sniffing, a month later.

"No, just pig feed."

Two pigs can't eat a hundred pounds of guts in a day, either. Once cooked, I discovered, guts had to be *stored*. In the *refrigerator*. Then, each morning, bleary-eyed, I would fish out a cold boiled lung or rumpled grey stomach lining, and I'd tote this to the pigpen. The pigs would grunt and oink and give my bare legs sloppy kisses, so grateful were they for another organ to devour. This makes a disturbing way, at best, to start out summer mornings.

Finally, one day in August, both the pigs took sick. They went off feed, groaned, and lay back in their muddy wallow with pained expressions. I guessed the cause was just one testicle or spleen too many — not that I had poisoned them, but my diet of expediency had, over time, resulted in profound malnutrition. A neighbor farmer, stopping by, confirmed this diagnosis.

"*That's* what you're feeding them?" he demanded, pointing to the trough where flies were making whoopee in the uneaten, gutty broth. "Pigs that size can't do too much with stomach linings, don't you know?"

"Cooked it," I assured him.

Incredulity is not a facial expression of which Yankee farmers are normally capable. But I'd say he managed nicely. "*Corn*," he told me. "Lord God, feed them corn!"

I changed my ways. Again. I patronized the feed store weekly, supplementing their corn mash with only the purest of table scraps and garden thinnings. I began to chauffeur lamb guts deep into my woodlot, dumping them beside a fallen tree and speeding off in the pickup truck. No more brilliant exercises in recycling, no whole earth. The pigs ate corn, recovered nicely, grew to hefty weights, and took their place, at length, in our well-packed freezer.

Vermont is a long way from the Corn Belt, sad to say. Pumping corn from Iowa into Vermont pigs is asking for a disappointing balance sheet. Against this I could not, in fairness, measure the high quality of the dietary components I had provided right off the farm. But I could fall back on the purity of pork produced: cured without nitrites. Healthful. Non-carcinogenic.

That is why I was so disappointed, a month or so after doing in our pigs, to sit down with the morning paper over a farm breakfast. Coffee, home fries, eggs and bacon — nitrite-free bacon. And big headlines:
SODIUM NITRITE NO LONGER SUSPECT. SWIFT, ARMOUR MUCH RELIEVED, announcing the results of a new study.

• Honeybees

One spring morning thirty years ago, a swarm of honeybees collected on a low branch of the elm tree just outside my parents' house in Illinois. I was six years old and appropriately fascinated. My father, who loved honey but had not formerly exhibited "the bee bug," called a local apiarist. Fate had struck. The two men sawed the branch clean off the tree and spent the morning carefully depositing the bees into a hastily acquired hive box. From then on, there were bees in our back yard.

Swarming bees are famous for docility, absorbed as they must be in mass transit, and in the socially cohesive work of house-hunting. A couple months later, though, I watched my father open up the hive to check his bees' progress in producing honey for him. *His* bees. For *him*. But the bees had their own idea, and they weren't in the least deterred by his homemade bee suit comprised of an old pith helmet, used porch screening, and mildewed canvas. The bees got hopping mad; one after another found a way to penetrate my father's armor and deliver a bee's ultimate punishment.

I witnessed this exhibition of man versus nature from the security of a hedge several yards away. My father was — and is — a man of iron will. A sting or two, or even many stings, would not prevent him from completing a task he had set his mind to doing. Here was a wild hive, and plainly his job was to domesticate it. On the spot. He pried each frame of comb from the angry hive, inspecting it for brood or honey. He searched till he found the queen, then clipped her wings so that she couldn't change her mind and fly off elsewhere. He installed new beeswax sheets for the workers to elaborate into comb, as they created their hexagonal storage cells. Throughout, he took his own sweet time.

When, at last, he closed the hive back up, I followed my

father back into the house. He was hurting — fact is, he was a walking pincushion that had accepted well over a hundred bee stings. I watched, nauseous but awed, as he sharpened a putty knife and scraped some thirty stingers from a single forearm. Bees had stung his neck, his lips, the corners of his eyes. Next time, though — he promised me — those bees would be tamer. Score: Bees 1; My Father 1.

That night, he had a raging fever. Doctors were consulted. But by morning he had made a miraculous recovery. His temperature was down; the swollen lumps had left his face. He breakfasted, then went out the front door to start the car. A bee was waiting — posted by the door — and stung him on the spot. Score: Bees 2; My Father 1.

I had forgotten all about that till a couple of years ago, when it all came back in a Proustian flood of memory as I stood uneasily over an open hive of bees. In *my own* back yard, right here in Vermont. Bee smells — honey, propolis, and sticky yellow wax — filled my nostrils. Draped around my head was a borrowed bee veil, which wasn't working. That is to say, one intrepid hive guard was busily burrowing his way under the veil's drawstring, and I had a hunch that his determination outstripped mine.

In my hand I held a borrowed bee smoker. A smoker is a can containing smouldering rags, with a bellows to direct smoke from them onto suspicious bees. Smoke *calms* bees. So I pointed this handy tool at the bee clawing near my throat, and deftly sent a puff of acrid smoke into my face. This did calm the bee, some-what, but it also brought tears to my eyes and a fit of coughing to my chest. When my head cleared, several *hundred* bees had poked their angry heads up from between the frames of honeycomb I had come to pry apart; in perfect unison, dancing to some unheard beat, they flexed their little insect torsos and beat their dainty wings. I had read about this boogie: it is the last thing one is apt to see before a bee battalion roars from the hive to sting one *en masse*.

Can bees smell human fear? I think they smelled mine that day. The lone bee I had calmed with smoke now found his way — calmly, calmly — inside my bonnet and poked his stinger in my neck. I howled. I dropped the smoker, dropped the hive cover with a thud, and fled. Score: Bees 1; My Father's Son 0.

But they were not *my* bees, after all. They belonged to my wife. The good Yankee farm wife, I had slowly helped her to understand, adopts a few useful hobbies on the homestead. Such as pruning apple trees, keeping the garden weeded, making dandelion wine — little things like that. Like managing an apiary. For a mere sixty dollars, I bought her a working hive; she had been gung ho at first, but when the honeymoon was over she found it required very little reason *not* to inspect her hive on any given day. The day had to be warm — but not *too* warm — with fair skies and rising barometer, and timed at least two days after the last storm. That rules out a lot of days. Plus things had to *feel* right, something only beekeepers can sense. She did not sense it often, and I never sensed it at all.

In our third year of beekeeping, my wife became pregnant. She asked: should a woman heavy with child risk getting stung by bees? Probably not, I agreed. But we had a hive chore pending, so *I* had to risk it. First of May, in these parts, is hive *requeening* time, and after two years with one queen we had been advised to do this. Beehives, it will be recalled, have one exalted member who lays eggs like mad — fifteen hundred eggs and up per day. This work wears a woman down, so old hives get a new lease on life when someone trades an old queen in for a new one.

When I stood awash in frightening memories by that open hive, I had come to swap queens. Where, the neophyte might ask, do new queens come from? They come from Sears Roebuck — believe it or not — by parcel post. Special handling, naturally. Each queen comes in a little wooden cage with a candy plug; the workers of the hive eat the candy off to liberate her. Problem is, the old queen. Two queens in a hive is one too many. The old queen might kill the new — a real waste of time and money — or they might choose up sides and divide the hive. No good. So the wise apiarist opens up his hive, finds the old queen, takes her into custody, and squashes her when no one's looking. Then he drops the new queen in.

Plainly, I had not gotten far with this important project. And a new Sears Roebuck queen won't wait forever, either. She has to get laying pronto to get the hive up to full strength for the nectar flow. So, smarting from my sting, and convinced the bees were on my case as devotedly as they had been on my dad's, I drove several miles to the farm of a skilled apiarist. Name of John Tatro. "Look," I said, "for ten bucks will you requeen my hive?"

He looked reluctant. "You got a new queen?"

"Just came today."

"She looks good?"

"She's fine."

"Then what's the problem?"

"Scared," I said, for now I know that truth is best. "Bees scare me, ever since I was a kid. My wife does this, usually, but —"

"Cut it in half," he said, making a slicing gesture with one hand.

"Cut *what* in half?"

"Those ten bucks."

So I gave him five and chauffeured him directly to my beehive. The old Yankee brought no smoker, wore no veil. He understood bees, and they certainly seemed to understand him. In two minutes — calm, surefooted — he took the hive apart and whisked the old queen away. Then he suspended the new queen, cage and all, in the hive. He watched to make sure the worker bees would accept her; satisfied they would, he closed the hive back up. In the cab of my pickup he dispatched the old queen.

Having thus revitalized the hive, I expected a whopping honey harvest by the time my wife could return to apiary duties. But it wasn't in the cards. Our typical nectar flow comes fast and furious in mid-June; that year, though, a brutal spring drought depressed the forage crops our bees rely on. Clover and alfalfa scarcely blossomed. And when they did, immediately they were baled up and fed to hungry livestock.

Come every September, a back-yard beekeeper has to balance sweet tooth versus hive survival prospects, and make an appropriate division of honey stores. A hive requires sixty pounds of honey, more or less, to make it through the winter; in the two years that my wife had managed the bees, our colony had produced about eighty pounds — allowing us to score twenty. No record, but not bad either. This year, under my command, I didn't think we had done as well.

"Listen," I told my now acutely expectant wife. "Let's just forget the honey, this year. Leave it all right in the hive. If there's any extra, *you* can take it out next spring."

She laughed at me. "Chicken?"

"That's right."

"Call John Tatro," she suggested. "Honey or no, someone ought to check the hive for winter."

So I returned to the experienced beeman's place and negotiated for his services again. "Terrible year," he told me as we drove back to my farm. "Much too dry for honey."

"Cuts into the income from your bees, huh?" I asked. For old Tatro had fifty hives; he was in the honey business.

"Income?!" He slapped the dashboard. "You think those bees care about my income? Shoot, no. They're working for themselves. And this year, the *bees* are short. Income? No, sir. This year it's the other way around."

"Meaning what?"

"You got to feed *them*, this year."

"Me feed them?"

"Else they'll starve, come winter."

"Me feed them, huh?" This was a new concept. "Feed them what?"

"What do you think?"

"Honey?"

"Honey's best. Though some get by with sugar syrup."

We reached my hive; he opened it and evaluated my bees' winter stores. Thirty pounds short, at least — a small fortune in honey. And cane sugar — for syrup — had just hit record prices, too. But worst of all, I could not stomach the thought of opening that hive on a regular schedule to offer sweets to honeybees.

"How would you like to buy another beehive?" I asked Tatro.

He shook his head. "Not this year. I'll be going to the bank just to feed the bees I've got."

"How'd you like to take this beehive off my hands?"

He looked at me carefully, gauging my resolve to be rid of bees. He shook his head again. He said, "Moving hives around is quite a bother."

"How much would I have to pay you to take this beehive off my hands?"

Now he smiled, faintly. "Ten dollars, maybe."

"Cut it in half," I said.

He grinned. "That's a deal."

So I paid five dollars to lose a sixty-dollar hive of bees with a new Sears Roebuck queen. Tatro must have calculated that he'd done all right, I reckon. But I toted up a different score: Bees 1, My Father's Son 1. Honey, when I buy it now, seems awfully cheap at any price.

II. VEGETABLE

• Mushrooms

When I was a college student, back in the heady Sixties, the only people I knew who went mushrooming were reckless types bent on serious tripping. Failing this, I recall they sometimes had to rush to get their stomachs pumped. I carried no brief, in those extraordinary days, against having a little psychedelic fun; but scouring the woods and fields for fungi of supposed psychotropic properties seemed to me a hazardous strategy for getting stoned.

Half a dozen years later, I had sworn off controversial intoxicants in favor of the Yankee ethos, having become a Vermontophile with a keen respect for flinty, stern New England values. So I was astonished when, one dazzling afternoon during my second October in Vermont, a white-haired woman with a classic, chiselled Yankee face drove her car into my driveway and rapped on my door. She carried a cane in one hand and a deep wicker basket in the other. She said: "You must be the new owner here. All right if I mushroom?"

It took me a few moments to comprehend this odd request. Seeing my confusion, the woman gestured toward the fields behind us. "I'm a neighbor, sort of. Been mushrooming here for years."

I understood now that she meant to hunt for mushrooms on my land — not blow up on the spot. I supposed she was not seeking mushrooms to get high on, either. "You mean *wild* mushrooms? Like — to eat?"

"Your back pasture," she said. "You've got scads of mushrooms, most years. This fall's been a good one — I've seen puffballs as big as your head."

"Is that a fact?"

"I'd be glad to show you. Got a basket?"

I did not have one. But I found a shopping bag and joined her for few pleasant hours of foraging; under her tutelage, I saw my fields with new eyes. Our primary quarry was *Agaricus campestris,* the "meadow mushroom" that she told me was a wild relative of the cultivated mushroom one buys in grocery stores for several dollars a pound. On that day we found them everywhere — free lunch, no less — nourished by the fresh, abundant cow manure that dotted the pasture. Here and there we found wide fairy rings comprised of scores of tender, pale fruiting bodies. I said, "I can't wait for supper."

"Try one now," my guide said, and she offered me one of the delicate caps. It was, simply, marvelous — like commercial mushrooms at their peak, only more flavorful.

"I never thought to pick these things before," I confessed, ecstatic. "I thought mushrooms were — well, dangerous."

She laughed. "I've been eating them for sixty-seven years."

"Never gotten sick? Or — or drugged, or —"

"Nonsense. I just stick to half a dozen I can recognize. People who get poisoned —" she wrinkled her nose contemptuously. "They're *experimenting*, like as not. Take these meadow mushrooms. They only grow out in the open, like this. Never in the woods. And they're always just about this size, and — well, there's just one mushroom you could possibly confuse them with."

"Which one is that?"

"The Death Angel."

I choked up the tasty morsel she had given me to chew. "Jesum!"

"But the Death Angel has white gills," she explained. Serenely. "*These* gills are pink. If you can't see the gills yet — if the cap hasn't opened — leave the mushroom be. Don't even touch it."

This added an intense new quality to my collecting. I noticed, then, that the woman's harvesting technique involved bending back each mushroom with her cane before stooping to pick it. If her cane revealed white gills, she could pass it by and not get deadly toxins on her fingers. I found a stick to use to make the same check; soon I had half a shopping bag full of mushrooms.

"That's enough of those," she announced. "Puffballs, next. They like to grow where pasture turns to woodlot — like up there, you see?" She pointed which direction we should walk, and we set off briskly. "*Giant* puffballs are the ones you want to stick with, starting out."

"Why is that?"

"Sometimes you can get the little ones confused. With *Amanita* buttons."

"*Amanita*," I repeated. "I think I've heard of that."

"Stay away from them," she warned me. "Wait — see *that*?"

"Where?"

She led me, pace quickening, to an old drainage ditch. In it were a half dozen giant puffballs; one was the size of a basketball, and heavier. Eighteen pounds, in fact. Pure white, with a skin like soft kid gloves. My guide drew a bread knife from her basket and sliced the puffball open to reveal solid, white flesh.

"Wow," I murmured.

"Half for you and half for me. Let's leave the others — if you overpick a mushroom, it's apt to die out on you. *Not* picking helps them spread."

She handed me my portion of the puffball, which looked as though it had just landed from outer space. "I can *eat* this thing?" I asked.

"Slice it like a loaf of bread, and fry it up in butter. Makes a meal. If there's any left, just freeze it. In a plastic bag. Come wintertime, you'll have a treat."

I said I might try that.

"Want to look for chanterelles, next?"

"Where do they live?"

"In the forest — if we're lucky." She stood abruptly and led me deep into my woodlot. "Check around those beech trees," she advised. "They look like little columns. Bright orange. Egg-yolk colored. *There* — you see?"

I could not see them, but she stooped to show me. And once we started finding chanterelles, we found an awful lot. Pounds. "This is wonderful," she told me. "Last year, there weren't hardly any. Too dry, I suppose."

"Now — there's nothing dangerous that I might confuse these with?"

"Nothing. Except Jack-o-Lanterns."

"What is that — a joke?"

"No, it's a mushroom. Looks a lot like chanterelles. But Jack-o-Lanterns glow in the dark, you understand? So when you bring your chanterelles home, take them in the closet. If they glow, don't eat them."

"Deadly?"

"No. But people wish they *were*, they get so nauseous."

Soon my bag and hers were overflowing, so we set off for our respective kitchens. I assured her she could come pick more, anytime she wanted. She said that the season was quite brief, but perhaps she would. I watched her get into her car and drive off, and I have not seen her in the eight years since that day. Maybe she has died — though not of mushrooms, I imagine. Maybe she's no longer mobile. Maybe she just felt that now that she had introduced me to mushrooming my own woods and fields, I would grow reluctant to share the annual October harvest.

Anyway, I have not seen her — for whatever reason. But on the evening of that golden afternoon, my wife came home from town to find several pans of mushrooms sizzling on the stove. And piles more of the raw goods spread across the kitchen counter.

"Look!" I crowed. "Wild mushrooms!"

My wife's personality does have a cautious aspect to it. She said, "You gone nuts?"

"This old Yankee woman came here. Took me foraging for mushrooms."

My wife has a sharp wit, too. "Mrs. Don Juan?" she sneered. "A Yankee way of knowledge?"

"Listen — these are basic, wild, edible mushrooms. Choice. Right off our own land, too. They're not dope, or deadly — they're just *food*." I lifted the lid on a twelve-inch skillet, beneath which thick puffball steaks were simmering. "See that? Smells fantastic, huh?"

"I'm not going to eat those mushrooms."

"That's okay. What I can't eat, I'll freeze. In little plastic bags. Then I'll have a treat, come winter."

So my wife watched me eat half a dozen pounds of sautéed mushrooms for dinner. "How're you feeling?" she had to inquire every several minutes.

"Hey," I said. "These things have been *identified*. This woman *taught* me. Like these here — *Agaricus*? If you didn't know, you might confuse them with the Death Angel. But these gills are pink —"

"You call that pink?"

"Well, but they've been *cooked* —"

"The Death Angel, huh?"

My wife left the room, then came back thumbing an encyclopedia of medical lore. " 'Mushroom poisoning,' " she read. " 'Victims often show no symptoms for twenty-four hours. Suddenly, violent nausea and diarrhea erupt. Victims often survive this phase and show marked improvement — even mild euphoria —

for several days. But damage to the heart, liver, and kidneys continues, until a sudden relapse causes death usually within five days of ingestion.' "

"Fair enough," I said. "What's for dessert?"

My wife went to the kitchen counter and began chucking my mushrooms — pile after pile — into the garbage.

"If you met this sweet old woman, who's been mushrooming for sixty-seven years —"

"How are you feeling?"

"Mildly euphoric," I assured her. But, truth be told, I began to feel confused. Caution, prudence, taking care — these were legitimate components of the Yankee ethos that I was aspiring to. But my mushroom lady — a quintessential Yankee — could calmly select baby puffballs from Amanitas without compromising these same values. The difference between us, I supposed, was simply confidence.

"You cannot learn to pick mushrooms with confidence," my wife said sternly, "in one afternoon."

"Right," I said. "You're right. I quit."

But that meal was a sort of Mushroom Apotheosis, and it did not harm me in the slightest. I remember it fondly. Nowadays I leave the fungi in my fields for the sheep, who nibble at them gingerly and shuffle off, unsatisfied. Gourmets they are not. One day, I tell myself, I will take a proper course of instruction — become an expert — and hunt mushrooms confidently. *Not* picking helps them spread? By then, at the rate I'm going, there should be a bumper crop.

• Christmas Trees

A decade ago, when I was thinking about buying this little chunk of Vermont, the realtor, smelling victory, groped for the winning phrase, the *bon mot* that would clinch the deal. "Something else," he said. "You buy this land, you'll never have to buy a Christmas tree again!"

I nodded soberly, although a lifetime's worth of store-boughten Christmas trees would have cost the merest fraction of his asking price. But I understood his message: owning a New England farm would bring me hitherto undreamed-of domestic economies, a cornucopia of goods that most folks had to pay hard cash for.

"Christmas trees are running ten, twelve bucks," he told me. "Down to Boston. Prices may go up, too."

I happened to know that they had *already* gone up, but I didn't tell him. I surveyed a dozen acres of scruffy trees in the middle distance, where abandoned pastures were attempting to return to forest. White pines, red cedars, here and there a spruce or hemlock. "Maybe," I said drily, "I should go into the business."

"Sure! Put in a tree plantation!"

"Couldn't I just harvest what's out there?"

He didn't argue with me. "Sure! Why not? Fine young stand of wild trees, there."

Actually, I wasn't much on Christmas trees. Gazing on those scrub pines, I recalled being the sort of snotty kid who would harangue his parents as the family searched for the ideal balsam fir on some suburban retail lot. "This is *sinful*," I would whine. "Look at all these trees they've murdered — innocent, baby trees. For what?"

"You want a plastic tree?"

"No — I don't want *any* tree. This is sick. This whole tradition —"

"Here, wise guy!" My dad would hold out a Scotch pine that was double-trunked, deformed, misshapen. "That's the tree for you — a cull. Wouldn't have amounted to anything, anyhow."

"God! No way!" my sisters would holler. "That runty thing? We want a *perfect* Christmas tree!"

And we usually got one.

The real-estate agent watched me, patient, till he feared the deal might slip away in reveries. "Yessir. Lot of money to be made in Christmas trees, nowadays."

This, I thought, was certainly baloney spewed for urban ears. Had I talked alfalfa or corn silage — had I seemed to know the first thing about agriculture — the man would have spared me this Christmas tree rap. Here was proof he took me for a city boy who didn't know what rural land was worth. But the farm — hopeful Christmas trees and all — was undeniably lovely. I bit. Minutes later, we were shaking hands on a price. Who am I to say the agent's Yuletide appeal might not have tipped the balance?

Come our first Christmas in Vermont, my wife and I tramped

the woodlot with a hatchet one December morning. After a couple hours, we had to conclude that we had bought a farm which lacked even one single perfect Christmas tree. We did find *something* to cut, however: a white pine with some fullness at the top and bottom, but a scraggly midriff. By cutting out a three-foot stretch of trunk and splinting what remained, we made an unusual but serviceable tree. Good enough for starry-eyed newcomers to Vermont. But why — I had to wonder — why, on this entire farm, was there no young conifer of consistent shape and fullness, no Christmas tree that my sisters would not have hooted at?

I did a bit of research. Twenty-five years ago, the preponderance of Christmas trees sold in North America were actually forest thinnings. This was not the eco-catastrophe, not the wanton rape of baby forests that I had imagined, either. Naturally seeded, wild tree stands *need* rigid culling to maximize ultimate timber growth per acre. Christmas tree markets were mere financial encouragement for forest owners to perform improvement tasks they should have done, anyway.

Trouble was — everybody wanted the perfect Christmas tree, and relatively few forest thinnings measured up. The ideal Christmas tree was at loggerheads with the foresters' purpose — thinning misshapen, cull trees from young stands of conifers. Twenty-five years ago, one tree in four bundled up and trucked to retail lots proved too ugly to be sold — and only two in four were of first quality. Wholesalers were howling, and the average farm price for Vermont balsam fir was 14¢ per tree. Nobody was getting rich.

The result has been a near-total shift of Christmas tree production — from authentic forests to straightforward plantations. These are as unlikely a variety of "farming" as plantations of tobacco or coffee or cane; the Christmas tree farmer turns perfectly good land into neat, even rows of baby trees. Two thousand can be grown to market size on a single acre. The "farmer" prunes every tree, once a year, to assure that each will have ideal shape. No culls allowed. He mows between the rows — to suppress competing flora — and he treats his trees to fertilizers, fungicides, and insecticides as necessary. After eight to fourteen years of handy tax losses — he can file as a farmer — he has a crop of Christmas trees to harvest. Every one is perfect.

When I learned how Christmas trees are grown nowadays, I knew this enterprise was not for me. But, in time, I made acquaintances among the ranks of those who own plantations. I am not a snob; I even went to visit one such planter as he toiled in his vineyard. How, I asked, could he justify converting a green meadow into this pygmy forest of identical trees, serving a bizarre and wasteful cultural tradition?

This is not a wise question to pose of a man who has been pruning balsam firs for five straight weeks, leaving only three weeks to go on this annual chore — because experience and skill have cut his pruning time to just one minute per tree. Ten acres — twenty thousand trees — make for a lot of happy minutes spent snipping misplaced branches. "Money, I should hope," he growled.

"It *can't* be that much money."

"Some years — when it all goes well — trees like these bring eight bucks at the roadside. Cut and bundled."

"What do you have *in* each tree?"

"Two, three dollars. Not counting the land. Or the taxes. But I had to pay them anyway."

"Fourteen years is a long wait to get your paycheck."

He grunted his agreement, moving on to the next tree. *Snip!* "That's not half the trouble," he said. "Christmas trees, they're just like Cinderella. You don't sell them by December twenty-fifth, they up and turn into pumpkins."

"Huh?"

"Just think about it. I cut four thousand trees and stack them by the road, and I had better sell them. Right? The wholesaler *knows* I've got to sell them. Christmas trees aren't worth much after Christmas."

"So you *don't* get eight dollars?"

"It depends. Depends how many trees get cut, in any year. Man could grow a million trees to the square mile, this way. A million trees! And no family buys more than one tree a year, either. Too many players start cutting trees, and it isn't hard to glut the market."

"Do you know," I asked, "what Vermont balsam firs bring in Boston? Retail? Glut or no?"

Snip! He said, "I'd just hate to know."

"*Someone's* making money."

"Probably." *Snip!*

I left him to his artistry, pruning trees to shapely perfection.

And I went home thinking, here was a classic Wrong Crop. No plantation for me. On the other hand, my homely patch of stunted conifers was not such a bad deal. I did not plant, or fertilize, or weed, or put in hours pruning; I could reap where I had never sown, if only one scraggly white pine per year.

With trees like I own here, the family does not need to argue out in the cold about which has the nicest shape. We ski into the woods — at dusk, most often, right on Christmas eve — and ski out minutes later dragging something that, with lavish use of tinsel and colored balls, we intend to make pass as a Christmas tree. The real thing: a thinning from our not-overly-managed forest.

Inevitably, some visitor from our former urban lives will drop in during the holidays. And will say: "You call that thing a Christmas tree?"

"For trees like that," I like to answer, "I moved to Vermont."

• Maple Syrup

When mud season — we don't call it spring — settles on Vermont, three of my five neighbors get busy making maple syrup. Not me, although I admit visions of boiling sap were prominent in the idyll of Yankee life that brought me here. Maple, I had read, was considered by Tom Jefferson to be the very sugar of agrarian democracy: dependent not on slaves sweating out their days on cane plantations, but on citizen-farmers putting in a few weeks of annual honest toil in their private woodlots. What, I thought, could be a more poetic and invigorating way to pass the end of winter?

Furthermore, it will be recalled that the old farm that my wife and I had acquired *had* a sugar house — a swaybacked shack of weathered clapboards nestled near a stand of maples. It was startlingly picturesque, even in spite of a length of rotten tree trunk that had collapsed onto its roof. The real-estate agent clearly sensed the sap rising in our veins the moment we saw the building.

My wife flung wide the door. Inside, we found a cast-iron, brick-lined arch and wood-fired evaporator, with a firebox capable of handling four-foot logs. Several flat, square pans for boiling down sap lay rusting in the runoff from the building's torn roof. I lifted one. Half a dozen rats scampered off, abandoning their cozy shelter. "This place needs some work," I murmured.

"Mebbe. But listen," cooed the realtor, "there's *gold* in maple syrup."

We knew. Hadn't we once paid two dollars for a mere half-pint of the stuff — enough for a single pancake breakfast? Somebody was making money. Why not us? We thought we'd try it, even after we tore down the sugar house.

So we conducted a census of our sugarbush, and discovered that all the biggest stumps in the forest were — maples. Stumps two feet across, three feet across — somebody had felled behemoths. There were other maples — up against the cliff, behind the swamp — enough to do some sugaring with, but the primary sugarbush convenient to the sugar house had been very largely timbered off.

I asked one of my sugaring neighbors where all my maples went.

"Sawmill."

"How come?"

"Well, old Hawkins owned the place. Back in the Sixties? He got awful sick of sugaring."

"Pity," I said. "With the arch right there, and the sap pans, and —"

"Those pans leaked fifteen years ago!"

"They *do* look rusty."

"Rust? He *burned* them."

"Honestly?" I asked. A man might dislike work, but such sabotage was difficult to comprehend.

"Hawkins never could get that arch exactly level. Once you get some dry spots in the boiling pan, the solder melts. Then you've got a burned pan. They cost a pretty penny, too."

"How much syrup was Hawkins making?"

"Eighty gallons, in a good year. Three hundred taps."

"Doesn't sound like much."

"*You* try it sometime."

I began to study — with increasing disinterest — sugar economics. I learned that, as a rule of thumb, a single tap in a maple tree in this valley should deliver ten gallons of sap during the four-to-eight-week sugaring season. That's about eighty-three pounds of sap, of which eighty-one pounds have to be boiled away to make about one quart of syrup. At current prices, that quart is worth $3.50 to its producer; so the modest, 300-tap sugarbush, producing thirteen *tons* of sap for somebody to deal with, yields roughly a thousand dollars of gross income annually.

Disappointing? In Vermont, a thousand dollars is nothing to sneeze at. But when I priced new evaporator pans, plus fixing the arch and rebuilding the sugar house, plus taps and buckets and gathering barrels, I found I was looking at over five thousand dollars of hard investment. What is more, I learned I could expect to burn as much cordwood firing the evaporator as I need to burn all winter long to heat my house. That would mean another week's work each summer cutting firewood.

Still, I wanted hands-on sugaring experience before deciding whether or not it was for me. Came the end of February, I invited my wife and myself to help a neighbor tap his maples. Free education, but I think in fifteen minutes I had learned all there is to know about drilling a hole into a tree, banging in a sap spile, and hanging a bucket on it. These are not difficult feats. After learning how, though, it was *work* — and the work went on all day, toting buckets by the score across a steep and snowy mountain. My neighbor is a canny man; he hates to miss the first good sap run, so he gets his buckets hung before the first real thaw. Well before it, that year. We walked home half-frozen, with no taste of syrup in sight. Sugaring, it seemed now, was about the coldest work on earth.

Ten days later, he called back. As we had asked him to. "Sap's running," he said.

"We'll be over."

It was the sort of day when spring first starts to arm-wrestle winter in earnest: thirty-eight degrees and bright all afternoon, but freezing in the shade of every rock and tree. With sunset, the mercury would plunge. This is sugar weather — this demoralizing season of one muddy step forward, two steps back — and Vermont is apt to get a couple months of it each year.

We drove the pickup to my neighbor's. "Maybe," my wife suggested, "that's why people sugar. To make the end of winter less dementing."

"Maybe they're demented already — and *that's* why they do it."

By day's end, she was ready to concede the point. If tapping trees had seemed like mindless grunt labor, it was white-collar work compared to gathering sap. Simply, we poured buckets into pails, pails into barrels, and then a John Deere tractor hauled the barrels down to the evaporator. One person boiling sap down in the steam-fogged sugar house kept four adults and two children busy on the mountain, staggering around with sap pails.

Sap is wet, and melting snow is slippery. These are elemental facts of life in the sugarbush. Soon enough I slipped and sloshed many cold gallons of the liquor of Yankee dreams all over myself. My down jacket metamorphosed into some cruel wetsuit.

"Hey, don't spill our sap," my neighbor hollered.

"Sorry. Lost my footing."

"There's *rocks* underneath that snow."

I knew that: hard, cold, slippery rocks. I toiled on, increasingly convinced that Tom Jefferson had never sugared a day in his life.

After many hours, all three hundred fifty buckets had been emptied for the day, and rehung on their spiles, and their contents transported down the mountain. Then we got to spend the waning daylight in the steamy sugarhouse — a veritable sauna. Here, bathed in sweat and sticky-sweet condensation, the operation's braumeister stood firing the evaporator. Its appetite for cordwood was frankly voracious. Somewhere, under clouds of rolling steam, I knew that sap was boiling, but I never glimpsed it through the fog. Now and then the master of this rig opened a brass gate to let a cup or two of finished maple syrup trickle out. We all sampled some.

"That'll go Fancy," my neighbor declared.

"Go where?"

"*Fancy*. The best grade. Better than Grade A, even. You can only make Fancy syrup early in the season."

"Good run?" asked the man in charge of boiling.

"You should make four gallons."

Somehow, this seemed precious small return for the ocean of sap that we had wrested from the sugarbush. And our day's work had been, after all, only *one* day's work. "How long will the sap run?" I asked.

"Till the nights stay warm. Warm nights, you start getting buddy sap."

"Buddy?"

"When the buds start swelling. On the trees." The man threw on another log. "Buddy syrup's pretty awful."

"Hey, it's milking time," my neighbor announced. He took another quick taste of syrup, then turned to me. "Want to come back tomorrow, learn some more?"

"No, thanks. I've learned enough."

The sap gathering crew tramped out toward the milkhouse, and my wife and I stood watching the sugar-maker fire the evaporator for a while longer. "How long does a day's boiling take you?" my wife asked.

"Midnight, like as not. It all depends."

"*Midnight!*"

"So," he said, "you want to start sugaring?"

"Less and less."

"It's quite a piece of work. Most folks, though, they get so sick of winter? Sugar season gets them up and moving. Helps the circulation."

Winters *are* long here, and perhaps my circulation suffers, but I continue not to sugar. One wall of my office is panelled in the weathered clapboards salvaged from the luckless sugar house. Picturesque. Now and then, gazing on those handsome boards, I think of the sugar of democracy and how I do not make it. And how much I *like* not making it.

Are these sentiments reproachable? I admit to worse: in recent years, I have become a modest maple landlord — turning my back utterly on citizen-farmer values. A while ago, one of my sugaring neighbors dropped by to make a sensible proposition. "You aren't *ever* going to sugar, are you?" he began.

"I sincerely doubt it."

"Would you let me tap a few of your trees down along our boundary?"

We went for a walk. He showed me maples — half a dozen, maybe more — that stand near his sugarbush. I would never tap them, I knew. "Help yourself," I told him.

"You want rent?"

"How about a gallon of syrup a year?"

"You've got it."

"*Fancy*," I added.

Eating pancakes drenched with syrup made from one's own

maple trees is a rich — an exquisite — pleasure on a bitter winter morning. But it need not be a democratic pleasure. For me, anyway, the sugar of democracy tastes all the sweeter knowing I've done absolutely nothing to produce the stuff.

• Corn

Corn, I recall being taught in school, is King. King of North American field crops, at any rate. Nothing else can match its yield of energy per acre, and the plant's indelicate size — from seed kernel to mature ear and stalk — lends itself admirably to the rough-and-tumble of mechanized farming. Equally important, though, is a simple human fact: any man who turns a bare field into waving corn — erect, stately, high as an elephant's eye — can't help feeling mighty proud.

I took note of this pride when, early in my tenure as a student Yankee, a neighbor came to pay a social visit toward the end of August. After some preliminary chat, he walked me to his car and opened up the trunk for me. There, folded back several times upon itself, was a single stalk of field corn. Reverently, he lifted it out and unfolded it across the lawn. "Sixteen feet," he told me.

"Wow! You grew that?"

"Down along the river bank. Stuff grows like a bastard."

Like a hybrid, I suppose he meant. As I congratulated him — one citizen-farmer to another — I thought: no one has ever brought a bale of hay around to show me. Nobody parades his oats or barley up and down the street. Corn, though — this is king. This is where Yankee farmers really prove their mettle.

Then I got a terrible, regrettable idea. I thought *I* should grow some corn.

I owned, at the time, ten sheep. Feeding corn to such a small flock — feeding corn *liberally* — my annual requirement might approach a single ton. Roughly $160 at the feed store. Looking back, I find it most extraordinary that I planned to grow one single ton of corn for less than $160. But I did — and, diseconomies of scale aside, I was fired with conviction. If a Vermonter's corn crop was a public statement, I was going to speak to my new neighbors in their own language.

Ninety bushels, I discovered, is the average local yield of

shelled corn per acre sown. On that basis — if I were a merely average corn grower — half an acre would produce the ton of corn that I desired. Half an acre, frankly, is not a major planting. Many farmers figure *fifty* acres is about the point where field corn recoups its costs; otherwise, the specialized machinery used to plant and cultivate and harvest and store the stuff is difficult to amortize.

This did not disturb me, for I had no corn machinery. I planned to substitute an array of garden tools and my own strong, eager back, but I got a whiff of the wild disparity between my half-acre cornfield and a typical plantation when I went to buy some hybrid corn seed. Three pounds, I asked for.

"Can't sell that. Comes by the bushel."

"Bushel?! I just want a *little* cornfield."

"Corn seed keeps. For several years, anyway."

"But a bushel — that's a lifetime supply."

They wouldn't sell less, though. So I visited the neighbor who had grown sixteen-foot-high corn and asked to purchase three pounds from the several bushels of seed he had ordered for the coming crop year. "Putting in some corn?" he asked.

"Just enough to get my feet wet. Get the hang of how to grow it."

"Corn for silage?"

"No. For grain."

"How are you going to plant it?"

"Little garden seeder, maybe."

"How're you going to cultivate it?"

"Garden tiller."

"How're you going to pick it?"

I flexed my muscles.

"Well, Lord God. Three pounds? God bless you, boy — I'll *give* that to you."

So I got my seed for nothing. Two or three weeks later, at a farm dispersal auction, I blew $100 on a set of ancient plows for the equally ancient tractor I had recently acquired. As plows go, this was a bargain. But the day I tried them out, I found I might as well have dropped an anchor into the good earth. My tractor could not pull the plows uphill, could not pull them on the contour; in fact, it could just barely pull those plows *down* a decent slope — a flagrant violation of the most basic principles of soil conservation.

Neighbors watch each other plow. Plowing is important work, a show of intelligent mastery over awesome horsepower. I actually stopped traffic on my quiet rural road, chugging downhill at an earthworm's pace to till my cornfield. It took seven hours — barely moving, and at full throttle — to turn my little plot over, and it cost me tractor wear and tear that was distinctly audible. Fact is, I got so damn sick of plowing that I scaled down my cropland from one-half an acre to one-third. Then I went to borrow some old harrows from another neighbor to prepare the seedbed.

"Putting in some corn?" the man asked.

"Some. But less than I expected. Plowing — boy, that's for the birds."

"Plowing takes a lot of iron. That old sod, especially. Hasn't been turned in many a year."

"Anything I need to know to run those old harrows?"

"Hell, no."

"Can my tractor pull them?"

"Should. You bring a clevis?"

"What's a clevis?"

"To hitch them up. You'll have to get a clevis."

So I drove to a farm equipment store and bought a clevis — a fairly simple, albeit beefy, hunk of steel. Twenty-three dollars. But I was, after all, getting free use of a disc harrow. Next morning, I began to run it over my plowed furrows. I disked for several hours, dragging those gangs of steel plates behind my tractor with very little effort; but then I realized that the harrow's pitch — its angle of attack on the soil — was adjustable. Infinitely. I had set the tool in its attitude of least resistance, so its tired discs were barely riffling up the earth. A man might harrow for a very long time this way, and never make a seedbed.

Once I got the harrows cutting properly, my tractor responded with a series of mechanical breakdowns. Work, after all, is work. But I had the job done by the following evening, in time to watch dark storm clouds brewing. Heavy rains destroy fresh seedbeds, so I left off harrowing and quickly wheeled out my corn planting machine — a precision seeder made for vegetable gardens. It is plastic; one pushes it. At $32.95, it had cost several thousand dollars less than the next cheapest corn planter.

Frantic, under darkening skies punctuated by forked lightning, I raced the seeding contraption back and forth across the field. Every few inches it deposited a seed, most often smack on the bare earth. Trouble. But this was clay soil, not a finely tilled garden loam. Dancing behind the seeder, I did my best to step each kernel into the hard ground. When I failed — often — hungry birds weren't far behind me. Unfortunately for them, my neighbor's seed came treated with a fungicide of respectable toxicity.

The real drawback to this instant seeding operation, though, was not revealed until the plants emerged. I had achieved dramatic variations in row spacing — the regular geometry that makes a cornfield so attractive. I had sown some rows six inches apart, and others six *feet* apart. Worse, a few rows crisscrossed or twined around each other. Such haphazard planting does not make a cornfield merely ugly; it makes weed control and fertilizing and eventual harvesting well nigh impossible. That is why I managed only fitful and sporadic efforts to cultivate my corn or to feed its growth with fertilizers. An astonishing array of vegetation burst from my little plot, each species battling to secure a bit of daylight. Toward the end, I had some twelve-foot corn stalks. I had twelve-foot weeds, too.

Twelve-foot weeds — setting fluffy seed aloft at the slightest puff of wind — did not much endear me to my neighbor citizen-farmers. No one came around to show their corn off to me, or to examine mine. I *did* have a crop, of sorts, and early in October I went forth to harvest it. I pushed a wheelbarrow down the rows, breaking off fat ears and trundling them over to the pickup truck where my wife sat husking them. This was slow, tedious — not to say boring — work; but it was not difficult. *Anyone* could do it. Every so often my wife would switch off with me — I would shuck, and she would pick. By afternoon, we had a modest pile of ear corn in the truck bed.

Now, my wife was pregnant at the time. Nine months pregnant, even. By two o'clock she announced she thought she was in labor.

"Honey — honestly?"

"It's okay. Let's get this done, then I'll go lie down."

"Don't you want to —"

"Not yet." She smiled gamely. "It's too nice a day."

So we worked. Then — having seen our quiet harvest from afar — the neighbor who had made me a present of corn seed stopped by to visit. Whatever his opinion of my field, he made an effort to be civil. "What's this — a husking bee?" he asked.

My wife sucked in a deep breath. Lamaze style. I said, "Guess what? Baby's coming."

"Well, Lord God!" He stared. "I read they do this over in Siberia."

"Do what?"

"Make their women give birth right out in the fields."

"We'll quit soon," my wife said. "He doesn't *make* me do this — promise."

But the man looked dubious. He shook his head and asked me: "Ninety bushel corn?"

"Not quite."

"Fifty?"

"Possibly." But in my heart I guessed what, when I quantified my efforts, I would find I had produced. Four hundred pounds of corn — or thirty bushels to the acre. Retail value: thirty dollars.

"This cornfield," he began — but then words failed him. "This is really something."

"Let's just say I grew enough to learn corn's not for me."

He studied my wife, holding her breath. He surveyed my golden ears — all several hundred of them. "Corn is king," he said. "To some."

I knew then the statement my little crop had made to my neighbors. Corn is king. But it is not everyone's crop.

III. MINERAL

• Natural Gas

I first heard of the Eastern Overthrust Belt a couple of years ago, in connection with a big, important natural-gas strike in West Virginia. Fat city. After paying Texans through the nose for decades, here was nature's most nearly perfect fossil fuel in the Northeast's own backyard. True, drilling the overthrust was complicated and expensive, given the twisted and broken nature of its rock formations. But the geologic structures bearing gas underground were apt to be vast. Sixty-eight *trillion* cubic feet of gas, perhaps. Now, what energy-starved Yankee wouldn't drink to that?

Some months later, I got wind of more exciting news. This same Eastern Overthrust Belt, though centered in Appalachia, nonetheless sent a long, slender finger up the Hudson River valley, brushing the entire western edge of Vermont. Where *I* live. Overnight, rumors were flying of the coming gas boom. Canny oilmen moving in, wildcatters plotting where to roll the dice and drill away. No more winters spent stoking hungry wood stoves; suddenly, Vermonters dreamed of sheikhdom.

Next thing I knew, a very large, aggressive, self-assured man was knocking on the door to my humble dwelling. Just at dusk — on a snowy December evening. When I opened up, he pushed his way in like he owned the place; next, he flashed a business card on which an oil rig was pictured. "Hey!" he said. "I'm Rick Ricetti. Landman. With Amalgamated Petro Consolidated. Heard of me?"

"I think I saw your picture," I said. "In the paper."

He strode to the fire, plopped himself down in my rocking chair and opened up a briefcase. He whipped out a legal document. He said: "Then I guess you know. About the gas." He pointed to the floor — no, *underneath* the floor. "There's a *lot* of gas down there."

I said, "I don't really think I'm interested. At this time."

"You know what it costs to drill one well? Listen — it costs millions. And it costs millions more to figure where's the *place* to drill it. Seismic testing, geologic mapping, all this stuff. *You* don't have that kind of money. Hey — *I* haven't got it, either. But Amalgamated does! But before we come into an area, we've got to lease enough land to make the testing worth our while. Right? So — you own 150 acres?"

"How did you know?"

He nodded, entering the information onto one of the blank lines in his contract. He said, "Town Clerk's office. Now, your full name's Donald Earl Mitchell?"

I stared at his contract, which was fast becoming filled in. It looked like the original fine print document. "I'm not signing that," I told him. "Not before a lawyer reads it, anyway."

"So who's your lawyer?"

"Never mind."

"Come on — you haven't *got* a lawyer. What's a lawyer, anyway? You know what he is? He's one more hand in your back pocket! Hey — you know, we *pay* to lease your land. For these drilling rights — whether we drill or not. A dollar per acre per year. For ten years."

"That," I said, "is not a lot of money."

"Hey! You think you're special? That's the going rate. But if we *drill* here — hey, if we hit gas you'll be on Easy Street. Because there's something called a Drilling Unit, see? Which is basically the 640 acres around a well. And if you got acres in the Unit, you get your share of the royalty. Which is one-eighth of the gas. Which should be —" He gestured expansively and named a dollar figure well into six digits. "That's every year," he added. "Till the well runs dry."

"Sorry. I'm not interested."

"What are you, crazy?"

"I don't want an oil rig out my window."

"Buddy, if we drill for oil out your window, you'll be able to afford some mighty fancy landscaping."

I said: "What's the rush, though? For one lousy dollar an acre — I figure, if you guys start drilling and hit gas around here, you'll be back to talk about a lot more than a dollar an acre. I can wait."

"Listen — you think you're so smart. But we've got leases right now with all your neighbors, see? All around you." He rattled off — accurately — several neighbors' names. "We could stick a well up there on Cuthbert's back cornfield and suck all the gas out from under *your* farm. If you aren't in our Drilling Unit, we won't owe you nothing."

"That sounds illegal," I said.

"Hey! *Illegal!* You know what you've got for oil and gas laws in the State of Vermont? *Zilch!* This is new territory, fella. Good luck! Sue us! Hey! — I don't want to fight. I came here to cut you *in* on this gas thing. If you're smart, sign here. Chance like this may never come again."

"Shucks," I said. "The story of my life. Just leave your contract here. I'll try to read it, maybe."

"Read it! Yeah, you read it! Right! I'll call you in a couple of days."

So I got my first landman out the door, and settled down to read his lengthy dissertation on the party of the first (Lessor) and the party of the second (Lessee). Soon enough, I knew that its complexities were well beyond me. In the morning, I ran my finger down a list of lawyers in the phone book. Choosing one of these to call, I said: "I've been trying to read Amalgamated Petro Consolidated's Oil and Gas Lease here, and —"

"Don't you sign that!" the man hollered in the telephone. "That lease is scandalous!"

"Oh, you've seen it?"

"Seen it! I should say! I'm working, on behalf of several clients, on some different language. Very important. If Amalgamated takes it, fine. If not, tough. I'll put your name on my list, and — in the meantime, don't let these landmen pressure you."

"Right," I told him. "Thanks for your advice." The call took thirty seconds.

Thus armed, I looked forward to Rick Ricetti's call. "Sorry," I said. "My lawyer doesn't like your lease."

"So who's your lawyer?"

I informed him.

"Fine! Fine! We'll get to work on him. We got lawyers, too. No problem. You keep in touch, hey? Bye!"

A few days later, the next landman came to visit. From a different company: Conglomerated Oil of America, say. He had a somewhat less muscular, somewhat more articulate presentation. I asked, "Can you really stick a well up on my neighbor's cornfield and suck the gas out from under my farm? And pay me nothing?"

"It is unlikely — but it's not impossible. This Eastern Overthrust — we expect to find some huge structures. Fifty square miles, maybe. So one well could draw in lots of gas outside its Drilling Unit. Drilling Units are pretty arbitrary."

"I'd have no recourse in law?"

"Well, you could try. But it would be our geologists against yours. And ours are pretty good."

I took his contract, which was twice as long as Amalgamated's. Finer type, too. And I called my lawyer.

"Don't you sign that lease!" he told me. "I've seen it. That lease is scurrilous!"

"Right," I told him. "Thanks for your advice."

A week later, the third landman made it up the driveway. Eager young fellow from North American Petroleum, Ltd. But I held my ground and turned him back long before he got inside the door. After that, the traffic stopped; I figure the landmen had worked the county's landowners pretty darn thoroughly, and now — so far as leasing was concerned — we were a dry hole. Some other tendril of the Eastern Overthrust must now be coping with their blitz.

Spring came. One day, the news reported that Amalgamated had sold all their leases in the county to another group. Global-Galactical Oil and Gas, Inc. This was big news, since it proved that Rick Ricetti and his like were just a bunch of leasehounds. Stories of elderly women being pushed into signing leases *while their husbands were out plowing* now began to circulate. Many folks had trusted Amalgamated's stated aim to drill for gas; now they felt upset, betrayed.

Shortly thereafter, though, a caravan of oversized trucks began to crawl along the country's roads, making seismic tests. The biggest truck would drive a few feet, hunker down on hydraulic arms and shake the earth. Violently. Instruments in the surrounding trucks would make sophisticated notes on the vibrations. The spot would be marked, then all the trucks would drive ahead a few feet and repeat the cycle.

I thought, now they're getting somewhere. This is exploration. But then one day the trucks disappeared, long before they could have plumbed the entire county.

One day, not much after this, I was cleaning the barn when Rick Ricetti stomped in. With an unpleasant companion whose job, it seemed, was to look as though he'd like to break my thumbs. I said, "What's this? I read that your company sold out."

"Oh, no. We sold to *us*. We're them, too."

"I see," I said.

"I'd like to have you sign that lease."

Aha! I thought. Those big trucks found gas on my land. They went away, because I hadn't signed. Eureka! I said coolly, "Gee, I'm sorry."

"Hey — everything's okay with your lawyer, now. We're giving you a seismic clause. Which is all he wanted, really. I suppose you've seen our trucks?"

"Seen them? I have *felt* them."

He dangled his document. "Well, you sign right here."

"How come my lawyer didn't call me about this?"

"Hey, I don't know. Don't ask me. Maybe he *forgot* you. He's told all his other clients."

"I don't think he'd —"

"Call him, buddy. Call him right this minute."

"I'm cleaning my barn."

"Boy, you're something. Dumb! You get in the oil business, you won't have to work knee-deep in crap with a pitchfork! I'll bet even your lawyer thinks you're pretty dumb. Here it is, now. Sign this?"

"No."

"Thanks a lot, dummy," said Ricetti. And his goon, or sidekick, sneered. But they turned around and left my barn.

A couple hours later, I called the lawyer. "Landmen again!" I told him. "Did you say it's fine to sign, now? Some new deal? A seismic clause?"

"Jesus, those bastards! Scoundrels! Goddamn liars! Did you sign it?"

"No. But almost. These guys are tigers."

"Don't sign anything, you hear?"

"Right," I told him. "Thanks for your advice."

Many months have passed since then. The seismic trucks are long gone, and there's not a drilling rig in sight. No more landmen come around. It puzzles me, and it puzzles even more the dozens of Vermont farmers who leased their drilling rights to one group or another. Is there gas beneath us? Will we ever get to drive Mercedeses? Live high? Go to OPEC meetings? In the meantime, nobody is chucking out his trusty woodstove. In the meantime, more and more folks think that the Eastern Overthrust Belt may screw a lot of people.

CHAPTER FOUR

The Right Crops

*L*IKE THE WRONG CROPS, THE right crops all presented certain initial challenges and even outright difficulties, but these were not, by and large, problems of production. One hallmark of a right crop is that it should require little conscious effort or attention to grow. The demanding aspect of a right crop is its harvest, or utilization; a hobby farmer must get tooled up — psychically and physically — to reap a right crop in timely and appropriate fashion.

The ultimate, unmistakable definition of a right crop is that it makes pocketbook sense. This, I must stress carefully, is not the same as income. I realize that cannier farmers than I have successfully found ways to convert their labors into coin of the realm, but I have not yet mastered this awesome feat. Still, growing the right crops can help a fellow squeeze what dollars he does have mighty hard; at the end of the day, this can amount to something very much like what my neighbors respectfully call "cash money."

After several years of freewheeling agricultural ventures with the wrong crops, cash money came to assume an unprecedented importance in my life. I was going broke, or, put better, going *land poor:* possessing substantial real estate, machinery, and livestock, but never able to discover five bucks in my pocket. Finding and becoming adept with the right crops did not change this unhappy condition overnight; little by little, though, such crops substantially reduced the need for cash money. That, in a place like rural Vermont, can seem very much like affluence.

I have followed closely the careers of several of my contemporaries who have fulfilled their promise and are rising steadily on corporate ladders of one sort or another. Striving to improve the quality of their lives, these individuals inevitably devise ways to earn more money. This is not our strategy up here; we devise ways to *need less* of the stuff. Whole categories of consumer goods that others pay plenty for — food, drink, and heating fuel come quickly to mind — we have in embarrassing abundance for a small investment in labor and smaller yet in cash. The cash costs of farming, too, can be cut back to the bone when one uses the manure of one's own livestock to fertilize fields growing the sort of hay that would have grown there *anyway* — the sort of hay that just comes up. Abandoning plows and harrows, one can use this system to recycle nutrients indefinitely through one's animals and one's fields — a profound savings in feed. And farmers, even those who in former careers required cash money to pay income taxes, quickly learn how to produce a dandy paper crop that completely obviates this boring drain on funds.

The right crops have helped us to survive relocation up-country, and even to prosper here — after a fashion. Without them, we would have long since sacrificed our dreams and hustled back to much better compensated, infinitely poorer lives.

• Firewood

Wood heat, until recently all but extinct, is now the basis of a booming industry in rural New England. We have our own stove foundries, we have wood dealers with commercial-scale businesses, and of course we have our own forests. In a region where few commodities are cheap, wood is regarded as an ace up the Yankee sleeve. A superbargain. I believe the case for wood heat is all too often, all too easily, overstated, and yet, after nine winters of heating my drafty old converted barn entirely with wood, I certainly qualify as a partisan.

The last time I bought a drop of heating oil was in the winter of 1972-73, when the price climbed an infuriating ten percent — from 19¢ to 21¢ a gallon — in a single heating season. Ah, the days of innocence. Nowadays, two-cent-per-gallon increases are too small to notice; the 20¢ gallon of fuel oil costs well over a buck.

Even a wood-heat partisan, however, must note with dismay that in this period when fuel-oil prices have skyrocketed, the price of a cord of dry hardwood delivered in Middlebury, Vermont, has also increased. From twenty to ninety-five dollars, in fact. Loggers and cordwood dealers have, as it were, ridden the coattails of oil sheiks to sudden prosperity, and this in spite of wood being, as we are reminded in an endless local litany, a *renewable* resource. As opposed, say, to petroleum.

Soon, economists may speak of cordodollars in the same breath as petrodollars. They *already* like to tell us what good sense it makes to keep this dough at home, allowing local timber magnates an arbitrarily high price for fuelwood that, in effect, is being set in the Persian Gulf. I am no economist, and I am a partisan; still, I say that paying ninety-five bucks a cord is a very questionable domestic economy — unless one just happens to love a crackling fire and the smell of woodsmoke.

One cord of dry hardwood, burned in an efficient stove, *may* yield as much heat as 150 gallons of fuel oil. And, then again, it may not. Oil can be measured with absolute precision and burned under measurable conditions; almost nothing about cordwood can be measured accurately. Item: dryness. Dry wood, when burned, can produce twice the B.T.U. output of green wood, but "dry" is a highly relative term. Item: species. Shagbark hickory is good for 25,000,000 B.T.U.'s per cord; butternut is good for scarcely half that.

Worst item of all: the actual-volume factor. A cord is a pile of wood four feet by four feet by eight feet — or 128 cubic feet. In fact, though, the *best* cords contain perhaps ninety cubic feet of wood; the balance of that volume is bark and air. Without much cunning on the stacker's part, a "cord" may contain only fifty cubic feet of wood. Charlatans can and do beat that. Every day. Buying fuel oil is a matter of measurement; buying cordwood is an act of faith. Cordwood does look, on paper, to be somewhat cheaper per available B.T.U. than fuel oil — but only the very driest and hardest of cords, sold by that rare creature, a truly honest dealer.

One class of Yankee, though, can be exempted from these calculations: those who own small woodlots and who are prepared to toil in them. And, I might add, who purchased these woodlots *before* the crunch. Thanks to blind luck and the vicissitudes of life, I fit all these categories. So I look on wood heat as a species of economy, though one cannot easily compare placing a check in the mail for Exxon to roaring through one's woodlot with a chainsaw for a week each summer. Or to the patient care and daily feeding of two wood stoves round the clock, five months of each year.

Let me *try* to compare. I own a woodlot of sixty acres, more or less. Throwing in the swamp, adding in the cliffs and rocky ledge on which no trees will grow, it may come to seventy acres of "forest." A mere drop in the bucket, but enough, I'm told, to produce an annual growth of nine cords of firewood. I harvest and burn roughly eight cords a year, so — with "prudent forest management" — I should be able to keep my stoves in fuel forever.

Nothing in my former life, however, had even remotely prepared me for becoming a "prudent forest manager." Not only could I not discern a wolf tree from a sawlog; I couldn't tell an oak tree from a sugar maple. So I was pleasantly surprised to learn that my government was *worried* about people like me — about naive, untrained, Johnny-come-lately owners of the nation's valuable timber resource — and was willing to spend tax dollars to make me a wise manager of my woodlot.

The government's principal agent in this enterprise turned out to be my County Forester, from the Co-operative Extension Service. He proved a perfect gentleman, and he spent a frustrating morning tramping through the forest with me, wincing involuntarily as I revealed an alarming lack of knowledge about forestry.

"I do believe you had a sugarbush here," he declared, examining old stumps. "Someone must have logged it pretty good, some years ago."

"Right," I said. "Former ower. Sick to hell of sugaring."

"Now it's mainly coming up to beech and basswood."

"Listen, I want firewood. Heat. Fuel. For free, like."

"Wouldn't be a bad idea to favor the remaining maples. Clean out all the junk around them."

"Maple — that's the three-pronged leaf?"

He looked mightily discouraged. But he took a sort of squirt gun full of yellow paint from his jacket pocket, and he marked a tree from fifteen paces. "That," he said, "is sugar maple."

This tool impressed me — I am easily impressed by tools — and, when he had left, I thought of marking trees throughout the forest. But I had no idea where to buy a logger's squirt gun, so I settled for an old paint brush and a can of paint. Yellow paint — oil base, enamel. I entered the woods with a field guide to trees in one hand, the open paint can in the other, and the simple strategy of marking the trunk of each tree that was *not* a maple. Then, once I had cut my fuel, I wouldn't have a forest full of unsightly yellow blazes.

It was autumn. Leaves were turning, and I despaired of being able to detect the maples once their branches were bare. So I worked with dedication, and three days later I had marked five acres of the woodlot. My paint can was empty. It seemed to me that five acres might yield the seven cords of wood I felt would heat the house that winter, so I left off painting and went out to buy a chainsaw.

This important purchase set me back nearly as much as a winter's fuel oil would have (this was 1973), but I took the long view, recognizing that certain capital costs were inevitable. The dealer, fellow name of Connors, had a missing finger that I feared to ask the cause of. Chainsaw accident? Misjudged tree? But I offered him at least as much to worry about. "Cutting firewood?" he asked.

"Some. I think I've marked five acres."

"Keep you out of trouble. Thirty, forty cords anyway."

"Forty!"

"Piece of work. Good money this year, though."

"Sure. Say — how, exactly, do you fell a tree?"

This question changed the whole tenor of our conversation. I imagined him telling his wife at dinner about the character who bought a chainsaw, proposed to cut forty cords of firewood in one breath, and asked him how to do it in the next. He recovered, though, enough to offer me a book on forestry practices. I believe he gave it to me. I believe he doubted he would see me alive again.

I read the book. Good reading. Soon I had trees dropping over backwards, falling sideways, hanging up on other trees, and showering heavy branches down onto the forest floor. I was young. The trees I chose to fell conformed to sound management criteria — which is to say they would have made terrible sawlogs for a lumber mill and were so large and misshapen as to be very difficult to fell in any direction with accuracy. The government would have been proud.

My fun ended the day I took my chainsaw back to Connors in four pieces. In a box. "Truck run over this?" he asked.

"Tree fell on it. Buckled, sort of. Slight miscalculation."

He grunted. "Glad you came in, anyway. I got to check the number of that saw."

"How come?"

"Warranty." He took the portion of my saw which bore a serial number, and checked it against a printed sheet. "Ayup — just as I thought. Got a bulletin about this? Says the clutch is no good."

"Seems to work all right."

"Says the clutch can blow up, sometimes. Hurts the saw. Even hurts the operator, sometimes."

"Fix it," I said. I was still in shock, I think, from having seen my mighty tool crushed like a popsicle at my feet.

"No charge to fix the clutch. We're like *De*-troit. You been gaining on your woodpile?"

"Slowly."

"Here's a tip," he told me. "Get the easy wood out, first."

When his repairs had been accomplished, I returned to the forest with less confidence in saw and self. I began to seek the easy wood — straight-trunked trees right at the forest's edge, trees with a clear and unambiguous line of fall. And I have been cutting out the easy wood ever since, forest management be damned.

Now — after nine years — I have finally cut forty cords of hardwood out of those five marked acres. And there must be forty more cords out there, because I still have hundreds of trees blazed in eyesore yellow. Visitors remark on this the minute they enter the woods; I tell them an interesting variation on the story of a leprechaun tracked to his pot of gold. The irony is, after my first few days cutting firewood, I could tell each tree in the forest by its shape, its bark, by its smell, its sapwood, buds, seeds — there is no confusing tree species once a person has felled a few and cut them up to stove length.

By going for the easy timber, I can cut, haul, split, and stack a cord of hardwood in a day. This would set no records, locally, but it does mean that I need to schedule only about a week of dogged work each year to fill my woodshed. That seems a just amount of time to devote to providing for winter heat in a cold climate. Indeed, when I consider what I'd have to pay in cash money for those B.T.U.'s, I rank that week of forestry as the highest-paid work I do all year. Worth a couple of thousand dollars, maybe — unless I consider wear and tear on my saw, the abuse of my pickup truck, the taxes on my forest land, a minimal wage commensurate with my talent, and much else.

On balance, though — even counting costs — there is value here. I *am* a wood heat partisan. And Connors, although he doesn't exactly consider me a lumberjack, at least no longer looks amazed when I stop in with hands and feet still intact. With the boom in wood heat, he has grown accustomed to selling saws to worse clowns than I was nine years ago. Just last week I bought a file from him to sharpen my tool; he was taking $400 from some flatlander for a new chainsaw. "Connors," I asked, "is that a bargain?"

"It all depends." He shrugged. "Do you like the smell of woodsmoke?"

Yes. It *is* a lovely smell.

• Vegetables

A friend of a friend of mine staggered into his garden with a loaded shotgun, early last August, and he blasted the zucchini plants. *Blam! Blam!* One can smell hot lead, one sees the empty shells. "Take that!" the fellow cried. "I've had zucchini up to *here*, already! Zucchini soup, zucchini bread, zucchini soufflé, zucchini spaghetti, zucchini casseroles, and *still*" — he picked a limp, shell-shocked baseball bat of an overgrown zucchini from the good earth, and harangued it — "still you monsters grow. Enough!" With a parting blast, he left the vegetable full of buckshot.

The typical Vermonter eats from the garden. Eats from it so

avidly — not to say obsessively — that only now and then is a rational perspective encountered, such as this zucchini-plugger's. Lay this to the legendary Yankee parsimony, which holds it a minor crime to pay cash money for vegetables one can grow for oneself. And to the brevity of our growing season, the frustration of working soils that lie frozen solid for five months of each year. No wonder when the growing is good, the Vermonter pigs out on whatever is growing.

I have seen the world, for a fortnight in midsummer, as a mad race to eat zucchini squash before they could balloon into outsized clubs. The full metamorphosis — from tasty lilliput to stringy, coarse brobdingnagian — takes only a couple of days. Who, having moved into a pastoral landscape, needs such gratuitous and unrelenting pressure? Who would seek such a harvest?

I did — for years. The novelty of being able to produce abundant vegetables dedicated me to gardening for bumper crops. Each May I would purchase the little seed packet that contains just six zucchini seeds for 69¢. Quite expensive, as seeds go. I would plant each one, then stand back, fate sealed, waiting for the inevitable explosion of zucchini. Luckily, this was only a stage. Now, I plant just one zucchini seed and invent creative ways — drowning, burning, pulverizing — to destroy the other five.

Most of the difficulties gardeners experience in growing vegetables have analogous solutions. In fact, there is a predictable progression of stages in garden management that flatlanders like us, transplanted upcountry, can be expected to pass through as they mature in wisdom. The first and most naive garden theory is that one can eat a normal, varied diet while the garden is in season, and freeze, can, or otherwise preserve all excess production. This turns out to be an awful lot of work. It also requires unnatural dependence on pressure canners, chest freezers, ten-tray dehydrators, and a drawer full of nifty, vegetable-specific gadgets like bean frenchers and corn shellers. None of these items, I must point out, is cheap. Nonetheless, I well recall throwing myself into "putting foods by" with the energy of a zealot — and with pen poised over checkbook.

This phase is soon succeeded by one less strenuous, which involves gorging oneself several times daily on whatever the garden happens to be producing at the time. One strives to have the garden plot producing *something* edible from, say, mid-April right up until Christmas.

We ran our garden according to this second school of thought for a good long time. It minimizes mindless bean-shelling orgies and entire September weekends lost to tomato canning. Besides, vegetables never taste so fresh — or are so nutritious — as when just plucked. The maturing gardener can sell off most of that fancy food-preserving gear to some bright-eyed newcomer.

There's just one small problem: the gardener's diet, on this eat-what's-growing theory, begs for comparison to serial monogamy. One finds one's metabolism wedded, for a fortnight, to asparagus; then asparagus disappears without a trace, and it's on to peas; then endless salads; then beans; and so it goes, through zucchini madness and the obligatory dozen ears of corn per dinner. The first hard frost is almost welcomed, because it kills off a mess of vegetables as surely as a loaded shotgun. This, though, heralds broccoli season, and then Brussels sprouts and cabbage — plants that thrive on frosty nights. And before the soil freezes, local custom is to cover rows of beets and carrots with moldy hay bales, everyman's free insulation. Thus protected, root crops can be harvested quite fresh deep into winter: one enters the garden with a strong, sharp shovel and digs to find the prize. Picturesque. Thoreau would love it. But one's stomach knows too well exactly how these roots will taste. One has dined on these same turnips for three weeks, or longer.

Finally — by New Year's Day — anybody's garden is *finis*. The gardener can at last walk into the A & P without a trace of shame, selecting his vegetables from the riotous assortment that has been there all along. People need these brief winter months when nothing grows, to straighten out their digestive tracts. Before one can turn around, though, Town Meeting Day arrives. First Tuesday in March. On Town Meeting Day the good Vermont citizen rises, plants tomato seeds, and marches off to vote down the coming year's school budget. An often-heard greeting, on that predictably frigid morn, is: "Did you start your sets?"

"Did I *what*?" I replied, the first time I was thus accosted.

"Start your sets. Tomatoes, peppers —"

"Should I have?"

My questioner led me to believe I'd shirked a civic duty as important as voting itself. I have come, I confess, to share this feeling — even though the plants I start in March invariably get fried in the hotbed, some May afternoon. Every year I grow — and kill — fine tomato sets; then I have to buy some. But I grow them anyway, out of civic duty, I suppose. We have this conceit: if everybody had a garden, there would be no poor. No welfare cases. No indigents. I know better, but I can't help liking the thought.

In any event, if our poor were made to garden, then they'd have the same weird dietary habits as all our eat-what's-growing theory gardeners. Serial monotony loves company.

Sooner or later, all gardeners court depression by pushing a pencil over their harvest's cash worth versus the money and human effort required to produce it. Theory-I gardeners — the food preservation nuts — might well avoid this exercise, because of their considerable investment in gear. But Theory-II, eat-what's-growing gardeners, have costs as well. Rototillers. Rakes and hoes and cultivators by the armful. As a Theory-II gardener, I finally pegged my garden's gross value at roughly $500 per year — based on supermarket prices. (The same produce would be cheaper at a roadside stand.) Amortizing my investment in tools at $100 per year, I could claim $400 return on roughly two hundred hours of family labor.

That, I noted soberly, was well under the minimum wage. But

— I asked myself — hadn't it all been great fun? I regretted asking. Some gardening work *is* fun, and satisfying too, but the great preponderance of it is boring by any standard, and much of it is actually distasteful. Such as picking slimy little slugs off the ripe tomatoes and squishing them between two fingers. People should get combat pay to do such work. Or buy tomatoes.

Is the Theory-II garden worth it? Eventually, its advocates throw out economics and rave instead about good health. Nourishment. Nutrition. Curiously, though, this attitude requires *more* expense: primarily for books and magazines hyping organic gardens. On reading these, a person can argue with conviction that his homegrown vegetables are transforming him into a superman, while those who shop in grocery stores are gradually dying of pesticidal residues. I used to make this case as well as anyone, but, with passing years, I note that I am not becoming a superman. Worse luck, I have urban friends who appear to be positively thriving on the poisoned produce of large-scale agribiz.

The Theory-II garden, I have come to feel, is a dubious exchange of labor for vegetables. In time, though, I discovered a third theory of gardening by watching carefully how some of my neighbors — with impeccable Yankee credentials — went about it. Theory III is *laissez-faire*, insofar as possible. One can't exactly reap a garden that has not been sown, but old-timers manage to skip most of the many stages in between — thinning, weeding, cultivating, dusting, watering, *grooming* — and still come out with something worth harvesting. Furthermore, they do not make an effort to eat personally all that grows. That is what a pig is for. Theory-III gardening is, in short, the triumph of common sense over ideology. I like this.

In contrast to the high purpose and eager muscles I make my family bring to gardening each year, these old-timers aim only for maximum return from minimum effort. We have a tortuously thought-out garden map, with staggered planting dates, companion crops, shrewd rotations, and a zillion marigolds inserted to discourage insect pests; our garden takes several days of hard labor just to plant. Still, the road to mature gardening is long, and it would be wrong to try to hurry our adolescence. But I am now aware that things work differently down the road.

Down the road, someone runs the sixteen-foot-wide disc harrow through the backyard on his way to the back forty some bright May morning, and that is called tillage. Someone else, in an idle moment a few days later, casually scatters seeds where the harrow has disturbed the earth. Some months later, whoever has time pokes through heavy weeds to harvest the goods. As one might expect, our garden vastly outproduces theirs; but I have come to be impressed by what I figure is their considerably greater return on investment.

The Theory-III gardener grows only those vegetables that really want to grow. That will do so without coddling. There are no eggplants, no green peppers, no lima beans in these unkempt plots; as one moves toward Theory III, I suppose one must expect a new round of dietary havoc due to a seriously circumscribed menu. This became clear when a dedicated gardener down along the Otter Creek showed me what he held to be the ideal vegetable for Vermont. The true free lunch. Horseradish. Horseradish, he proved to me, is darn close to something for nothing — if you want it. He pulled a fat white root out of the ground, cut a generous hunk off it with his penknife, and pocketed it. Then he threw what was left back into the soil. Then he walked away, confident that the root would take hold and grow up again.

"Wow!" I said, realizing just what this feat represented. "And you're sure that plant won't die, now?"

"Die?" He laughed at me. "Horseradish? You can't kill it with a blowtorch."

• Vino

Near my bathtub hangs a photograph of Robert E. Lee's wine cellar: a musty and capacious and inviting room for tippling in his Arlington, Virginia, home. Scores of cobwebbed bottles line the cool brick walls, and casks and kegs of what look like home-brewed potables are arrayed along a counter. A fruit press and wooden stools stand near a three-legged table; plainly, one could spend some time here. "Not the sort of storage space," the photo caption reads, "likely to be found in today's house or apartment."

No? I clipped that photo from *The New York Times Magazine* and tacked it to the bathroom wall while I was in the throes of the barn conversion project. Barns enclose a great deal of space, much of it of questionable value on account of low beams and massive framing members. What better use for a fourteen-by-six-foot corner rife with architectural booby traps than as a place to lay down wine?

I lined the wine room with rough lumber shelves and counters, and scarcely compromised its intended purpose by placing our water pump and pressure tank in one corner. These throw condensation, after all, which would create an agreeably cool, moist — not to say moldy — atmosphere. Handhewn timbers, spattered with bird droppings and host to a horde of busy spiders, loomed overhead — ambience worthy of Robert E. Lee himself.

As built, my ample cellar would doubtless have accommodated fifty-odd cases of wine — but I never dreamed of purchasing the stuff on such a scale. Rather, I would *make* wine, following a time-honored homesteading tradition. Simple matter of growing some grapes and fermenting them. Absolutely legal, too — Congress, in its wisdom, grants all heads of households the right to make two hundred gallons of wine per year. *That's* Jeffersonian democracy in action!

I did not enter winemaking as a total novice. I confess to having brewed several hundred gallons of beer in my youthful, pre-Vermont days — at a time when homebrew was frankly illegal. That's not why I quit, though. I quit the day a ten-gallon batch, prematurely bottled, exploded in the closet of a friend's apartment where I was a guest. Every single quart. This made an expensive mess of all his clothes and left *me* on the street. Beer is the beverage of impatient youth, but impatient youth ought not, perhaps, be making significant decisions such as When To Bottle.

Despite this sad experience in the fermentation biz, I decided to embark upon winemaking as an activity befitting a dedicated and maturing citizen-farmer. Not a matter of brew today, imbibe tomorrow, wine required time: months of fermentation, years of aging. Success at winemaking would symbolize adulthood, sober acceptance of delayed gratification, and refined values.

To my neighbors, however, wine had different symbolic meanings. Their taste in booze, I learned soon enough, ran more to Seven 'N' Seven, rum and Coke, or various sour-mash bourbons served straight up. Wine meant *effete* to them. Wine meant *foreigners*. Wine meant *snobs*, and *city slickers*.

I recall a picnic supper that one of these neighbors dropped in on, our first summer here. My wife and I were not yet familiar with local custom which sanctions neighborly visits at mealtimes — because then one is certain of catching someone who otherwise would be off on a tractor somewhere — but discourages offering the visitor a plate. The visitor would not be so *gauche* as to come to eat; he has come to watch *you* eat, and form impressions of your diet.

We offered the man a plate.

"Oh, no," he said, offended. We were new, and dumb; we had misread his intentions.

"Glass of wine?"

He shook his head, he made a distasteful face. And sat. We carried on. Some minutes later, when I realized he felt no urge to either leave or make conversation, I poured *myself* another glass.

"I see you're wine-goers," he commented.

Wine-goers? I was reared on the Biblical pejorative, *wine-bibber*, and the urban vernacular *wino*, but here was a brand new epithet. Wine-goer. So be it. "Matter of fact," I said, "I've thought of putting grapes in. Think they'd grow here?"

He stared, and shrugged. "Fox grapes grow. Like a bastard. They don't ripen every year, though."

"Why not?"

"It takes heat."

"Maybe the soil here isn't right?"

He scratched his beard. "I wouldn't know."

But I vowed I would find out. Since, after all, I could expect to now be recognized as the local wine-goer, I might as well get on with it. Research. The world's great wine soils, I discovered, are actually *poor* by conventional agricultural standards. They are stony and relatively infertile lands, exposed on south-facing hills to the baking sun; these conditions force the roots of vines to forage deep for water and nutrients, creating hardy plants and noble wines. Where soils are notoriously rich, on the other hand, vintners can produce only *vins ordinaires*.

My farm boasts soils of bottomless clay. *Fine* clay. It is demonstrably fertile, poorly drained, and extremely difficult for roots of plants to penetrate at all, much less forage around in.

I got on the phone and ordered a truckload of gravel from the local pit.

My neighbors, I am certain, have a lasting recollection of me shovelling clay and gravel into my concrete mixer, then dumping the stuff back into holes dug deep into the earth — trying to make each small core of Vermont more like, say, Bordeaux. Most of my neighbors' lifelong efforts have been directed toward the opposite goal; stony soils exasperate those who try to farm them. So it was reasonable that one of these dairymen should stop in to demand what the hell I was up to.

"Grapes," I answered, pointing to five wrapped plants fresh from W. Atlee Burpee's. "French wine varietals crossed with hardy, wild American types. The latest thing."

"What the hell you up to?" he repeated.

"Grapes like stony soil. Nothing too fertile, either."

"Well, Lord God. You *make* wine?"

"I am going to try."

But I couldn't make wine that year, for the vines had to become established. This process actually required several years, though by the third summer we had a few bunches of grapes to grace our table. Not enough to ferment, though. Year four, the birds got them — untimely vacation. Year five — and by now we had the vines tied to horizontal wires on the four-arm Kniffen system — we harvested a quantity of grapes that, mashed together, amounted to roughly three quarts of liquid. A slender yield, yet perhaps auspicious. I pitched yeast into it.

To call the resulting beverage *astonishing* would not be inappropriate, were I to rate this wine. Nor *surprising*. Nor *unexpected*. Unfortunately, I am sorry to report that it was also *undrinkable*. Worst foul swill I ever tasted in my life.

Making wine, it turns out, is a rather more delicate affair than making homebrewed beer. Complex chemistry. Tannins, acids, invert sugars, good and bad and "wild" yeasts, trace nutrients — people go to *school* for this. I did not want to go to school. I wanted to slosh about, barefoot, in a tub of grapes, without fear of abominable consequences for the palate.

I gave the vines another year of dedicated pruning, tripling my yield of nasty wine. By now, though, I had discovered I could give the bottled stuff away. As Christmas presents, no less. A certain type of person will accept such a gift with genuine enthusiasm, then lay it down for a cool decade or so. Waiting for the right occasion. Should he ever actually uncork the gift hooch, I can always attribute its remarkable qualities to extended storage.

These delicate wines, I am prepared to say, are all too easily bruised and best drunk very young.

For myself, I gave up the vineyard *per se* and fooled a bit with lesser juices. Strawberries, elderberries, blackberries, plums — even tomatoes, in a fit of desperation. These efforts did produce some palatable potables, but they were not cost-effective for a man attempting to fill an empty cellar. And, let's face it, weird fruits and berries are not the main event in civilized oenology. Grapes are what it's all about.

Then one day — a few autumns ago — my wife returned from visiting a neighbor who was making grape juice. "Out of *wild* grapes," she told me excitedly. "*Fox* grapes. They grow *every-where*."

I recollected that fox grapes grow like a bastard.

"You just throw a bunch of grapes into a quart Mason jar, add a quarter cup of sugar, and fill the jar with boiling water. Then you cap it. Come back in a month, and you've got grape juice."

"That easy?"

"The boiling water kills any yeasts or bacteria."

"So it won't ferment?"

"Won't sour." My wife had come to use these two terms interchangeably.

I thought hard — after all, fox grapes grew abundantly all around me, with absolutely no human attention required. No pruning, no four-arm Kniffen support systems. I said: "But you *could* ferment the same juice later, couldn't you? Just by adding wine yeast?"

We tried it.

I am not so arrogant or self-serving as to extol the virtues of this simple *vin du pays Yankee*. Truth be told, I would not launch an evening's fellowship with a bottle of the stuff. But it can be entertaining after drinking better wines, and the cellar — what is left of it, for now it doubles as a mud room — looks a damn sight better lined with dusty bottles of this sturdy, honest little potable. It costs me nothing, and its supply is inexhaustible. *In vino*, I have come to feel, *veritas* is where one finds it.

• Hay

I used to get a summer suntan loafing poolside, book in hand, or frolicking on sandy beaches. I have lost, forever, those sybaritic days, but my skin still turns aboriginal brown each summer as a minor side effect of driving my old tractor round and round rank fields, making hay. Haymaking is hard work. Demanding work. Sweaty work. And, for tens of thousands of rural Yankees, it is an unrivaled agricultural crapshoot. I am proud to be a player.

When I moved to Vermont, I frankly was not sure what hay *was*. Green stuff in bales, sure, but there my understanding ended. All around me, neighbors hayed, but I paid scant attention to their earnest labors until I bought a few sheep and wondered what to feed them. Hay, I then discovered, ain't hay. It can be expensive. Buying several tons at once could make a person wish he grew the stuff.

Imagine my surprise to learn I *was* growing the stuff — on twenty-odd acres — without even trying. For hay, it turns out, is merely grass — or grass and legumes, such as clover — that is allowed to grow approximately to its flowering stage, then mowed and sun-cured in the field until it is dry enough for storage. I was growing hay, but I was not *making* hay, because I lacked haying machinery. Instead, the neighbor's heifers in my meadow were harvesting the crop directly. They seemed to love it, too.

Is hay good feed? The best hay approaches *grain* in energy per pound and actually exceeds most grains in protein content — if, of course, an animal has four stomachs to digest it with. One or two won't do the job. But grassland farming — hay production — coupled with the raising of ruminant animals like cattle or goats or sheep is a model of sensible, non-intensive agriculture and wise soil conservation practice. It can be sustained for, literally, centuries.

When I learned these facts, I was impressed. Good-bye, heifers — I would harvest hay, and get good exercise, and prosper. I eagerly began acquiring a fleet of second- and third-hand machines for low capacity, small volume haymaking. Thirty-year-old machines, sound but too slow for today's high-acreage, fast-paced farmers. Mower, rake, baler, wagon — I bought these machines for what seemed like a pittance. I cleaned them up, I greased them conscientiously, I watched my hayfields grow. And then I learned the big catch in haymaking.

The catch is: it takes three consecutive days of perfect summer weather to dry hay sufficiently that it can be safely baled up and stored.

Safely?

Well, for starters, hay baled too green will mold, and animals may then refuse to eat it. Or worse, perhaps, they'll eat it and get sick. Bummer, either way. What's worse than a barn full of hay that can't be fed? It's a barn that one morning bursts into flames from — you guessed it — spontaneous combustion in improperly cured hay. The valley that I live in hosts a few such fires every year, and they are spectacular affairs. Hay burns nicely. People come from far and wide to watch. Firemen can scarcely save the structure, but they do their best to drive the cattle out of the inferno. And then *keep* them out; cows, for some reason, simply hate to leave a burning barn.

When I started haying, I swore to myself — my wife, too — that I'd never be so rash, so harried, so sunstruck as to put anything less than bone-dry hay into my barn. Why flirt with catastrophe? All a person had to do was postpone mowing until three days of cloudless skies were confidently predicted. June came, and I waited. All around me, neighbors started haying. Some made out okay, some didn't; still I waited for a green light from the weatherperson.

Having noticed my array of machines such as he'd quit cursing twenty years ago, one of my prosperous neighbor farmers stopped to visit. "Going to do some haying?" he asked.

"Waiting on the weather," I said.

"Wait too long, the hay will lose its good."

"Is that a fact?" I asked him.

"Hay for sheep, especially. Once it gets all coarse and stemmy, once it sets seed —" He gestured with the palm of his hand. "Junk. Not worth the work of digesting it."

I said, "I'd be damned embarrassed to burn my barn down. I'm waiting for the weatherman to forecast three fine days."

Now he laughed. He genuinely laughed. "In June?" he asked me. "You may have to wait a while."

He was right. Soon I learned no weatherperson in a haying region would hazard such a forecast in the month of June or late in August — peak haymaking seasons in the Northeast. Weatherpersons are sick of getting blamed for ruined hay — millions and millions of dollars worth, in any year — so they will not make the forecast novice hayers long to hear. The most senior weatherpersons put in for vacation during haying weeks, and their understudies get adept at variations on a masterfully equivocal forecast: "Warm today, fair skies, maybe a cloud or two, with just a chance of showers." Having touched all bases, such a forecast entertains no lawsuits.

In self-defense, each haymaker becomes his own weatherperson. Those who don't get better at it than, say, the National Weather Service give up haying pretty quickly. So I studied weather patterns — warm fronts, cold fronts, highs and lows — and I learned an interesting fact. The chance of three consecutive rain-free days in June is roughly only one in four. Come July, the weather tends to stabilize, but come July, the hay crop is well past its prime. By the first of September — second cut time — storms are fewer and more predictable, but cooler nights bring heavy dews that soak mown grass as thoroughly as summer showers.

The catch in Yankee haying is: when you've got the primo hay, you haven't got the weather. And when you've got the weather right, the hay's most likely gone to seed.

This state of affairs has, I suspect, plenty to do with the sour temperament of the archetypal Yankee farmer. Like as not, his haying is not going well. He mows on Monday, into clear skies and soaring expectations; by Tuesday night his meadow full of grass may be approaching hay. Wilted, but still damp — one could wring water from it. Not right for baling yet. If it rains on Wednesday, though, the crop will need two more days drying — and will risk two more days of rain. Once hay has "been down" for five or six days, and rained on twice, its color and flavor and nutritive properties have very largely leached away. What, when mowed on Monday, was superior livestock feed can quickly end up garden mulch. Few crops on earth can be so difficult to harvest in a timely fashion.

I mowed. My hay got rained on. But it dried, in time, with constant raking, and I got it baled up and sheltered in the barn. I mowed some more. And then I started noticing the days on which my neighbors mowed, raked, and baled. They were well ahead of me. They must, I decided, be putting hay into their barns greener than I thought was wise. But then again, they had been farming longer than I had been alive.

So I dropped by a neighbor's barn one humid afternoon, with storm clouds gathering, and watched his bales streaming up a long conveyor to the hay mow. Dairymen make a lot of hay, sometimes twenty thousand bales a year; none of my neighbors have burned their barns down yet.

"Gaining on your hay?" the man asked me.

"Not much. I think I'm too cautious. Too conservative."

"Something to be said for that."

"That hay there — that's not too wet?"

He shrugged. "Maybe."

"Ever had hay heat up on you in the barn?"

"Have to keep an eye on it."

I shook my head — the man's hay mow was easily 200 feet long, 20 feet deep, and 36 feet across. "How do you keep an eye on hay in a mow that size?"

He pointed to an iron rod leaning up against the barn. Sixteen-footer. "I just take a sledge and drive that rod into the pile of hay. Smack into the center. Leave it there for half an hour. If it comes out too hot to hold —"

"Too hot to hold?!"

"Well, then I'd worry. Then I guess I'd call the fire department. Hay can heat up quite a little bit, though."

This brought a new and, frankly, disturbing level of assessment to my haying efforts. Green is green and dry is dry, but trying to guess what point between the two is time to get the baler running makes for sleepless nights. I have panicked and hustled hot bales from the barn on more than one occasion, wrecking tidy stacks of hay; other times, when I have restrained myself from panic, I have found the doubtful bales perfectly cured, come winter.

Experience at haymaking does obviate a degree of frenzy. But things still go wrong, mechanically, and the weather seldom goes exactly right, so that haying becomes a public demonstration of the quality of each farmer's standing with The Man Upstairs. Mowing is a prognostication and an act of faith, and everybody notices. Neighbors wave and nod and tell themselves: "Just watch that hay get rained on." When it doesn't — when, against all odds, a person gets his crop into the barn in three rain-free days, dry and green and leafy and smelling as only fresh hay can smell — that person feels like a king.

I have rarely known that feeling, though I spend a good five weeks each year making hay. But without the bargain feed that one's own hay represents, scarcely a farmer in Vermont could stay in business. Counting every cost in sight, my hay goes in the barn for only $25 per ton; purchased hay costs three to six times as much. And if, sometimes, I feel I can cause rain to fall by merely climbing on my tractor with intent to mow — well, rain falls on the just and the unjust, too. On any given afternoon in June, I'm not the only luckless soul whose hay got rained upon. My life as a haymaker has taught me to approach success with frank, sensible attitudes: succeeding, when one does, is nice — but the misfortunes and failings of one's peers can be equally enjoyable.

• Manure

There is money in manure — for better or for worse. Although Yankee farmers have always realized this truth, several new advances in manure technology have managed to increase the value of this inevitable crop; manure lagoons and huge slurry storage tanks and even methane digesters have begun to appear, changing methods of manure application and reshaping agricultural landscapes. These new technologies are sold — and sold hard — by various industrial giants who produce their highly mechanized components. They are also sold by the government, whose agricultural agents consider it important to get farmers to make the very most of their basic resource.

Students of manure — or, as they like to call it, *fecal matter* — have long since finished quantifying everything in sight. For example, the sharp young government man who came to discuss manure with me, recently, took no time in pegging my ewes' production at 0.1 cubic foot per head per day. After allowing for their lambs' fecal matter, too, he told me we were talking two cubic yards per head per year. By now, I had a hundred sheep; so he informed me that my flock produced two hundred cubic yards of manure per year.

"That's like hard to visualize," I said.

"Think of it this way: your basic dump truck holds around seven cubic yards. You're talking thirty truckloads per year."

"Holy cow!" I cried out, anguished. "That's a lot of — of fecal matter."

"No," he contradicted me. "It's not."

"It is for one guy and his pitchfork. And his wheelbarrow."

"That," he sniffed, "is hardly a manure-handling system."

I expected he would say this. I had planned to argue the point: at the end of a day of barn cleaning, my hands are *coated* with manure. He had his agenda, though, and moved along now into quantifying the precise *value* of my crop. Twenty pounds of nitrogen per ton, six pounds of phosphorus, and twenty pounds of potash. These things all cost money — plenty — when one buys them in a bag from a fertilizer dealer. Each costs 25¢ per pound, give or take a little. Just a few quick calculations later, my visitor had placed a fertilizer value of roughly $2000 on my fecal matter.

"Holy excrement!" I shouted. "That's a lot more money than those sheep make for *me*."

"But," he added — these guys always have a "but" — "you have to *handle* it properly. In storage, in spreading, in incorporating it into your soil. Else you're going to lose a good deal of that value."

So I explained to him how I handled my manure: once a year, I would set aside a week to shovel out the barn. With a pitchfork. Into a wheelbarrow. I would dump the stuff just uphill from the vegetable garden, creating a veritable mountain of steaming dung. Then — much later, and sometimes never — I could rototill it into the garden soil. In addition, anyone who wished was invited to drop by and haul some off to nourish *his* garden. This reduced my workload, somewhat; a greater reduction came about in consequence of leaving the manure pile exposed to the elements for several years. Given time, the stuff would cook and compact and compost itself till it occupied only a fraction of its original volume. "It like disappears," I told the government man happily.

He was not happy to hear it. "This," he said, "is costing you some sixty percent of potential nitrogen. A good bit of potash, too. It's costing you five hundred dollars a year, in round numbers."

I nodded. "*Plus* all the stuff I let my friends haul off. Don't forget that."

"Right. And — frankly, your garden must be mighty well fertilized by now."

"Oh, it is. It is."

He thumped a clean hand on his pad of calculations. "You need a way to put those nutrients back on your fields," he told me sternly. "Where they *came* from, after all."

That gave me ideas. "When my sheep are out on pasture — grazing — they're like *spreading their own* fecal matter, right?"

He didn't say yes; he said, "That's not incorrect. They don't, however, do a good job of soil incorporation."

"Meaning?"

"It just sits there, losing nutrients into the atmosphere. Or we get a bad storm and it runs off, polluting rivers. *Modern* technologies work manure into the soil at the time of spreading."

"Well, tough —" I sputtered. "Tough — fecal matter! I mean, this pasture system is pretty old. Pasture has worked for a good long time."

"It's not the *best* system."

"Suppose," I said, "I never let my sheep into the barn. Then I'd have no manure to spread, right? It would like start and end right there on the pasture. I could drag their hay out to them, through the snow, and —"

"Why have a barn, then?"

"Lambing," I admitted. "They do have to be inside at lambing."

But he let me follow this train of thought. "What's the least barn housing period you could cut them back to?"

I pushed a pencil. I said, "Fifty days a year."

"That would cut your manure chore to just twenty-five tons. Worth two hundred and eighty dollars."

"Twenty-five tons," I said, "is still one hell of a lot of fecal matter."

"No," he contradicted me. "It's not. A hundred-cow dairy herd makes fifteen hundred tons per year — not counting calves, even." He snapped his briefcase open and began showing me manure handling systems for family-sized dairy farms. He showed me steel tanks up to 118 feet in diameter, and up to 24 feet high, for holding well over a million gallons of slurried fecal matter. With massive pumps and agitators to place solids in suspension. He showed me liquid manure spreaders holding over three thousand gallons per load, attached to chisel plows that could inject the perfectly shredded and blended manure into the soil. One could store up a year's supply of fecal matter at a time —

fresh as a daisy — then squirt it all into the soil just at planting time. "That," said the government man, "is a manure-handling system."

"*That* looks expensive," I said.

He shrugged. "On a big dairy, five hundred bucks per cow. Total investment. It saves a bit on labor, but the real payback comes from fertilizer quality in the manure. No lost nitrogen. The guy who's spending ten thousand a year on fertilizer can afford to look at these improved manure systems."

"I don't spend that much," I confessed. "Not on fertilizer."

"Well, *whatever* you spend is too much if you haven't started utilizing your manure. That big pile by the garden is simply wasteful."

I realized that, honestly. "What would you suggest?" I asked. "For twenty-five tons of volume per year?"

"Buy a used manure spreader. Old-fashioned, beater type — there are lots of them around. Then you'll have a way to put the money in that fecal matter back onto your land."

Used machinery is the only kind a lot of farmers can afford; I went to visit one of several local used machinery dealers and asked him to keep an eye out for a manure spreader for me. Bargain basement. Something no one bids on at an auction.

"What kind of spreader?"

"Old-fashioned, beater type. Aren't there lots of them around?"

"How much do you want to spend?"

I thought. I thought a one-year payback made a lot of sense. I said, "Oh, about two eighty."

"That doesn't buy much in a spreader, these days," he said. "But I'll see what I can do."

A couple months later he called back; he had acquired a spreader — $275. I went to see it and nodded eagerly as he showed me its fine points. Basically, it was a low-sided wagon that slowly conveyed its load back to a whirling drum with welded steel teeth. These teeth would tear apart the packed bedding from my barn floor and fling it — manure and all — into dark, wide swaths as I drove around my fields. The machine was to be powered by my tractor's power take-off shaft; we discussed the horsepower requirement of the spreader and agreed that my old Allis-Chalmers could pull it. Not surprisingly, the spreader was rusty and worn and thoroughly caked with old fecal matter. But I judged it service-able and strong enough to handle my relatively modest manure chore.

Came time to clean the barn, and I pitched the first whopping load of fecal matter into my spreader. It could hold considerably more than my old wheelbarrow, and — since it would unload *itself* — I saw that this tool would reduce my chore considerably even as it made me money. Not without a certain pride of ownership, I mounted my tractor and drove the spreader to my hayfield. I engaged the power take-off shaft, and gently eased the clutch out. A whir of machinery came to life behind me.

I turned round, naturally, to watch the spreader find its load and settle down to work. Immediately a large chunk of wet fecal matter slapped into my eager face. And another. More. In fact, the old spreader was pelting me with crap. I turned away; I opened wide the tractor's throttle, hoping to outrun the barrage. This was not successful. I slumped down, I crouched beneath the steering column of my tractor like an Apache warrior slung astride his mount, attacking. Something like a battle cry escaped my lips, too. And then, miraculously, the spreader all at once commenced to spread its load properly.

I spread seven loads that day, and each time the same thing happened. In the evening — blackened head to toe, and emanat-ing a fantastic aroma — I visited the used-machinery dealer. I asked, "Is there something you forgot to tell me?"

"About what?"

"That spreader throws manure at *me*, the start of every run."

He smiled. "That can happen, when the load's not packed tight up against the beater."

"How do I do that?"

"I guess it's hard," he said. "With sheep manure. All these spreaders are designed for dairy cattle. Cow manure."

I shook fecal matter from my arms, my neck and shoulders. I said, "This is a hell of a thing. And all because the government —"

"Maybe you should build some kind of baffle."

"A baffle, sure."

"Or set up a big umbrella."

"Umbrella!"

"Or — you got an old raincoat?"

I *do* have an old raincoat; now that the barn is clean, it looks considerably older. However, I feel great knowing I have prudently returned those many cubic feet of nutrients to my soils. To be sure, the government is right. There is money in manure. Whether it is any way to get rich, however, is quite another matter.

• Schedule F (Form 1040)

Before I started trying to be a farmer, I used to hate doing my income taxes. Part of me complained — as W. H. Auden did — that the government seemed determined to graft an accountant's mentality on my sensitive, creative spirit. And every year, as I riffled through the myriad tax forms arrayed on the counter at the local bank, I was haunted by the feeling that I must be losing out on countless loopholes for reducing my taxable income. Work Incentive Program Credits, Depletion Allowances, Tax-Free Involuntary Conversions, Multiple Support Agreements — how could an ordinary person get in on these?

Then I purchased a dozen sheep. I cared for them — fed them, housed them, trimmed their dirty little hoofs — and by the year's end I was sure I'd lost a bit of money at it. Curious as to the tax status of this venture, I peeked at a marvelous form which has since changed my life: Schedule F (Form 1040). F stands for Farming. By the time I had filled in most of the important blanks, I knew that farming was for me. I had racked up — wow! — $1200 in deductions versus $35 worth of farm products sold. Plus $800 in straight-line and accelerated first-year depreciation. Plus an investment tax credit of $77, directly cancelling out other taxes due.

This, I thought, had great potential.

So I filed as a farmer, hoping the computer wouldn't hoot and jeer and ridicule my painstaking declarations. It did not. In fact, in what I took to be a signal of its appreciation, it fired back a complimentary copy of the *Farmer's Tax Guide*. This 82-page, fine-print book is published by the Internal Revenue Service to assist farmers in calculating their losses to the last nickel; I received it gratefully. But, broaching its contents with idealism and high purpose, I was dismayed to find my reading skills were frankly not up to the task. No doubt my neighbors, though — real farmers all — had no difficulty digesting sentences like: "A special rule applies to determine whether or not a net operating loss (NOL) carryback is taken into account in determining the recapture amount resulting from disposing of an asset before the end of its useful life used in figuring the credit."

I would not have tried so hard to comprehend each nugget of lore contained in this *Farmer's Tax Guide* had I known then that the volume is revised and reissued annually. Tax laws come and go; times change, and of course the IRS wants America's proud farmers to keep right abreast of things.

Just as an example, I built barns of modest size in 1976 and again in 1979. Though nearly identical in design and materials, the first barn is a "building" and the second is not — according to the government. A "building" is depreciable but, sadly, is not eligible for the nifty tax write-off called Investment Credit. In 1976, see, all barns were "buildings" and a "building" meant "generally any structure or edifice enclosing space within its walls, and usually covered by a roof . . . " But in 1979 the *single purpose livestock structure* — not to be confused with a mere "building" — came into being.

I nearly dropped the *Farmer's Tax Guide* in my excitement. What, I asked aloud, was a single purpose livestock structure? I read on — mouth watering — and, by gum, it turned out to be a *barn* — so long as the barn's function in housing animals was not adulterated by, say, storing grain or hay. Meeting this condition would allow a man to claim Investment Credit on his new barn. It would make his new barn not a "building."

Clearing all the hay and grain out of the new barn was mighty inconvenient, but it turned out to be well-paid labor. I moved the grain into an Investment Credit-qualifying "storage facility used principally for the bulk storage of fungible commodities" — that is to say, a grain bin — and, had I wanted to push the point, I could have built an Investment Credit-qualifying silo to store the hay in, as haylage. Feed *and* livestock in the barn, though, made the barn a "building" rather than "a structure that is essentially an item of machinery or equipment." The two might be architecturally indistinguishable; but a "single purpose livestock structure" beats hell out of a mere "building" when it comes to taxes.

This Investment Tax Credit is no small potatoes. Everyone should know about it. When the tax-law writers throw a freebie to the general public, they're apt to create some new mechanism for reducing a person's *taxable income*. That, friends, is the short end of the stick. When they decide to do something nice for business — farmers, for example — they get right to the point and reduce a fellow's *tax*. Directly. If he owed $1000 tax but built a $10,000 single purpose livestock structure — presto! No tax due. A farmer who manages new investment in his business with any care or forethought holds the ultimate tax-cutting weapon in his hands.

I never know just what I'll turn up when I sit down with a new *Farmer's Tax Guide*, but it's a game that's good for several winter evenings of Byzantine fun each year. Last time around, though, I became utterly distraught at reading certain fine points involved in distinguishing farming activities presumed to be engaged in for *profit*, from those deemed merely recreational or "hobby" farming. The difference had a pulse-quickening gravity: "hobby" farmers, the *Farmer's Tax Guide* sternly threatened, could not deduct net farm-operating losses from other income.

I was alarmed. A few days later, I went to seek advice and counsel from a farm economist in the employ of the government — that is to say, the taxpayers. "These rules in here could shut me down!" I moaned. "It says that I have to show a *profit* two years out of five!" By now I had been losing a few thousand bucks for three or four years straight, and visions of future handy losses had been dancing in my head.

The economist smiled wanly — I could see he was a man of wisdom. "Showing a profit," he declared in reasonable tones, "*is* a convincing demonstration of the profit motive. But *not* showing a profit creates no inference that you *lack* the profit motive."

"Hey," I said. "That's great!"

"It does, however, shift the burden onto the taxpayer to *prove* a profit motive."

"Just the motive, huh?"

He nodded. "Lots of people stumble into farm enterprises thinking they can make some money," he assured me. "Certainly it's unfortunate when someone's intent to make a profit turns out to be unreasonable — but the important test is, were those intentions *genuine*?"

"Are you kidding me?" I asked. "That's just terrific news! They couldn't ask for a more genuine guy."

"The amount of your losses has some bearing, too. Couple thousand bucks a year — on most farms today, this is peanuts."

"Right! Right!"

"One dairy cow can be worth more than you lost last year. Easily."

"Yeah! And cows are dying every day, too!" I reminded him. I had caught with happy enthusiasm the farm economist's lofty perspective. The kind of losses I was busily racking up were too measly to notice.

"Looking down the road, though," he wondered. "Five, ten years from now — do you *ever* see a profit?"

"Do I have to?"

"Well, it might be nice. Most folks can *create* one, too," he suggested. "Like by buying next year's feed in *this* tax year. Or their fertilizer, seeds — they take a bigger loss for this year, angling for a small profit next."

"Good thinking," I said.

"An occasional profit is awfully hard to argue with. Keep abreast of tax law changes, too."

I thanked the man for his free advice (at taxpayers' expense) and went back to my budding farm enterprise with the secure feeling that I could continue losing money for a long, long time. To nail down this privilege, though, I did endeavor mightily to show a small profit on this past year's Schedule F. Since first filing as a farmer, my flock of sheep had grown tenfold; my farm cash flow was no longer miniscule, and managing it over twelve months to put me in the black should not have been an insurmountable problem.

Enter Mssrs. Reagan, Stockman, Kemp-Roth *et al*. These public servants may be good for business, but they have derailed my small hopes for coming up with even meager and contrived profits from my farming operation. Thinking big — thinking of G.M., and U.S. Steel, and Exxon — these men have rewritten the rules of accounting. Now, long after my farm has started making money, I can expect to keep splashing red ink on my tax forms. More of it, in fact, each year.

Nowadays we no longer, for example, depreciate capital items like machinery. We *recover* their *cost* nowadays, by the Accelerated Cost Recovery System. Pickup trucks, as one example, are now "cost recovered" in just three years — a sobering testament to their putative engineering. Tractors good for twenty years are "cost recovered" in just five. *Silos*, even — although a good silo can be expected to last a lifetime.

Even more interesting, I am now supposed to save up unused Investment Credits for fifteen whole years — just in case, by 1996, I might be getting near a positive bottom line on my Schedule F. This is like having money in the bank. And the credits now apply in full to the decrepit, twenty-year-old machines that I am wont to spring for, just as though they were brand new models.

In short, I no longer resent the hours required of me to fill out my government's income-tax forms. The accountant that the IRS so patiently nourished in my breast has come to love his labor, and the agricultural enterprise that I stumbled into has proven to be an inexhaustible source of Net Operating Losses (NOL's). Enough to make a person love the soil, all right. I only wish I had a greater income to farm away.

CHAPTER FIVE

The Pleasures of Technology

*L*ATE IN MY URBAN PERIOD, A DEC-
ade or so ago, I recall an outright loathing of machines. Slowly, inexorably, life
had come to depend on a host of nifty mechanical servants whose
inner workings I could neither comprehend nor fix. They were not
built to last, and, whenever they ceased to function, I paid through
the nose in money and time and general aggravation. Broken
espresso makers, pulsating carving knives, stereo headphones all
had to be set out with the garbage; even a rather fancy typewriter
and a certain kitchen range turned out to be troublesome posses-
sions not worth fixing. That is to say, they proved more expensive
to fix than to replace.

On one level, therefore, I saw moving upcountry as a grand
liberation from the heartless tyranny of machines. Simplify, simplify, I told my wife, quoting Thoreau — and, for a time, I swear
we lived with few mechanical devices more complex than kero-
sene lamps and wood stoves. This seemed, at first, in tune with
what I perceived to be the Vermont ethos, but I was dead wrong.

The simple life turned out to be anything but simple. We soon
became aware of the extent to which we had relied upon a quiet

priesthood of "service" personnel. We *missed* this faceless army: those who made pure water flow through pipes into our faucets, and those who saw to it that the noxious wastes we flushed away *went* somewhere; those who provided infinite amounts of electricity from the nearest double outlet; those who routed melting snow and rain washed down from hillsides away from human habitations; those who kept the heating system in tolerable working order and replenished the fuel tank as required; not to mention the vast number of workers who took care of other people's cars — my own included — whether those cars had been built in Detroit or Bavaria.

Of course, even in rural Vermont it is possible to find others who will take these responsibilities off one's hands, but it costs a great deal of money and can be damned inconvenient as well. The man who cannot make his car start has no business living at the end of a long, snowy driveway several miles from the nearest town. When a siege of numbing cold grips our wide valley, freezing pipes on dozens of farms simultaneously, much damage can be done by simply waiting for a plumber; one is better served by learning how to plumb, oneself. Up here, happiness and comfort depend on one's own mastery of the range of mechanical skills required to make things work and keep them working.

The simple life? It turned out that my neighbors *loved* machines; Vermonters all (real ones, they had a way of mentioning pointedly), they kept more machines than I could number, much less name. Their farms were predicated on machinery; their yards were littered with tons of steel representing thousands of dollars invested per milking cow. An endless source of trouble? No. My neighbors exuded a serene, quiet confidence that they could make machines serve them, and not the other way around.

For me, though, an undertaking such as, say, design, construction, and maintenance of a septic system posed an awesome challenge. So did keeping a 400-foot driveway passable in winter. So was coming to terms with the assorted internal-combustion engines that my life required, and keeping each in reasonably efficient tune. But the satisfaction gained from solving such problems dwarfed any achieved in my former life of mental, ostensibly creative, work. When some pipe or valve or wire hidden in the walls of one's dwelling screws up, there simply is nothing like the feeling of knowing what lies back there. How it works. How the walls were put together. What fastens to what, and how.

As I came to feel at home in this landscape, I realized that the joy of making things work, of personally solving the practical problems of our complex, machine-dependent standard of living — had created an important common bond between me and my fellow citizen-farmers. True, most of them painted on a vastly larger canvas than I either dared or had the means to. While I would be rigging up a gravity water line to tap a pair of nearby springs, my neighbor would be getting set to pump a good portion of a river half a mile away into his dairy barn. While I would be learning how to change the muffler on my tractor, his boys would be building one from the ground up — out of scrap. And yet, comparisons of scale aside, I have come to adopt my neighbors' frame of reference. And some of their mechanical competence, too.

Here, then, are some of the reasons behind my growing fondness for the pleasures of technology.

• Burning Gas

One day a neighbor's kid — barely in his teens at the time — came roaring past the tent we had pitched outside the barn we were converting to our present dwelling. I say roaring — he drove an amazing homemade vehicle incorporating an old auto chassis, an unmuffled Volkswagen drive train, two used tractor seats, and wheels and accessories from various junk implements. The whole thing was held together with so much used baling twine.

"What do you call *that*?" I asked him, when he shut the motor off.

"Just something we threw together."

"Street legal?"

"No — we just ride it round the pasture. Check to see if any heifers have calved."

The mere sight of it would make me calve, were I a bred heifer. I mentioned the contraption to the boy's dad, next time I saw him. "Your kids build that crazy go-cart all by themselves?" I asked.

"You know boys," he offered with a twinkle in his eye. A peaceful smile, such as passeth understanding. "Boys love anything that burns gasoline."

That was news to me, but in time I began to burn a bit of gasoline myself — in the concrete mixer, then the chainsaw, and eventually in a Rototiller. Much to my astonishment, each of these machines acquitted itself very well. When they broke — what tool doesn't? — repairs were inexpensive, easily obtained, and actually effective. Often even I could make them. I began to see Technology in a different, warmer light.

My neighbor's kid smiled when he saw, some months later, that I had acquired a tractor. Quite a plunge. Ford-Ferguson, made in 1946. A recent, sloppy paint job failed to conceal an alarming amount of rust; but I'd had to pay only $800, or very nearly what the machine had cost brand new, some thirty years before. I liked the thought of inflation and depreciation running at a dead heat for so long.

"What you going to do with that?" my neighbor's boy asked.

"Plow my driveway," I answered decisively. "Maybe I'll plow up the garden, too, come spring."

"What's it, twenty horse?"

"Eighteen, I think."

He hooted.

"I don't *need* much tractor."

"How's it run?"

"I drove it home," I said. "Seemed to do just fine. But since then, I can't get it started. I think maybe that's why the price was right."

"Shoot," he said. "Gasoline engine? It'll start." The lad climbed on my tractor's seat and cranked the engine over, listening. "Either no spark or no gas," he informed me. In a matter of two minutes' fiddling, he announced I had a *wicked* spark. The problem must be gas. He tore the filter off the tractor's fuel line, and cleaned its several orifices for me — to this cause, I sacrificed a toothbrush. Unlike automobiles, I noted, every bolt or wire that might need attention on this sturdy vehicle was sitting right in broad daylight. Soon the motor sprang to life, coaxed by a savvy fourteen-year-old with ten spare minutes.

"Runs," he judged. The muffler belched out rust and smoke. "*Wicked.*"

But why a grown man would want to own an eighteen-horsepower tractor — such as his grandfather might have had — remained a mystery to this boy. He was perfectly at home commanding 100-horsepower behemoths, wading with a corn chopper into fields of ripened grain. I don't think he realized as keenly as I did our differences of scale; even now, his family's farm produces 8000 pounds of milk each day, while mine produces 8000 pounds of meat each *year*. But notwithstanding this disparity, I have become just one more farmer with a shed full of machines.

One might think a 30-year-old tractor would be difficult to purchase parts for. I certainly feared so, having found parts unavailable for last year's yogurt maker. Visiting a local Ford tractor dealer, I explored the point. "I've bought an old 9N," I told him, stating the model number. "Think you maybe could turn up an owner's manual for me? If it's still in print, or —"

He turned around and picked the very volume off a shelf behind him. "Dollar fifty, please," he told me. Then I went on to buy a radiator cap, oil dipstick, and a complete set of tune-up parts — all right in stock. The course of loving a machine, I thought, has never run so smoothly.

I began to frequent farm dispersal auctions, ogling tractor implements and even coveting a few. Dour Yankees in old, faded coveralls would hunker down around some tired plow or harrow, nodding scarcely perceptible bids to canny auctioneers; I stood, wide-eyed, on the fringes. Bargains seemed ubiquitous — they always are, when farms go under — but I thought I should invest a half dozen afternoons as a mere spectator, learning what I ought to pay for what I ought to want.

Two old farmers — each an auction buff — generously furthered my education by letting me in on their separate but tried-and-tested pricing mechanisms for used machinery at auction. One would guess the tool's *weight*, then multiply it by some constant — 40¢ a pound for "old steel," and up to a dollar a pound for late model, "new steel." On this system, my tractor — some two thousand pounds of "old steel" — was worth exactly what I had paid for it.

The other Yankee farmer would count up how many things on an implement *turned around*. This was a tricky calculation, subject to a few adjustments, but he would reach a sum of significant turning parts and multiply that figure by $50. Time and time again — so long as the machine involved was reasonably well aged — his pricing system pegged the tool at darn close to what it sold for.

These same mentors helped me overcome an instinctual aversion to rust, honed by countless bitter memories. Rust on an auto-mobile spells danger, and expensive trouble; rust on the simplest hand tool can render it scrap metal. But on a farm machine — an older one, anyway — rust is but a fine patina of respectability, a badge for years of honest service. The engineering geniuses who designed these tools *expected* rust. They *planned* for it — or so my handlers told me at these farm dispersal auctions.

I remember looking, with mixed desire and apprehension, at a hay baler. An important tool. The old-timers liked it. I said, "Look at that corrosion, though! How am I going to work on that? Every bolt looks frozen up with rust."

"Propane torch will free that."

"But — look at the frame! It isn't weakened?"

"Hell, no. That steel's *thick*. Rust is just skin-deep. Take a hacksaw to it, you'll see plenty of steel left."

To test this proposition, I had to buy the baler first. But the price on it was particularly right; the last item the machine had tried to bale was an old fence post. A mistake. A minor error in the operator's judgment. Had this done any important damage, though? None, so far as my handlers and I could tell. Whoever bought the tool owed a day's work jimmying the splintered cedar post from where it was wedged among various moving parts.

Thirteen hundred pounds of "old steel"; four hundred bucks. A bargain, right? And balers have many, many turning parts. I bid, and I bought, and I drove the baler home. I freed that hapless fence post, and since that day the old machine has tied a cool ten thousand bales of hay for me. And scarcely missed a single knot.

I realize that our mechanized civilization is a mixed success. Technology has given, and technology exacts its price, and the bargain we have struck appears to many to become more Faustian each passing year. I know these things. But, hitching my old, rusty baler to my old, rusty tractor, and fully expecting that these odd, unlikely, outlandish contraptions are apt to work for one more haying day exactly as intended, I have to offer this small part of the Machine Age my unqualified support. Will they last forever? I don't know, but they were built to last. Would that my truck — even my toothbrush, for that matter — would perform as long and as reliably. It's enough to make one think technology is wicked useful.

• A Pastured Porsche

When my wife and I escaped our palmy, upwardly mobile lives in southeastern Pennsylvania, our family car was a sleek, canary Porsche. A Porsche! Looking back, now that I have driven a pickup truck into a state of near-terminal corrosion, I can scarcely believe I once owned such a car. Gone for me — forever — is the status and upscale *camaraderie* derived from cruising in Sunday morning auto rallies, winking headlights at the other Porsches on the road, and blithely checking in for $100 tune-ups. Gone is the thrill of having utter control of a vehicle at frightening speeds; in contrast, my pickup can be frightening at *legal* speeds. Gone is the pride of owning a car that is, frankly, a work of art.

No one up here had ever seen a Porsche, and my new neighbors were wholly unaware of its important sociological connotations. In fact, they tended to dismiss this guerdon of my youthful success as "that noisy little foreign job." It seemed to me that *tractors* were their Porsches. Fair enough. Hydrostatic drive trains and two-stage power take-off shafts — I thought that these must be the rough equivalents of torsion bars and torque tubes in the worldview of my neighbors. I was wrong, though. Tractors are eminently, manifestly useful machines. Sports cars are not.

I was wrong, though it took me a while to find out. I embarked on an embarrassing transition phase, during which I owned a Porsche but was no longer *into* Porsches. The car was a white elephant in the new pastoral life. A dangerous state of affairs: to own a Porsche requires dedication to a certain ethos, else it's one expensive bother.

At first, I always parked the Porsche outside the farm gate and barely off the road, but I grew lazy, and before long I was driving the car onto our premises as far toward the construction site as its low-slung, racing suspension would permit.

One morning, crack of dawn, I rose to find two dozen of my neighbor's heifers gathered around the Porsche, shuffling their heavy feet and licking off the carnauba wax. "Hey!" I hollered. "Stop!" They didn't bat an eyelash. I leaped into my jeans, dashed outside with a shovel in hand, and drove the obnoxious cows uphill, into the woodlot. One of them shuffled off with a windshield wiper in her mouth, like a long stem of coarse, West German grass. I stared at my car: a couple of reflectors gone, a bumper

pushed askew, the chrome nozzles of the windshield washer eaten clean off the hood. And warm saliva everywhere.

I was damned upset, for five A.M. And I figured it would be a waste of breath calling the car's insurer; my comprehensive coverage might contemplate acts of God and urban vandals, but not casually destructive Holsteins. Replacing the lost bits of car wouldn't kill me, but I expected a certain quotient of pocketbook outrage — everything I ever bought with the word Porsche on it cost three times what I expected.

In the midst of my tantrum, who should stop by but the cows' owner. He was headed for his milking parlor; my frenzy over heifers slurping up my little foreign job had animated morning coffee at his breakfast table. Had he come now to apologize on the cows' behalf? No. A Porsche was utterly without value for him. He said: "Oughtn't give those cows a chance to chew on metal."

"No?"

"Cows *like* metal, see? Tastes *sweet* to 'em. Cows start eating metal, first thing you know they're down with hardware."

"Down with what?"

"Hardware disease. It's killed many a cow."

I thought of my windshield wiper, masticated to a pulp and probably even now lolling in some heifer's paunch. I did not report this, though; our values were in open conflict. He thought his bred heifers were worth more than my Porsche! Still, I did not seek to be party to a cow's demise. So I asked him, guardedly: "Is there any cure?"

"Well, they used to operate. But now we all use rumen magnets. Works pretty well."

"What are they?"

"Stubby little permanent magnet. Size of your thumb. Get one down a cow's throat, and it sits right there in her rumen all her life. Just collecting metal. It's too big, see, to pass on through her gut."

"Wow! What a great idea!"

"You ought to fence in some place where you could park that little foreign job."

"But—fencing? Me? It sounds like so much work, and bother—"

"Hell, no. Go electric. Do it in an afternoon."

'Going electric' had not occurred to me, since the barn was nowhere near being wired yet. But my neighbor told me I could run a twelve-volt electric fence charger off an automobile battery, and that a single strand of hot barbed wire ought to hold even his rowdiest stock at bay. It made sense to me. A couple of days later, I had fenced in about an acre between our construction project and the road. Nifty. Cows respect a nice, hot electric fence even though it may have very little mechanical strength. And people can easily crawl beneath a single strand of waist-high wire.

Breeze, the large dog who had adopted us, could glide beneath the fence and never catch a shock, but he learned about electricity anyway, from the Porsche. One afternoon, my wife returned from a shopping foray and backed the car up dangerously close to the electric fence. In fact, the rear bumper actually touched it by the time she killed the engine.

"Whoa!" I shouted to her from across the lawn. "Don't step out!" Because, as I had learned from a recent study of basic electricity, a vehicle on rubber tires has no ground connection. My wife might be in contact with the fencing circuit, but she would feel nothing till her foot stepped out onto the damp earth. Then she would be hot-wired.

"Start it up and pull ahead," I told her. "You're on the fence."

She did turn the ignition key and pull ahead to safety, but not before our eager and welcoming dog had bounded up to lift his leg and water a gleaming chrome wheel cover. A thick stream of urine is not an inefficient conductor of electric current; Breeze leapt four feet in the air — every hair on end — and howled off to hide beneath the bed for several hours.

That canary Porsche just never was the same for him. When he heard it coming — and he could hear its throaty whine from half a mile away — he would whimper and cower and look for a place to hide. This is unattractive behavior in an otherwise handsome canine; we considered how it might be changed. Inevitably, we considered life after Porsche — not simply in the dog's behalf, but we saw a bellwether of sorts in his outright fear and loathing of the car.

Winter hardened this assessment. However marvellously well-engineered were Porsches of that era, they were not designed to start well at fifteen below. In fact, they hardly start at all. Though each cylinder is individually carbureted, I was surprised to learn no choke was felt to be required. Chokes, the engineers had felt, had simply no place on a fine racing engine. I felt otherwise after umpteen winter mornings when the car simply refused to start. Cars that start always — even parked outdoors, in driving blizzards — are authentic status items up here; what good was my snob car if I couldn't get it on the road?

I was no longer helpless at machinery. What, I asked myself, does a choke amount to? Nothing more than a way to restrict the flow of air to a carburetor, which creates a richer starting mixture. Damn, I thought — a self-reliant Yankee ought to be able to make such a device. It wouldn't have the word *Porsche* stamped on it, but a cable to a flap controlling access to the air filter ought to do the job.

I purchased the materials I thought I would need, then got the car as far as the farm of a neighbor one wintry Sunday morning. The man had a large, heated garage and shop, a facility that I had admired in midsummer when it was in constant use for repair of tractors and harvesting machinery; now I asked my neighbor if he'd let me fix my car inside it.

"Ayup," he said. "If you can find space among the snow-mobiles."

I thought he was joking, but in fact seven family members — *seven* of them, near and distant — were all busily repairing their snowmobiles on that morning in the shop. Just another Sunday. A twelve-year-old girl had her entire engine torn down and was earnestly honing out its cylinder walls. Her older cousin, a beefy young man, was replacing his muscular machines's broad drive track — and crying the blues about the cost of high-performance parts. Everybody shifted work stations just a bit, creating enough room for me to drive in my equally impractical, noisy, uneconomical conveyance.

Suddenly I realized: my neighbors' sports cars were not tractors. Tractors were too useful, too practical, too necessary. No — their Porsches were, so help me, snowmobiles. Now, I do not *like* snowmobiles. Like any self-righteous flatlander transplanted here, I consider snowmobiles an invention of the devil, a paradigm of technology run amok. Now I saw, though: these machines were to my neighbors what my sports car was to me.

A greasy-fingered lad I did not know sidled up to me and asked to see my engine. I showed him. He was impressed, I think. He said, "Damn! Look at that! Four carburetors!"

"And not one choke!" I blurted out. *"No choke,* can you believe that?"

He grunted to tell me: you've got your absurd mechanical toy, pal, and I've got mine. Which was true — except that mine was supposed to be doubling as basic transportation. And mine cost more. In fact, I could have traded it for several snowmobiles and change.

"Heck," said the greasy fellow. "Don't gripe. Put a choke on it."

"I was going to, actually. But *now* —" I slammed the engine lid shut. I backed out of their garage. I roared back home, and told my wife: "We own a snowmobile of a car, you understand? A snowmobile! Stupid! Silly! Let's sell it quick and get a pickup truck — before the next cold snap."

Across the room, the dog barked approvingly.

So we came to own a vehicle more appropriate for up-and-coming hobby farmers. Now and then, when I go clunking around a curve that my Porsche used to take at sixty, or when I pull out to pass and floor the gas and nothing happens, I do miss the sports-car days. But I'll bet my little sports car — cow-licked and cussed at and shockingly disrespected in this rural, Yankee kingdom — I'll bet my yellow Porsche doesn't miss life here at all.

• A Good, Hard Pull

It is not hard to imagine the origin of pulling contests. I have a horse, say, and you have a horse, and I say mine can out-pull yours. I say mine can move a greater dead load. But, you say, mine's *bigger*. After dickering a bit, we decide to weigh each horse and then see which can pull more weight *per pound*. We throw a pile of bricks onto a sled, and weigh that, and then whip the horses into action. If each pulls the sled, we throw more bricks on. All day, if need be — until neither horse can budge it. Then we calculate who won.

That making such comparisons should have become a species of rural entertainment — a sporting event — was probably inevitable. And in modern times, when tractors did horses out of their former honest labor, it was reasonable to extend the competition to include the new, mechanical beasts of burden. Tractor pulling, then. The stuff of bustling county fairs. *Our* county fair, held each August a scant mile from my little farm, offers a complete historical perspective on pulling contests. We have ox pulling, pony pulling, horse pulling, tractor pulling, modified-tractor pulling, and lawn-and-garden-tractor pulling. Some have even advocated *wife* pulling contests, though we don't have them as yet. There are pulling competitions every day and night of our four-day revels.

The first tractor pull I witnessed did not interest me nearly so much as, say, watching grass grow. Or as much as contemplating the sociological dynamic that had assembled several thousand farmers in the long, tall grandstand, rapt and absorbed watching other farmers pull a load of concrete with their farm tractors. Six feet, they had to pull it — no big deal — and each contestant had three tries to achieve this seemingly modest task. After each attempt, two strong men with brooms swept burned rubber off the concrete pulling pad, to preserve its tractive properties. In short, this was one slow — not to say boring — competition. But to a community of people intimately acquainted with asking tractors to perform feats at the outer limits of their design capabilities — to such a community, tractor pulling can be the most interesting sport on earth.

To catch the fever, though, I had to step back in time by watching a few horse and pony pulls. Not for the squeamish, and not for the S.P.C.A., either, these proved to be intense affairs, with sweat and spit and foam awash on huge, high-spirited creatures sorely tested by apparently heartless keepers. Generally, three men were required to back a team up to the weight sled, and then to connect the hitch. As the contest wore them down, some teams would simply refuse to be backed up to the groaning sled. Their keepers would then shout, and smack them; dust and dirt would fly. Once I saw an openly rebellious team drag its handlers, face-down, across the nearest chain link fence. And First Prize — lest one think the point of all this effort might be filthy lucre — amounted to $60.

My next step was to watch a lawn-and-garden tractor competition. Effete, suburban, bourgeois — but the tractive capabilities of riding lawnmowers were something I well understood. They are almost nonexistent. Even in the Open Class which permitted special tires, wheel weights, and souped-up engines, these machines were well within my frame of reference. This pull proved a microcosm, almost a Little League, replete with eight-year-old contestants and cheering, overwrought parents.

Having studied these related contests, by my third year in Vermont I felt ready to appreciate watching the big boys pull. And by now I could discern a universe of subtleties. True, most tractors at first glance look alike, but there are fine distinctions between even apparent twins. Tires — and the way tires are "loaded" — vary widely. Racks of cast steel weights, fore and aft and on the wheels, offer myriad possibilities to alter tractive force. There are many ways to let a clutch out, or to open wide a throttle; and the skill of thinking with machines is not equally distributed even among farm populations.

"Hey-hey-hey!" a boisterous announcer would bark into the P.A. system. "Class Five, tractors weighing fifteen thousand pounds and up! First contestant: Eugene Desabrais on his International Turbo Nine-Eighty-Six! Eugene, get on up here!"

It would be nighttime, like as not; somewhere in the dark a big tractor would rev into life and wheel toward the brightly lit pulling pad. Onlookers would sip surreptitiously from pints of booze, which our county fair prohibits. All would study critically the Desabrais rig as it backed up to the weight sled. This would be Eugene's big moment: the whole county watching, and the county would never forget what Eugene could or could not pull.

"He can't pull that," somebody remarks behind me.

"Look at that front end. He isn't weighted right."

"Watch him jerk it."

Sure enough, Eugene would jerk it — which is to say, he popped the clutch — hoping to get a quick jump on inertia and walk the weight sled home from there. But jerking the weight sled corresponds to a tilt in pinball, and there is a litmus test to prove the crime: a small American flag on a wooden block sits atop the weight sled, right on all that concrete. If the flag falls over — as it did — the pull is disqualified.

On his second try — more cunning, now — Eugene might slip the clutch out slowly. Very slowly. Everyone would watch his gargantuan tires ripple, squat down, almost buckle as the tractor found the load, and then, as he throttled up, a pound or two of rubber would be laid down on the pulling pad. The weight sled would not move an inch. Busted? No. Eugene has been learning, has been studying his big machine's response. Now he would jump down and move a few hundred pounds of "suitcase" weights from the front axle to the rear. Three hundred pounds, say, on a tractor weighing fifteen thousand.

Then he would climb back up and pull the weight six feet. Like child's play.

Well, for those who think *baseball* a slow-paced sport, a ten-hour tractor pull can make it seem like *jai alai*. But pulling is not a gross, indelicate affair, for all its brawn and hard, cold steel. One can grow to like it. Just as I had grown to like it, though, the sport took off in a wild new direction influenced, doubtless, by the snowmobile set. This new type of pull is called a Class A Super-Stock/Modified Tractor Pull on The Vermonster Weight-Transfer Sled. Catchy. In a few short years it has become, for better or for worse, the most exciting public entertainment that my county has to offer.

My front porch, the reader will recall, is one mile from the fairgrounds; that is, as the crow flies. A low-slung mountain lies between the pulling track and my place, so the smoke and noise and cheering of an old-fashioned pull never impinged on our tranquil domestic scene. A few summers ago, however, I was sitting in the living room and ran to see if a locomotive weren't perhaps grinding up the driveway. What I was hearing was The Vermonster's maiden voyage, as it were, and the tractor pulls of yore now seem like so much arm-wrestling.

The Vermonster's pulling track is three hundred feet long — not a measly six, as in the old, dead-weight pulls. And whereas tractors in a dead-weight pull can generally either budge the sled or not budge it — go or no go — a weight-transfer sled is set up so that every tractor can get the thing moving. How *far* they move it is a different matter, though, and few indeed can drag it the full hundred yards.

The Vermonster looks something like the back half of a flat-bed truck, with wheels on the rear axles but only a steel skid plate where the front axle would be. The weight — a large, decorated concrete block — rides up and down a rail from the rear axle to the skid plate. As each contestant begins his pull, the weight rides on the wheels: a rolling load. But as the wheels turn, they drive the weight block forward toward the skid plate: a progressively deader load. The rate of the weight's progress can be adjusted through a gearbox, to adapt The Vermonster to the quality of any competition.

Now, having such an exotic — such a high-tech — weight to pull made people yearn for something more interesting than the same old farm tractors to pull it. First, folks took authentic tractors and rebuilt, or "super-stocked" them, expressly for these pulling events; before very long, they were creating "modified" tractors — which are hardly tractors at all — for the sole purpose of competing in tractor pulls.

The "modified" tractor is an astounding testament to the excess of technological and mechanical skills on American farms today, not to mention the wealth of spare parts in agricultural junkyards. When winter is at its most deadly boring, the competitive Vermont farmer evaluates his machinery dump; he finds a chassis, axles, "trans," an engine or two perhaps, and he hauls these to his shop and goes to work. By county fair time he will have wrought a unique, handcrafted, customized pulling tractor. One can barely start the thing; it won't idle, won't keep cool; it hasn't any muffler; it will not do any farm work whatsoever; but it will — or might just — pull The Vermonster a hundred yards, making a culture hero out of its creator.

It is common, now, to see two V-8 automotive engines mounted in tandem on a single "modified" pulling tractor. I have also seen such rigs powered by engines lifted from P.T. boats and medium-sized aircraft. Beer kegs are popular as fuel tanks — who knows *what* the fuel is — and very tall, very wide exhaust headers guarantee an unrestricted flow of smoke and noise and, sometimes, flames. Elaborate precautions are required to contain these engines, to prevent them from injuring spectators in the event of an explosion — a surprisingly unremote possibility. The drivers are all *men;* they wear street clothes and crash helmets and expressions of grim determination. And each tractor has a name: Agent Orange, Bionic Rooster, Widowmaker III.

This is not just a bigger and grander and more earsplitting sport than dead-weight pulling; it is also *faster,* making it more interesting to non-farm types. Not too fast, though. For example, two huge road-building machines — a grader and a steamroller — have to resurface the pulling track after each contestant's efforts. The analog to men with brooms in old-fashioned tractor pulls. Also these homemade, "modified" pulling tractors, inspired but largely unproven machines that they are, not infrequently break down completely in mid-pull. Clutches fry, transmissions cook; unable to be rolled without provoking further damage, such machines must then be *lifted* — by a pair of backhoes, say — onto a flatbed trailer, which carts them off. One or two such mishaps can really slow an evening down.

On the whole, though, there is nothing like a Class A Super-Stock/Modified Tractor Pull. I particularly like taking urban friends to such a sporting event — the people who venture northward to my farm in search of the pastoral, the peaceful, the bucolic. Modified tractor pulling offers a powerful corrective to their idealized notions about rural life.

I took one such fellow — an accomplished high-technology engineer, from Boston — to last year's Class A Pull at the county fair; the event proved almost too much for his scientific mind to grasp, let alone accept. Wild, ear-splitting machines shrieking in the night. I sought out one puller whom I know to shake hands with (he lives not far down the road), and arranged for my urban visitor to examine his machine up close.

"You build this all yourself?" my stunned friend asked the tractor's creator.

"Ayup."

"What did it *cost*?"

"Oh, quite a little bit."

"And will it — is there any farm work you can do with a tractor like this?"

The Vermonter thought, and scratched his ear, then ventured: "Could spread manure at sixty miles an hour."

• Against the Grain

Even the back roads of Vermont are kept passable year-round, because dairy farmers must have milk trucked out and grain trucked in every few days. The rigs that haul around these precious commodities have legendary traction; they barrel along through snow and sleet with a nonchalance that terrorizes drivers of mere automobiles. The planning of a farmstead, too, requires giving thought to passable truck access in any weather. Dairy barns are mostly built quite near to the road, so that their self-unloading grain bins and stainless steel milk tanks can usually be filled or unfilled even in a howling blizzard.

Grain is big business up here. New England farmers like to grow their own forage crops — hay and silage, mainly — but they buy in almost all their grain from the Midwest. Folks can grow it cheaper there. An average-sized dairy herd can eat a ton of grain a day, though — costing up to $200 — while a farm-sized steel bin holds only about six tons. So the grain trade is a huge materials-handling enterprise, involving the continual resupply of thousands of customers. Deliveries must come off without a hitch.

As I have explained, I was something of an ideologue when I started sheep farming. I thought, *à la* Frances Moore Lappé, that feeding grain to livestock was just one more lamentable American evil, and a prime cause of third-world poverty and hunger. I thought, too, that my barn would look more picturesque tucked into a grassy hollow some five hundred feet back from the road. So I built it there. Since I wasn't planning to buy morally tainted grain — or sell so perishable a commodity as milk — it didn't matter that my barn would be not much accessible between Thanksgiving and, say, Easter.

Time, however, has tempered my enthusiasm for grain-free sheep production. Particularly when a ewe devotes herself to lactating for a pair of hungry lambs, treating her to daily grain avoids metabolic stress and pays its way in pounds of flesh. It can be a bargain. What is not a bargain, though, is a self-unloading steel grain bin — $2000 is the going price. Lacking that sum, small farmers usually buy their grain in 100-pound sacks at the feed store. This is a time-consuming, back-breaking proposition; worse yet, bagged grain costs twenty percent more than grain bought in bulk and blown into one's grain bin from a dealer's truck.

I could not afford a grain bin, and for years I was unhappy. I could not *not* afford one. As my little flock grew, I found myself feeding an entire sack of grain per day at certain times of the year — too much to heft on tired shoulders to the barn from the place where the driveway peters out into lawn.

Then, I got the bright idea to *build* a grain bin. Nothing too substantial, but with plywood and two-by-fours I managed to construct a large open box just inside my barn and roughly the size of a powder room. Or an ice-fishing shanty. It would hold three tons of grain — the minimum truck order — and it cost barely $100 in materials, a sum I figured to recoup the very first time the bin was filled.

Proud of myself, I called up half a dozen grain merchants for quotations. Crimped oats, $185 a ton. Sixteen-percent-protein dairy pellets, $205. Soybean meal, $280. This was heady business, shopping for an appropriate and affordable grain to balance out my feeding program. Just like real farmers do, I thought. Finally I settled on plain old corn — a cheap source of energy, though somewhat shy on protein.

"One sixty-nine the ton," the pleasant salesman told me. "Whole."

"Whole?"

"Or, we can grind it for you."

Whole corn sounded like rough going for my ewes' little teeth; but I couldn't see them lapping up a dry meal, either. So I asked, "Isn't there something in between?"

"Sure. Cracked corn."

"That sounds great."

"You want this brought tomorrow?"

Now, we were early into Vermont's famous mud season. All our snow had melted, but cold nights usually left the ground frozen till midmorning each day — after which things softened up. Bare, frozen ground can offer reasonable traction; by noon, though, sunshine could make the going slick and messy. So I warned the grain man to send his truck out my way early. "See, my bin's a little ways off the road," I told him. "Can you get here first thing in the morning?"

"Why?"

"I'd hate to get you stuck."

"Hey," he told me huskily. "These are *grain* trucks. They can get around."

By eight A.M., next morning, the ground had firmed up nicely and I looked forward to the convenience and efficiency of bulk-delivered grain. Just like the neighbors got. But by ten o'clock the expected truck had not arrived. The sun shone down brightly, and ice was quicky melting out of the ground. By eleven o'clock, alarmed, I decided to play safe and call to postpone my corn for a day. I had just picked up the phone when a large, heavy truck crawled up the driveway.

I went to meet the driver. Lanky fellow. Young. Cleanshaven. "Where's your bin?" he asked me.

"In the sheep barn. Back there —" I pointed, searching his face for some response. There was none. I said, "I sure wish you'd gotten here sooner. Things are getting slippery."

He shrugged. "Guess I ought to make it. You go get the barn door open."

I did as he told me, then watched him back the truck around and aim it toward me. He gunned past the end of the driveway, out onto the lawn — and, considering, his rig performed remarkably well on the slick brown sod. He crabbed and slithered to within eighty feet of the barn. And there he stopped, wheels spinning hopelessly in mud.

He climbed out with a pail of road salt. This he sprinkled, generously, underneath his tires. I said, "Maybe we should just forget about this. Till another day."

"I believe I'll make it. Just you watch me."

I watched. Ten minutes later, he was mired past his axles. I said, "Look, forget it. You can't get there from here."

"It's some slippery," he admitted.

"Maybe you should think about just getting *out* of here."

He nodded, and tried going forward. No way. He was badly stuck.

I said, "Let me start my tractor."

Now, I had recently traded up to a bigger tractor than my old Ford-Ferguson. The new machine was no behemoth, but it wasn't a toy, either. It had forty-three horsepower, weighted lugs, and locking differential — it could pull significant loads. I backed it up to his truck and hitched a chain between us. Moments later I was wallowed in a mudhole just as deep as his.

"What now?" I asked.

"That your only tractor?"

"I'm afraid."

"How about your neighbors?"

So I jogged up the road to beg help from a substantial, well-equipped dairy farm. "Stuck *where?*" my neighbor asked me.

"I built a little wooden grain bin in my sheep barn."

The man raised his eyebrows. "Better get the John Deere," he muttered.

The John Deere proved to be well over twice my tractor's size. Four-wheel drive, too. Thirty minutes later, we had that one stuck as well.

My neighbor farmer lit a cigarette and studied the grain truck's tractive difficulties. "How much you got on?" he asked the driver.

"Three ton for this guy — in the back compartment. And nine ton for Elmer Danyow in the front compartment. I was going there next."

"That's why your *front* axle's sinking — you're not weighted right."

"I was thinking that," he said. "Don't know how I *will* get out."

I felt sick — for him, and for my lawn, which was fast becoming a rutted machinery dump. "This is like the worst day of my life," I told them.

"Better get Elmer on down here with his Allis-Chalmers," said my neighbor. "If he wants his grain today."

"What's Elmer's big iron?"

"Got a Landhandler. Dual wheels on it, too."

We got on the telephone, and soon the biggest tractor for miles around was in my back yard, too, chained to our two tractors and all spinning turf into muck. And then the grain truck finally budged. We towed it back out to the gravel portion of my driveway.

"Now what?" asked the driver. "Can I make another try for it?"

"Not unless you're crazy," I said. "Can't you take that cracked corn back and — I don't know, store it? Sell it?"

"Cracked corn?" asked Elmer Danyow.

"*Plain* cracked corn?" asked my neighbor.

"That's what he ordered," the driver told them. "Listen — in the eighteen years we've been in business, no one's ever ordered that before."

I was badly shaken. "So, like — no one else would buy it?"

"I can't take it back there."

"Then let's pull you backwards to his barn," said Elmer. And I watched, aghast, as he and my neighbor turned their big tractors around, hitched them to the truck's rear axle and dragged it, kicking and screaming, back across the lawn. They nearly knocked the barn down when they got there, too, but they settled for snapping several fenceposts off like toothpicks and scoring the north wall with a casually aimed loader bucket. They made it, though. Then they came to see my new grain bin.

"Not bad," said Elmer. "Got no top on it, though."

"I'm going to build that later."

"Got no filler pipe," my neighbor commented. The truck driver busied himself unwinding a flexible six-inch pipe through which grain usually blew from his truck to the filler pipe on a customer's bin. Two such pipes mate perfectly, for nifty plumbing.

"I'm just going to *hold* his pipe," I said. "And aim it in the bin."

My neighbor digested this news. "Cracked corn," he remarked. "That might be some dusty."

"Oh?"

"Guess I'd best be leaving, now," said Elmer.

"Me, too," said my neighbor.

They remounted their tractors and rode off. I climbed halfway up my bin, and the driver handed me the end of his blower pipe. It was surprisingly heavy. Then, with just a trace of pleasure, he tossed me something else: a little white mask. Unsure what it was — or what for — I stuffed it in my pocket. Then he switched his blower on.

There was a rising roar behind me; suddenly the pipe I held became a noisy Gatling gun spewing forth bits of corn and yellow-white flour at very high velocity. It filled the air. I couldn't see, or hear; pretty soon I couldn't breathe, either, and that is when I realized what I had pocketed. I grabbed for the dust mask, losing aim with the blower pipe as I slapped it on my face. Fifty pounds of grain shot toward the barn roof in one second, then showered down upon me. Here, I realized, was the truck driver's revenge. But I guessed I had begged for it. No longer certain where the grain was going — and past caring — I dug in my heels and shut my eyes and clutched the rattling grain pipe till the last cracked kernel had been fired from it.

Then, slowly, the dust cleared. Every horizontal surface in my barn was painted with cornmeal. I was a floury snowman, dust sifting from my eyebrows every time I blinked. The grain bin was filled and, unfortunately, overflowing. It looked like Thanksgiving for half the rodents in the county.

"How'd you do?" the driver asked me pleasantly.

"I think," I said, "I'll have to refine this bin design."

"Don't do that for *me*." He grinned. "I'm not *ever* coming back here."

But there are many grain merchants in this valley, and I still can get my bin filled. I have roofed it over, now, and moved it outside somewhat closer to the road; I have also equipped it with a regular supply pipe. When the ground is good and firm, I get it filled without a hitch.

One time, though, a grain truck's driver asked about my lawn. The ruts — even now — are of heroic proportions. "That?" I replied, nonchalantly. "That's just where I held a little tractor-pulling contest."

• Warning: Poison

I once thought quitting urban life to try out farming in Vermont would offer escape from dangerously polluted environments. I might not get rich, but I would breath clean, fresh air, drink water pure as newly fallen snow, and nourish my body on foods not laced with chemicals. Benefits like these, I felt, were hard to put a price tag on.

But we hadn't been upcountry long when our water started tasting funny. My wife remarked about it to me over several days, and I made a note to check it. I had much else to do and did not fully understand the complex, arcane, hundred-year-old system that brought water from a large dug well into our country kitchen. So I let it wait.

Some days later, the water no longer tasted funny. It tasted rotten. So I took a hike and found, I swear to God, a full-grown deer floating in the well. This deer was not alive. In fact, my neighbor thought he must have drowned a couple of weeks before. The neighbor got involved because I couldn't get the dead deer *out*. He drove his tractor down and spooned it up with (I am sorry to report) the manure bucket on his loader.

"That well needs a new cover," he suggested to me.

I agreed. No argument. I made a note to place this item high on my list of projects.

"Say you drink this water?" he asked.

"I guess we can't drink it now. Who should I call — is there a Poison Center? Health Department?"

"They won't tell you much," he said. "What you want to get is bleach."

"*Bleach*?"

He studied the old well, estimating its capacity. "Two, three gallons of laundry bleach," he said. "Like Clorox. Pour it right down in there — now, you'll smell it at the faucet for the next few days. When the smelling stops, your water should be all cleaned up."

I checked the man's advice in a reference book I had acquired — *How To Live in Rural Splendor*, or some such — and, yes, laundry bleach *was* rated an inexpensive source of chlorine for purifying water. Or for cleaning out polluted systems. But I think it must have bleached our bodily plumbing, too; for weeks after the smell was gone, our water tasted as though it had just come from the laundromat. Coffee — even *bad* coffee — could not hide the stuff.

I realized, thus drunk on Clorox, that my objections to urban pollution had more to do with style than substance. Nameless strangers doctor urban water and pollute the air; one is helpless, one can hardly pick out who to blame. In the country things are different. Here one knows one's enemy too well, and he can usually be caught red-handed wreaking ecologic havoc. But one does not prosecute oneself. What's a little poisoned water among friends?

Indeed, as I grew in wisdom at the farming game, I was struck by the variety of noxious substances that chemical companies hoped I would buy and use. Chemicals to make plants grow, chemicals to make certain other plants *not* grow, chemicals to ward off animal diseases or improve digestive processes or foster thrifty growth. I am philosophically opposed to such things, but the point becomes moot when one's neighbors hire crop-dusting planes to spray poison on a windy afternoon. Real men in these parts all wear caps emblazoned with the logo of their favorite commercial poison — ROUND-UP, BICEP, LASSO, et cetera — as proof of deep affection.

There is no escaping.

In the sheep biz, orphan lambs can now be raised on artificial milk replacers that mimic the nutritional characteristics of the ewe's own milk. This is a terrific boon to sheep producers everywhere, for lambs are apt to starve on cow's milk. It just isn't rich enough. I do not consider milk replacer an egregious chemical intrusion into my generally natural style of farming; it comes as a powder in a fifty-pound bag, and I go through two or three bags a year.

The best tool for mixing this powder into liquid milk is the kitchen blender, and economy of effort dictates that one mix up several gallons at a clip and store them in the refrigerator until needed. This system served us well for several years, until one groggy morning when I poured some on the family's oatmeal. For breakfast. Thinking it was real milk.

First I served my son, who was then two and would drink anything. Then I had a bowl myself and noticed that the oats seemed stale. Pure, organic oats from the natural foods co-op. Then my wife sat down to breakfast.

"What have you — my God, that's milk replacer!"

"Where?"

"You've *eaten* this? Both of you?"

I woke up then, and found the bag of powder. Its list of ingredients would fill pages and included a variety of drugs to counteract diseases common to orphan lambs. None sounded toxic, but none sounded like ordinary components of a human diet. My wife got on the phone to the nearest Poison Center, where somebody took a history of our Incident and copied down the names of some of the more interesting substances in our breakfast. But — and this was cheering news — he could not locate Lamb Milk Replacer in his compendium of common poisons. He promised to get back to us; *we* promised to wait anxiously.

Several days later, he called. "You the folks who drank the milk replacer?"

"Right!"

"Well, how are you doing?"

"Fine, I guess. You learn some more about it?"

"Nope. But we have to do a follow-up. Regulations. Has to go in our statistics. So — nobody died?"

"No thanks to you!" I said, and hung the phone up. As my neighbor had indicated to me at the well, the mild, everyday toxicities of rural life must be faced alone.

Not long thereafter, I had an adventure with a really toxic substance. All my sheep got lice. Sheep lice are ugly little creatures that spend their whole lives crawling over their poor hosts' backs, sucking blood for sustenance. To achieve an infestation, all one has to do is buy one sheep that has one louse. Then wait — it's a time bomb. And once lice get into a flock, it's damned hard to get them out.

The time-honored weapon against external parasites is the sheep dip, essentially a bath of mild insecticide in which each sheep is immersed. Baptism. It's an awful bother, and it isn't totally effective. Worse, the odd sheep can panic and drown. And the farmer supervising this activity can scarcely avoid getting splashed — even soaked — with sheep dip. Sheep dips are not good for people, even if they have a few external parasites themselves.

Enter a marvellous new drug: fenthion (0, 0-Dimethyl 0- 4-methylthio-m-tolyl phosphorothioate). Poison. In a twenty-percent solution, it is approved for killing cattle lice. Throw out the sheep dip; a shepherd only needs to part the wool on each sheep's back and pour a measly two or three cc's of 20% fenthion onto the spine. The skin absorbs this chemical, creating in the sheep a systemic toxicity for the bugs that suck their blood.

I must say, I was surprised that a mail-order drug house

would sell me such a poison sight unseen. Without a note from my mother, even. When the vial arrived, its label warned straightforwardly: "May be fatal if swallowed, inhaled, or absorbed through the skin." Discussion of this product with a knowledgeable vet confirmed these dangers and resulted in my buying heavy-duty rubber gloves to wear while handling the fenthion. Even small amounts spilled on the skin, he informed me, were apt to cause in humans symptoms like those of muscular dystrophy. These might last a week or longer. He admired its efficacy at killing lice, but he urged me to use the stuff with great caution.

I arranged a large pen in the open barnyard for maximum ventilation and drove the sheep into it. Then I built a working chute to handle them in little groups, dosing each with deadly poison and turning them out to pasture. But the last sheep — there is always a last sheep — came into the chute alone and squirmed and kicked to avoid my grasp. She hated to be alone. And then somehow, as I was about to reach out for the fenthion, she jumped squarely at my head. I heard a loud crack and realized my nose was broken. Next moment, she leaped over the side of the chute, and I slumped to the ground, unconscious.

I don't think I lay there very long. But when I came to, blood streaming from each nostril and in stunning pain, there was the bottle of fenthion on the ground beside me. Spilled. Had it spilled on me?

I staggered to the house; my wife packed me in the car and drove me to the hospital. Emergency room. The doctor who saw me there was mightily impressed with my clean, forceful break. "Should mend nicely," he assured me. "Looks just like a chisel did it. I'm surprised a sheep could do that."

"I can't wait," I said, "to help *her* lamb next spring."

"Say you were treating them for lice?"

"There's this new poison," I began — but I didn't want to overly alarm him. Or myself. "It's dangerous to get it on yourself. But I might have, maybe."

"You *might* have?"

"I don't know. I blacked out when she hit me."

"But if you — were you wet? Your clothes, or —"

"No." I wanted to add, *But it soaks right in! It only takes a couple of cc's!* But he was cramming nasal packing up my nose, and the pain was excruciating.

"We do have an excellent Poison Center," he informed me. "Perhaps you should call them."

"Yes, perhaps."

"They're very thorough. Research, follow-ups —"

"I'm familiar with their work."

"In the absence, though, of any evidence you spilled this on you — well, I wouldn't worry much."

He sent me home, nose set and stuffed, and in fact I was spared death and noticed no symptoms of muscular dystrophy. Luck, of course. I do have a square foot of barnyard now where nothing will grow — not ever, I suppose. It is my mini-Love Canal, a hazardous waste disposal site right on my little farmstead; I detour around it with respect, doing my daily chores. It is an enduring symbol, quietly giving the lie to my youthful hopes that ecotopia was to be found down on the farm.

• Less Is Less

If getting by with less ranks high on our national agenda for the 1980s, rural Vermonters are in step with the times. In fact, for once we are *ahead* of the times. On my farm and others in a tight little radius, I have experienced the energy-efficient future as interpreted by self-reliant folks with a hand to tinker. In many novel ways, the future is bad news. Herewith, a brief tour of some self-sufficient installations.

Not far up the road lies a farmstead whose electricity is generated right on the premises. By a windmill. Cost: a cool $12,000 — installed, including forty-foot steel tower and a massive bank of lead-acid storage batteries, for when the wind's not blowing. Or for when it's blowing too *hard*. Yes, high winds can spin this owner-engineered mill so fast that it would self-destruct; someone has to climb that tower every time a good blow threatens and apply the brakes. A fine place to be when the sky crackles with bolts of lightning.

How do parsimonious Yankees justify such a capital outlay to produce their own kilowatts? To begin with, they have built their dwelling half a mile from the nearest utility pole. The cost of "bringing in" electric would have been $4000, and this gave them a flying start toward doing something self-sufficient. Then, of course, they receive no monthly bill from the power company. Forty bucks a month — a safe figure — for twenty years comes to $9600, putting them ahead of the game if their system lasts that long. And it might, it might. On the other hand, they have some fixed expenses of their own — notably battery replacement. Arguably, though, they may at least break even over the long haul.

Life with home-produced power is not the same as life on the corporate stuff. The power supply is unforgivingly finite, and governed by the weather, a notoriously fickle source. These windmill owners have come to know intimately the wattage requirements of their various household gadgets and appliances. Is the refrigerator running? And the television? Then don't use the vacuum cleaner. That's when the breeze is blowing; if the windmill stands becalmed, forget the television, too.

Dedicated homesteaders can adjust. Right in their living room, next to the stereo, these pioneers have mounted meters that report the wind's speed, its direction, and the state of charge of their storage batteries. A glance or two each day keeps the fuses from blowing — until, that is, city friends come to see the future.

"They just won't believe the lights can go *out!*" raved the owner of one such power system after a recent long weekend. "Everybody *loves* the windmill — then they go and do things like stand before the open refrigerator for ten minutes! *Looking* for something!"

I said, "Well, it sounds self-limiting. When the power goes, so do the guests — right?"

"They go, and they leave me with a half-thawed freezer! And no water! Pump won't work — I can't even flush the toilet!" He licked a finger and raised it to the wind. Nothing. "Nice day if it don't rain!" he muttered.

It sounded like some fuses of the spirit had burned, too. Urban visitors have long been famous for straining humble, rural lives. City mouse and country mouse. Another area where dreadful abuse occurs is Hot Water — particularly when the precious stuff depends on home-grown solar heating.

Solar hot water is *in*, here in Vermont — but not the kind one buys from a New Age engineering outfit. No, here we make our own; I have seen a couple of dozen solar hot water heaters, no two of which were alike, and no one but their ingenious builders had better try to troubleshoot or fix them. They work, much of the time. A spell of clear, bright days puts their owners in fat city, but there are entire weeks when the sun plays peek-a-boo, or disappears entirely behind thick clouds. Times like these, a person can be lucky just to get his face washed. Times like these, a person does not need company calling.

I went to a dinner party in a nearby house boasting solar hot water, to celebrate the visit of some old friends from New York City. After dessert and coffee, the urban couple volunteered to do the dishes.

"No, that's fine, I'll get them," said the host.

The guests insisted.

"Well, okay," he said. Reluctantly. "Easy on the water, though — okay?"

This is Greek to real New Yorkers. The visitors proceeded to do dishes Manhattan-style, in which one takes the drain plug out of the sink, turns the hot tap on full blast, squirts dish soap onto a sponge and rubs it, slowly, over every dish in turn — every pot and pan, too, and each utensil — while holding each beneath the steaming jet of water. Not for one second is its flow interrupted.

After several cheerful minutes, during which time the solar hot water heater, Yankee ingenuity, and the sun itself were lavishly praised, the water ceased to steam. In fact, before very long the water was not even warm. "Now what?" the New Yorkers asked.

"Now we wait for sunshine."

"But it's night!"

"Yes, I know that."

"You're — you're kidding! Don't you have some sort of backup?"

"Ayup." The host put a kettle of cold water on the stove and turned the burner on. Pointing down the sink, he said: "That was my shower, pal. And yours."

The best catastrophe I know of self-sufficient, energy-efficient living deserves its own headline: COMPOSTING TOILET EXPLODES; FIRE GUTS HOUSE. What, one might ask, is a composting toilet? Simply the ultimate in recycling homestead waste, especially appropriate to modest water supplies — every conventional flush, after all, requires seven gallons — and to poorly drained soils that cannot absorb the effluent from a conventional septic tank.

Several types of composting toilet are now marketed; the usual arrangement is to have a large fiberglass tank sitting in one's basement underneath the chute one calls one's toilet. Such tanks are sloped, baffled, vented, and otherwise engineered to speedily cook human manure down to humus for the vegetable garden. Organic, to a fault. Once a year, the homeowner opens a little door and shovels out this precious crop. When such systems work as advertised, they are indeed odorless and trouble-free and, obviously, use no water.

Enter the self-sufficient, energy-efficient Vermont homesteader. He heats his place with a wood furnace, well across the basement from his composing toilet's tank. As winter creeps in, he becomes dismayed that warm air from the house is whistling up the toilet's vent stack. Waste of precious heat from the firewood he cut himself. So he finds the cracks — around the cleanout door, around the seams — where house air is entering the system, and he seals these. Carefully. With gobs of butyl caulk.

Several days pass. The composting toilet no longer robs his house of heat, but now things start to smell. Faintly, at first; then not so faintly. The toilet, apparently, *needed* all that air to vent itself. And something else has changed: a gingerly examination of the system shows that liquids in the tank are no longer being evaporated.

What to do? The homesteader frets and thinks. He's loath to let his toilet vent itself on heated air; winter is too long and cold to tolerate an undamped chimney. So he buys a couple of bales of peat moss from a nursery and dumps these down the chute to soak up the excess moisture. Several more days pass — days of apparent improvement — until a new inspection shows that the peat moss arrived too late. The foul liquids ceased to smell only because they ceased to be liquids. They have frozen.

The homesteader does not *want* a frozen cesspool in his basement. He considers how he might best thaw things out, so that the peat moss can wick up the mess and speed its digestion into compost for his garden. Now, perhaps, he wonders if he's placed an energy-efficient monster in his home and castle. But — undaunted, ever self-reliant — he obtains a heat lamp and suspends it down the toilet chute to warm the innards of the fiberglass tank below. And shuts the toilet lid.

Evening comes. Vermonters often retire early in the winter,

but this night his wife has difficulty sleeping. She keeps smelling something funny. Finally, around ten-thirty, she follows her nose into the bathroom and lifts the sealed lid. Suddenly provided with a rush of oxygen, the composting toilet explodes in flames.

The fire which ensued did not, in fact, burn down the house. Nor was anybody hurt. But the fire did do substantial damage — particularly in the basement where the handsome fiberglass tank melted and left a pile of warm guess what? Organic fertilizer is where one finds it.

The future beckons — making do with less — and we self-reliant Vermonters step boldly forward. I count on Murphy's law to hold. And someone else's law, too. More dour. More Yankee. *That* law holds that Murphy was an optimist.

CHAPTER SIX

The Sociology of Rural Life

*A*TTRACTION TO A ROMANTIC landscape was the reason we decided to uproot ourselves and relocate to the country, creating a life very different from that for which society had earmarked us. Time, however, and intimate acquaintance with *any* landscape, no matter how spectacular, renders one nearly incapable of noticing one's surroundings. One becomes — well, not exactly blind, but definitely inattentive; appreciation of glorious pastoral scenery is not enough to *keep* a person in Vermont, though in our case it *got* us there.

In its place, we came to substitute a growing involvement in the web of interdependence that is rural society. As the landscape paled with familiarity, its inhabitants began to loom large. Living in the country meant living with these natives far more than living with fields and mountains, lakes and forests. The natives, beyond any shadow of a doubt, were here to stay; to join their society eventually became of greater interest to us than the scenery.

Vermonters do not live on the cutting edge of social change. We have a traditional society; the way we live, the work we do, the values that we cherish are anything but novel. How could I —

arriving here fresh from the social battles of the late 1960s — how did I so easily exchange an angry, strident radicalism for the life of a farmer — what I used to term an agrarian peasant?

I have no real answer. But as propinquity causes the glories of a landscape to pale, a growing awareness of the coherence of the society around one can take the place of landscape as a source of beauty and attraction. And, too, as a phenomenon to try to fathom.

Many forces, certainly, have undermined tradition elsewhere; unglueing whatever mastics cause social cohesion, these forces have rendered much of modern life inchoate and uncivilized. Somehow, my neighbors have managed to keep these dark forces at bay. Lack of wealth — and also of actual impoverishment — helps. So does the lack of population. Mobility up here can be difficult and costly; anyway, a farmer always has to be home in time for chores.

These conditions should not perhaps be praised as blessings; after all, they cause a degree of human misery, and vastly limit the range of choice that a young person is able to make about his life. Thus rural sociology runs against the modern ethos of personal fulfillment and self-realization. And yet, and yet — what best nurtures "individual growth" may be positively destructive for societies. Without societies, individuals could scarcely grow at all.

Against this contradiction lies another: Vermont is, after all, a last bastion of rugged individualism. People here can be profoundly independent, irascibly self-reliant — always, though, within the context of deep allegiance to one's family, to one's neighbors, and to one's town as the fundamental civic institutions. In the battle between individual and society, shrewd Yankees know how to keep a fine creative tension. I like to think that, in casting my lot with theirs, I've found how to have my libertarian cake. And eat it, too.

• Political Process

I came to Vermont from a city where the body politic had been cunningly dissected into scores of wards and precincts, so that the act of voting always had struck me as abstracted and impersonal. Yet I would vote, standing in a long line of "neighbors" I had never seen. Total strangers filled my pockets with partisan road maps to the multi-levered steel machines on which my votes were cast and counted; half a dozen "checkers" on the lookout for funny business made me feel I needed not a registration card but a note from my mother. Perhaps this atmosphere of persuasion and suspicion indicates a healthy, two-party system, in which either side might plausibly win. But it is a far cry, I suspect, from the political process one might expect in an ideal democracy. It is also a far cry from the way we do things in Vermont.

Nowadays, I relish being one of the five hundred voters — or, as we say, *polls* — in the Town of New Haven, which boasts several cows per citizen. We polls cast our ballots at the Town Hall, where we also gather once a year to brawl about the town budget, and rather more often to kick up our heels at volunteer fire department dances, wedding parties, and school plays. Town Hall feels like a church basement, the sort of public space that intimidates no one. It's a friendly place to vote, and, voting, one can savor citizenship in a coherent political entity: the rural town.

"Downtown" New Haven is a good seven miles from my farm, over winding and traffic-free country roads. Half a dozen houses cluster round an elementary school, a general store, and our Town Hall. Newer, busier highways have rendered this village somewhat off the beaten track, so I had to ask a neighbor where to go to register to vote, shortly after we moved up here.

He gave me directions. "Ever taken Freeman's Oath?" he asked.

"Never even heard of it."

"Well, you can't vote here unless you go and take the Freeman's Oath."

The idea of some tiresome pledge of loyalty offended me, as though citizenship up here needed the trappings of a fraternal order. As though allegiance to the state could be secured through some verbal formula. "What's this oath about?" I asked.

"Says you won't let anybody ever tell you how to vote."

"No kidding — that's it?"

"Says your vote's your own. You won't listen to nobody."

"Hey — I like it!"

I liked taking the oath, too, in the unimposing basement office of our Town Clerk. We swore, my wife and I, something very much like what my neighbor had represented: that, as Vermonters, we would cast our ballots "without fear or favor of any person." We walked out into crisp sunlight, glowing with civic pride.

Come our first election day, we followed our urban habit of arriving to vote early — before work — to avoid long, discouraging lines late in the day. We reached Town Hall at eight-thirty, but found to our dismay that it was locked. Nobody about. Puzzled, we crossed the street and went inside the general store.

"Aren't they pretty late getting the polls opened up?"

"Not till ten o'clock."

"Ten!"

"Ten to six, like always." The grocer shrugged. "It's a small town. People *milk*."

We bought doughnuts and stood on the wooden porch eating them, killing time. My wife saw a bulletin board nailed to one wall and went to read it. A mimeographed list of the town's voters had been prominently posted on it.

"Hey," she said. "Our names aren't on here."

I came over to check. She was right. "Well, damn," I scowled. "Now what?" Years of megalopolized voting led me to expect I'd have to forego casting this first ballot — or else spend an arduous morning battling assorted electoral bureaucrats. I could see trips to the county seat, allegations and complaints, ultimate frustration. I asked, "How badly do you want to vote today?"

Before my wife could answer, another car pulled up alongside ours at the general store; the Town Clerk emerged from it. Buying coffee for the election workers. She waved to us: "Morning, folks — see your names right up there?"

"No," I said darkly. "As a matter of fact, we don't."

"Really?" She joined us on the porch and squinted at the list. *Her* list, after all. "Funny! Wonder how that happened."

"We did come to vote," I told her. "Now who do we have to see to get onto the list?"

"*See?*" She opened her purse, took a pencil from it, and wrote our names on the list. "Don't have to see anyone."

This, I thought, getting in my car, is democracy.

By quarter to ten, the election committee had arrived, set up their percolator, and unpacked their ballots. We sat outside quietly, resigned to waiting until ten; but now an old farmer joined us, and he hadn't come to wait. "Open up! Open up!" he shouted, rattling the doors. "I'm late for my nap!"

They let us in. They took our names and handed us sheaves of folded paper — a different color for each electoral race. I walked to a booth made of someone's faded curtains and worked my way casually through this wadded rainbow of choices. Remarkable, how voting on paper ballots cut candidates down to size. Down to human scale. Why, it was as though famous national leaders were all running for some student council.

In the next booth to mine, the farmer who had opened up the place stood pawing through his paper ballots. He proved a noisy voter with his own techniques for humbling candidates, for dealing with them on his level. He would read each name aloud, then mutter some brief phrase of character assassination. "X for Lister? Skunk! And Y —? Thinks his shit don't smell." Then he'd mark a name. "Ah, Z —, it's the kiss of death. I can never pick a winner."

No one tells a Freeman how to vote; no one has to, since they're nearly all Republicans. Perhaps it is knowing which party will win — year in, year out — that fosters the warm complacency I so admire in our polling place. In a national election year, I distinguished myself by attending our town's Democratic Caucus, announced in the local newspaper. Now, I thought, I'll get a chance to meet my true compatriots.

Four other Democrats showed up. A dismal turnout? No — this Democratic Caucus broke all prior attendance records.

"Our purpose tonight," intoned the Democratic Chairperson, "is to elect three delegates and two alternates to our State Convention."

Two of those present in the room quickly disqualified themselves in accordance with the Hatch Political Activity Acts. Which meant, simply, that every other person who attended the Caucus was suddenly a Delegate. Plus we had to scare up two more Democrats in town, to serve as our alternates.

"Wait a minute," I said. "I just moved here recently. How do you folks know *what* I believe? I could be *anything*, for all you know. Anarchist, Republican — doesn't that bother you?"

"Nope. Does it bother you?"

It didn't, and yet it did. Where I had come from, a person would have had to lick a lot of envelopes and ring an awful lot of doorbells — do some *work*, in short — in order to get tapped to go to a State Convention. It seemed mighty strange to be given the job just for showing up at one caucus.

"Next order of business: Will the Delegates be pledged? And to whom?" This wasn't hard, either — we had a virtual one man, one vote situation. Each Delegate was entitled to his own decision, unfettered by any democratic process.

"Just a minute," I objected. "When I go to this Convention — like, who should I be representing?"

"Represent yourself," the Chairperson shrugged. "Who else?"

Who else indeed? I did — or tried to — but the State Convention, whose nominal purpose was to elect delegates to the *National* Democratic Convention, was of a character that frustrated consensus. Roughly half of my two thousand fellow delegates placed themselves in the running. Without commitment to any one candidate, most sought to be wooed and wined and dined, keeping their options open. When it came to voting, most candidates received a single vote — their own. Here in Vermont, even the Party of the People is in the hands of rugged individualists.

After this Convention I had planned to meet my wife at a wedding party being held at our Town Hall. I came late; the affair was in full swing, and I quickly found myself facing a neighbor citizen-farmer over stiff drinks.

"Well," he asked, "did you Democrats get everything straightened out up there today?"

I was startled. Apart from attending a non-attended caucus, I hadn't talked politics to a soul in town. But I deadpanned. "We sure did," I told him. "Everything's all taken care of."

"Have any trouble?"

"Only trouble is, not enough Democrats!"

"Oh," he said, "there must be twenty-three in town. Counting you and your wife."

"Then how come only *five* come to a caucus, where they get to — "

"Democrats in Vermont waste their gasoline voting. Sooner or later, most of them realize it."

At the time, I bridled at this, but after years of watching the political landscape — with increasing detachment — I'm ready to concede the point. I still vote — it's so much *fun*, here — but I expect no surprises when the ballots are tallied. In this small town, every person's politics are known; Republicans are destined to lead us onward. Realizing this no longer fills me with defeat, however. Our one-party system strikes me less and less as cruel fate, and more and more as a benign, enduring feature that permits public issues to be debated with minimal appeal to ideologies. A one-party system thus becomes a no-party system — liberating people to consider questions on their merits.

Is this agrarian democracy? Is this what Tom Jefferson had in mind? Maybe not; but we must be closer to the grand ideal than the bodies politic of the cities where I came from. And I think the architects of our system of self-government would feel utterly at home with the way we get the job done, here. I'll bet they would love to meet my neighbor and to hear him say: "Don't you tell me how to vote! I've taken the Freeman's Oath!"

• Onymity

An acquaintance in a nearby town, newly transplanted to Vermont from northern New Jersey, visited his town clerk to register to vote.

"I live on the Swamp Road," my friend volunteered.

"I know that," replied the clerk.

"You *do*?"

"Bought the old Irving place, didn't you? Looks like you're fixing to spruce it up a bit."

"Yeah?"

"See where you fixed some shutters. Put a new wood stove in old Irving's fireplace. Hear you bought a brand new refrigerator, too."

At this point, the newcomer felt vaguely disturbed. He'd been unaware he was a guppy in a goldfish bowl. He cleared his throat and said he'd come to register to vote.

The town clerk reached for a spiffy new quadruplicate form that the State of Vermont has produced recently to streamline voter registration. Multi-colored, pressure-sensitive carbons with questions about date of birth, place of birth, place of prior registration — all a person might expect. First, the clerk administered the Freeman's Oath; then he uncapped his pen to fill out the official form.

"Last name?"

"Adamson."

"First name?"

"Roger."

"Middle initial?"

"D."

The town clerk entered this onto the application, bearing down hard so as to penetrate through all the copies. Blue for the voter, white for the town's records, pink to be sent to the registrant's previous polling district — to remove him from its rolls — and yellow to report the decision of the Board of Civil Authority regarding the citizen's application. Now, however — having merely entered my friend's name — the clerk tore off the original copy of the form and handed it over to Adamson. "There, that's for you," he said.

"Wait a minute," Adamson protested. "There's eight more lines to be filled out, here."

"Ayup. But they don't make no never-mind." The clerk took the three pressure-sensitive carbons of the state's form, and he tossed them into the nearest wastebasket. "That's what we do with those," he said.

"Now, *wait!*" In his hand Adamson held a form that had his name on it, period. The fancy copies lay with used Styrofoam coffee cups and sundry office waste. "First you don't complete this form — then you throw your copies in the trash! What's going to happen to me when I come in here to vote?"

"Beg pardon?"

"How are you going to know who I am?"

"Oh — don't worry about that!" The town clerk smiled disarmingly. *"We know who you are!"*

Urban folk are known to complain, from time to time, about the anonymity in which they're forced to live the great bulk of their lives. Daily transactions with shopkeepers, grocers, waiters, bus drivers, public servants of every stripe, mechanics, bakers, bankers, barbers — all have a faceless quality. Even neighbors, inhabitants of the same apartment building, pass like strangers in the hall every day for years. Lamentable? Listen: there is something to be said for anonymity.

In a rural place, one lives with the opposite condition: I propose the term *onymity*. It means, simply, that everyone is known entirely too well. When a person drives to town, say, every human being he passes will honk or nod or wave — and think: Now, what's he up to? Where's his wife? Why hasn't he fixed that muffler? Who's doing his chores, back home? Was he crocked the other night? People who may rarely meet to have a real conversation take scrupulous notice of each other's activities, building composite impressions of character that last and last.

In a city, if one behaves regrettably or one's projects come to naught, there are uncounted ways to cover the shame. One can *move*. Take on new friends, find new work, join a different set or circle. All right, so one pays a price in *anomie* and *angst*, and one pays it to a shrink, as like as not. Here, we have few shrinks — damn little *angst*, too — but one's mistakes are in the open, for better or worse. And a community of natural peers can recollect forever.

Our Town Report, published annually, lists the marriages that have taken place in the past year. Generally, our young people wed upon completing high school; of the dozen or so marriages in a given year, eight are bound to be between youths who have known each other ever since kindergarten. Except for one token outside-the-county marriage every year, the balance of these unions are only across neighboring town lines.

At first, it depressed me mightily to think how limited are rural kids' social horizons. And *my* kids are rural kids. Nowadays, though, I think: after seventeen or eighteen years, those kids must know each other *well*. Onymity must reign. One might fall in love with the homecoming queen, but littered round her pedestal would be recollections of the day she dropped her tray in fifth grade, the time she tossed her cookies on the school bus thirteen years ago. Where everyone is so meticulously *known*, people harbor very few illusions about their fellows.

Furthermore, most of our town's *families* are reasonably well known quantities — with family traits that have been faithfully observed for generations. Youth of Family A, say, are apt to be hellions; those of Family B are finicky and nervous types. Crossing one of each in matrimony is a simple genetic exercise, like mating a Hereford with a Shorthorn. When Vermonters mention their relatives — and ancestors — each surname is a kind of shorthand for half a dozen adjectives describing personality. It *sounds* like genealogy, but actually it's character explanation. Or assassination, sometimes.

Imagine the havoc wreaked by newcomers settling here without firmly established traits and long-standing social histories. The uncertainty is unnerving. It even happens to *me*, now, after a decade here; someone new moves in, and I can scarcely contain my curiosity. It requires months of dedicated observation — earnest gossip, too — before the newcomers are known well enough that old-timers can behave comfortably in their presence.

I met a woman from Pennsylvania who, after several years of the standard probation accorded new arrivals, was asked to serve on her town's Recreation Board. The town in question had no recreation to speak of. They had created this committee to care for a park — a patch of lawn, really — between the Town Hall and the general store. The park boasted half a dozen dying elms; the committee had ambitious plans to build a park bench or two. It was a joke, in short, but the newcomer correctly perceived that being asked to serve on *any* town board was a signal honor. She accepted.

Couple of weeks later, the committee chairman came to visit. Just to get to know her better. "Saw your car was in LaFlamme's shop the other day," he ventured. "You been having car trouble?"

"Yes, I — I had to get a new transmission."

"Trouble. Cost you plenty, did it?"

Now why, she thought, should I have to tell this Recreation Chairman what I paid the garage? She said, "I guess I forget."

"Oh. Well." The guest smiled to suggest that whatever she had paid, she had probably paid too much. He pointed to a chair, now, across the room. "I see how your husband sits there every night, about eight-thirty? Watching TV? What is it he watches?"

Now how, she wondered, does he know where my husband sits? Snooping in the bushes? She said, "I don't know. Some show, I guess."

"Ayup. By the way, is that your dog out there?"

"Of course. That's Skipper."

"Think that dog's related to my brother-in-law's coon hound."

"No, he's not. We brought him up here with us. From Pennsylvania."

"Funny. I could swear — you got any papers on him?"

By what right, the woman wondered, does this neighbor call my dog a mongrel? She said, "Yes, in fact we do have papers."

"Papers aren't hardly worth a damn, nowadays. Folks can fake up pedigrees so easy —"

"May I ask," the woman interrupted, "why you want me on this Recreation Committee?"

"Sure. You been here a while. Folks would like to know you better."

"Well," she said. "I've changed my mind. I can't serve. Folks know quite enough!"

The road to onymity — the newcomer's inevitable destination — is paved with such mistakes and embarrassments and impositions, and an overriding sense of being spied upon. But, once one is *known*, certain privileges and honors are conferred on one that do make life convenient. Neighbors can sense each other's needs and respond to them before even being asked. Should one's car run out of gas, any farm along the road would gladly lend a few gallons. If one needs to make a phone call, no questions are asked. At nearly every business, credit is freely and cheerfully extended to citizens who are, after all, known entities in a small, well-known community. Rarely does one need to feel financial embarrassment.

In nearby Middlebury — our county's Shire Town — a local entrepreneur brings a truckload of fresh Maine seafood to the town green every Friday; he sells it right off his pickup's tailgate. The price is right. Citizens queue up to buy fresh fish from him. Not long ago, my wife stood in this line but came up several dollars short on a swordfish purchase — until the next person in line handed her the money. They were strangers, formally; but each had seen the other's face around town more than once, and that can be enough to offer somebody the protective umbrella of onymity. They arranged to meet the same time next week — in the same fish line — for the loan's repayment. And they did. Now, do such things happen in suburban shopping malls?

Up here, in short, no one suffers from anonymity. Our intercourse is founded on the nosiest sort of curiosity and the shameless exchange of gossip. But it works, for those who do not hunger for privacy. To those who *do*, the facelessness of modern urban living seems — well, heavenly. To each his own.

• Swimming Holes

In the South Jersey suburb where I lived through adolescence, "swimming" was an unusually intense social ordeal played out in chlorinated neighborhood pools or in the salty Atlantic. Bodily display, and noting *other* bodily displays, so overwhelmed the experience of getting wet that swimming seemed the merest excuse for self-presentation rituals. Which is to say that twenty years ago, I would never have confused "swimming" with simple recreation.

Here in Vermont, however, things are somewhat different. Here there are few pools and no vast, democratic ocean beaches whatsoever. Swimming is more nearly a private sport, conducted at countless unguarded swimming holes. Some are quiet lakes and ponds, others are swift brooks and bracing mountain streams, lazy rivers or deep quarries. One goes swimming *en famille* — or with a few good friends, perhaps — and one rarely needs to interact with anyone else. There are swimming holes enough for everyone to beat the heat in wonderful and simultaneous privacy.

Fact is, I've acquired half a dozen favorite swimming places; none of them seems in danger of becoming overrun in consequence of advertising. Creeping middle age has caused me more and more to choose calm, warm water and idyllic surroundings over the tricky currents that I used to love to master. Nowadays I mostly head for any of several protected bays that convolute the shoreline of Lake Champlain, some ten miles away.

My current first choice, Kingsland Bay, was once the site of a summer camp for upper-crust girls bent on learning French; later it was a Sixties-style intentional community. It is now an undeveloped, unlisted State Park, known primarily by word of mouth. A scorching weekday in July might bring fifty people to enjoy its hundred-odd acres: room for all, and then some. The bay is slung like a narrow pouch from the lake's broad hip; one can scarcely see the vast expanses of water just around the bend. Plunging in off baking slabs of bedrock, or from an unused yachting pier, I generally execute a casual backstroke and drink in the harmony of blue skies, shady lawns, and outcropping granite ledges that melt into the cool, fresh water. By the standards of the suburban pools I used to frequent, this lake's water is not very clear or even clean, but, afloat in Kingsland Bay, concrete pools with decks and chaises seem ludicrously sterile.

Flying over this pastoral valley, one sees almost more ponds than one can count. Ponds to water livestock, ponds to stave off summer drought, ponds for irrigation — and, of course, ponds for swimming. In my experience, the value of farm ponds for swimming is, well, debatable. True, most ponds are still and warm, but runoff of fertilizers, soil, and manure can turn these reservoirs into lagoons choked with weeds and algae. Some have water no better than the nearest cesspool, and the slippery, mushy clay that underlies most farm ponds gives one ample cause to fear being sucked down for good. But the abandoned quarry, surprisingly common in this landscape veined with lime and marble, provides first-class swimming.

Open-pit quarries are typically worked until the water runs in faster than it pays to pump it out; then the extractors go dig elsewhere, leaving one hell of a swimming pool. For the land's eventual owner, quarries can present hazards of privacy and liability. But for the intrepid swimmer guided by a U.S. Geological Survey topographic quadrangle map, they offer adventures.

Why is skinny-dipping the time-honored custom at quarries? There's no wading pool, for starters — no shallow end for strutting about, for chitchat. These holes are *deep*; their sides are straight and sheer, and splashing about in one is serious business. Dangerous business, too; perhaps the risk is nicely complemented by exposure. Finally, since quarry swimming often requires an arduous hike over difficult terrain, one is not apt to arrive wearing the latest poolside fashions.

I have a friend whose farm includes some incidental quarries, so I no longer have to trespass to gain access to one. Still, a little of their excitement goes a long way; the owner scarcely uses them at all, preferring to swim in places where he can at least in principle touch bottom. Nudity does not appeal to him nearly so much as safety — a common symptom of lost youth.

An older gentleman of my acquaintance, on the other hand, owns his own nude beach. It is a minor attraction of the island which he also owns — and lives on — in Lake Champlain. Last July, my family enjoyed a memorable picnic on his spit of fine, white sand, whose usual inhabitants are just the owner and his wife. They cherish their privacy.

Sandy beaches up here are a rarity. On a summer's day, when

the lake hosts thousands of small craft, his retreat can look mighty attractive from the water.

"I used to post the island?" he recounted for me on that dazzling afternoon. "Worse than worthless. 'No Trespassing' *invites* folks. So then I used to walk around with a shotgun? Macho. But you really can't just open fire on people, and they know it. So I started walking up stark naked — now, *that's* apt to drive them off. Quick, too. Your average Vermonter — well, he hasn't been to California." The man laughed as only someone can who no longer cares what anybody thinks of him. "Word spreads, too," he added.

"Hey," his wife interrupted. "See that? Down the beach?"

We squinted. Even now, a frumpy woman of indeterminate age was picking over shells or driftwood two hundred yards away.

"Well!" Our host leaped up. "Looks like you'll get to see a demonstration!"

So we closed the picnic basket and set off to walk the beach: me, my wife, my son and infant daughter, our host and his wife. All profoundly naked. When we closed within some fifty yards, the unwelcome visitor looked up. I still can see her face, taking in The Worst Thing She Ever Saw. She dropped her shells and fled

into the water, fully clothed. When she'd waded in up to her neck, staring steadfastly toward the mainland, she cupped her hand to shout: "I've been marooned! My husband's gone to fix the boat! He's going to be right back! He ought to be here now!"

"Private island," my host told her. Softly. Pleasantly. We continued walking down the beach, engaged in conversation; when we returned, the woman was no longer there. I doubt she will return — not ever.

Still water is fine, but there are times when I long to be brutalized, or, at least, massaged, by vicious currents. When this mood infects me, I trek fifteen miles to where the New Haven River drops off the front range of the Green Mountains into the Champlain Valley. This is crystal clear, pure water — cold enough to make one squeal; the sport is to float downstream a mile or two by inner tube or — for experts — on one's back, legs splayed out in front to fend off passing boulders.

People die each year this way, it's true. After a thunderstorm, the whirlpools and eddies in the river can be lethal. But the risks must be measured against the sheerest exhilaration. When one has navigated the small craft of one's body through this torrent, to climb ashore again in one piece — one knows one is alive.

To tell the truth, I have not much indulged this urge in recent years. My last trip was the best, however. I had just finished the entire summer's haying, which creates a feeling much like that following high-school graduation. Dazed, perhaps, by over-exposure to high-decibel machinery and unrelenting sunshine, I set off down a stretch of river without first emptying the pockets of my cut-off Levi's. A few delightful bends downstream, I noticed something like a plastic fish bobbing in the water several yards ahead of me. Interesting. Not a fish at all. I maneuvered toward it, reached to grab it and turned up — a credit card!

Piece of luck, I thought. Some poor fellow has lost his credit card in the river, but I've snatched it back for him. Simple matter of looking him up in the telephone book — it is great, I thought, how effortlessly neighbors in a rural place can help each other out.

I turned the credit card over to check the name. Damn, I thought. Incredible coincidence. Don Mitchell. Same name as mine, even. Then —

Then I reached for my wallet, which was not there.

The feeling I recall was much like noticing one's image in an unexpected mirror and wondering: who is that person? for a fleeting moment before recognition hits one. Suddenly the river was alive with little bobbing scraps of selfhood — driver's license, draft card, health insurance card — and even folded paper money, although not a lot of it. The current hurtled us onward, downstream, and while navigating around rocks and bends and broken branches I had the additional, extraordinary challenge of recapturing these soggy proofs of my identity.

Half an hour later I lay panting on a pebbled beach, sorting through the fish I'd caught. I had done fantastically well, considering — the only major losses were my wallet itself, a dollar bill or two, and my Social Security card. This latter was a bit upsetting, but I knew there were bureaucratic channels through which it could be replaced. I napped, letting my papers dry in the warm sun, and then I trekked back upstream to where I had left my car. Quite a swim. Memorable.

Two days later, the phone rang. "This Don Mitchell?"

"Yes."

"I found your Social Security card. In the New Haven River."

"No fooling?"

"Washed up on the beach. Down at New Haven Mills."

New Haven Mills is a swimming hole. I used to go there, but the place seemed dominated by an aggressive pack of neighborhood dogs. "That's great!" I said. "I'll come get it — where do you live?"

He described his house to me. "I know the one," I said. "Tell you what — I'll stop in the next time I go there for a dip."

"I'm putting your card right in the hall bureau," the caller told me. "First drawer on the right hand side. If you come around and no one's home, walk right in and get it."

"Thanks," I said. "That's very kind."

"Glad to help."

But I haven't made it to New Haven Mills to swim since that conversation, and it was already three years ago. Like I said, my taste in swimming holes has changed somewhat. So, in consequence, I carry no Social Security card, but I cannot exactly claim I've lost it. I know right where it is, waiting for me whenever the day comes that I get the urge for river swimming. Like so much here in the country, it should keep indefinitely.

• Saturday Night in Vergennes

Refugees from urban life, relocating upcountry, all too often choose to settle twenty long miles from the nearest town. Or *forty* miles from the nearest town worth going to. They are, after all, running from civilization. Pioneering can delight — for several months, anyway, but sooner or later the urge arrives to step out. Come Saturday night, say. Many learn too late that rural New England comprises entire counties where stepping out is mighty hard.

Consider my poor friends who endured three winters in a remote corner of northeastern Vermont. The nearest movie house was a numbing 27-mile trek — no joke, on dark back roads adrift with blowing snow. And what if, on a given night, fewer than a dozen souls showed up to enjoy the flick? Why, then the theatre's owner would simply refuse to show it. After all, he had his costs to meet. As many customers who came could shell out for a dozen tickets, or they could drive back home.

Things are not so bad in Vergennes — our local burg — although the town's one theatre, in an ancient gambrel-roofed barn, quit doing business several years ago. This "city" of 2,273 boasts several bars, two sit-down restaurants, two Italian grinder shops, a laundromat, a liquor-and-sporting-goods store, and a small, dingy games arcade. Compared to most Vermont towns, this array of choices makes Vergennes a sort of entertainment Mecca, which just happens to lie five miles up the road from our farm. On any classically boring, cabin-feverish Saturday night, my wife and I can step out and do the town in style for twenty-five bucks — and that *includes* the price of a week's laundry.

Vergennes vaunts itself as the smallest little city in the U.S.A., which claim is essentially a quirk of history. That a burg of less than two square miles chose to become a *city*, back in 1788 — when only two other cities had been chartered in all of New England — suggests grandiose dreams, dreams never fully realized and now in considerable disarray. Vergennes is, first of all, a working-class town, its major employer being a single plant where precision aircraft instruments are assembled. It is, secondly, a poor town, crammed with public-assistance clients living within walking distance of the county welfare office.

Only a minority succeed in perceiving Vergennes as an attractive and prosperous mercantile center — much less a metropolis. Still, on a black and chilly Saturday evening deep in winter, the amber lights of town beckon across our frozen landscape with the promise of excitement. Night on the town. At times like this, a city's throbbing soul may be discerned beneath the surface of this humble burg.

Everything worth stepping out for in downtown Vergennes lies within a block of Main Street — and the commercial part of Main Street is only three blocks long. You can park right on the street, for free. No meters. Never crowded. The premier parking spots are right next to the laundromat. Park here — because, with minimal effort, you can amalgamate a week's wash with Saturday night fever. You have, of course, your own washer-dryer right at home, but Vermont likes two-tier electric rates that drastically penalize winter consumption of niceties like electric hot water (the washer) and hot air (the dryer). In winter, you come out ahead each time you use the laundromat. The laundromat relies on some more sensible, cheaper fuel.

Crime is not rampant in Vergennes. They publish the entire police blotter right in the *Citizen*, the local weekly paper. Item: Returned runaway subject to nursing home. Item: Intoxicated subject removed from local restaurant. Item: Subject arrested for throwing glass on highway. A dozen such crimes give the cops a busy week; things are not so bad, though, that you have to stand guard over your clothing at the laundromat. You can set a few machines whirling, then go out to dinner. Dinner — no matter which establishment you choose to patronize — is a scant two blocks away.

You will *not* have an Italian grinder. You're not slumming, after all. So you have to choose between the fancy place — Painter's Tavern, in the handsomely restored old Stevens House — or the decidedly unfancy Park Restaurant. Since you will enjoy a late-night drink at Painter's Tavern anyway, enjoying its ambience for far less than the price of a meal there, you head for the Park.

Like nearly everything else downtown, the Park looks out on Vergennes' town green. No table by the window? Never mind. While not unattractive, this green is cluttered with too many benches and monuments, bandstands, information booths. Besides, it is dark and cold outside. Sit up near the cash register and smell the hot, home-cooked food wafting from the kitchen. Note the yokes for teams of oxen hanging from the north wall, but note, at the same time, that no serious attempt at Atmosphere is made. The Park Restaurant is not about Atmosphere. The Park is about dinner.

Open the astounding menu. Honey-dipped chicken dinner, $3.95 including salad, potato, vegetable, fresh baked rolls and butter. Steak dinner? $5. And you may luck into something special, like complete spaghetti-and-meatballs dinner for $2.75. This is just the kind of place you tried to find in rural France — or Belgium, or in New York State — simple, honest, quietly delicious food, plentiful and dirt cheap, served in modest but clean surroundings. Wine? No dice. You can have bottled beer, though, for another dollar. Or linger over pie and coffee.

All totalled, dinner at the Park should set two grownups back about $12, tip included. Now, back to the laundromat to transfer clothes into the dryer. You must decide whether to hang out here in overheated splendor, waiting for your clothes to dry, or step across the street to Vergennes' he-man bar for a drink. Perhaps you and your wife will split up, briefly, over this issue. Hey — you came for night life, right? So spurn those chrome-and-plastic laundromat chairs, those stacks of magazines, and go for the gusto. You can reunite in twenty minutes.

Because the he-man bar changes names frequently, I'll call it Kelly's Tavern; it has a big red door out through which unruly patrons are occasionally escorted. When you enter, everybody will look up at you from the battered bar, the hockey game, the pool table. You will not succeed in passing for one of these farmhands; you *can* find a common ground of thirst, though, and unslakable thirst is something they will understand. Take a seat. Everything is cheap, but Canadian bottled ales are especially popular. Moosehead, for example. Have a Moosehead at the bar — you can appear to be watching the T.V. while actually surveying the room behind you through the long mirror.

Anyone for trouble? A very large and well-muscled young man falls off his chair abruptly. He sprawls for some time on the floor and then rises to brandish a heavy barstool at the tall, lean bouncer moving in to attempt an expulsion. Join the general conversation on the topic of When Is Drinking Drunk? This may call for another Moosehead ale — another dollar. No one seems to *know* when drinking's drunk. The large young man insists — too loudly — that he's only drinking, not drunk, but the bouncer snatches the barstool from his arms with surprisingly little difficulty and shows him out the door.

"Thing about Vermont," your neighbor may explain to you. "Nights when bars get rough, they never seem to call the cops. They call the Fish and Game Warden."

You are unsure how to take this. *Wham!* The door flies open, and the young man just expelled is back. He grabs someone's pool cue, tries to join a game. There are protests. Insults. Just in time, you remember that your clothes are dry. You slouch out, inconspicuous. But leave a nice tip on the bar — Kelly's may need it.

Now — laundry stacked and sorted, reunited with your wife — you are ready for the Player Lounge. A classy bar, with music. Dancing. It fills a large basement room beneath a florist shop; long tables, low lights, lots of exposed brickwork. And if eighty people pack it, sixty will be chain-smoking. Such poor ventilation as exists is quickly overwhelmed.

Player Lounge attracts a nice crowd: farmers and their wives, young marrieds, decent rural folks. They like to dance. The band plays classic rock, as though the Fifties never died. "Oh, Donna." "Rock Around the Clock." "Walk, Don't Run." Okay, so it's not the Talking Heads. But not only does Player's have no cover charge and no minimum; if your very life depended on obtaining a drink in less than half an hour, you would likely be a goner. The place is so vastly overcrowded and understaffed that it is possible to spend an entire evening dancing and carrying on without once being accosted by a waitress.

Should you *seek* the bar, though, you're in for an arduous test of human will and ability at jostling. Should you succeed, the best way to amortize your investment in time and effort is to demand a giant pitcher of beer. This will set you back $3.50, but it is apt to be more beer than two of you can drink. So take it to an empty spot at one of the long tables, slap it down, and seize the chance to meet rural Vermonters at play.

Player Lounge rocks, in its unselfconscious fashion, until one A.M. Long before that, though, you'll experience difficulty breathing the smoke-filled air. So leave in time to have a nightcap at the lovely, peaceful upstairs bar in Painter's Tavern. This, you will recall, is the fancy restaurant. It occupies a major portion of the masterfully renovated Stevens House, an inn built in 1793. The restaurant and bar surround a two-story atrium with trees — real, indoor trees — growing toward the skylights. You can take a comfy booth overlooking this winter garden, or overlooking honest-to-goodness winter through frosty panes high above the town green. Erik Kilburn, folk guitarist, solicits requests. Live entertainment, see? If you've still got five bucks, order two fancy coffees, generously endowed with liqueurs and awash in whipped cream. By the time you finish them, you'll both be laughing at the snow, the bitter cold, the endless winter.

That's it. That's a big night in the nation's smallest little city. Not high culture, nor particularly varied; certainly not a patch on Boston, Montreal, New York. But, when winter overwhelms our rural world, I'm mighty glad to have Vergennes five miles up the road.

• Ice Fishing

In Vermont, our climatic extremes exact extreme responses. Such as racing over, up, and down snow-covered mountains — on skis, for some, on whining snowmobiles for others. Manic activities like these are symptoms of a vast, maddening reservoir of seasonal boredom. Cabin fever.

After several years here, I became aware that many fellow citizens battled the phenomenal monotony of winter with a far less strenuous pastime. They went ice fishing. All around me, people were stealing away to little plywood shanties dragged out onto Lake Champlain. There they drank and swapped lies all day long, kissing the beast of winter as they hauled up hapless smelt.

One does not go ice fishing alone, and one's choice of a fishing partner has all the gravity of choosing a spouse. So it was not easy for me to break into the society of fishermen. I managed, finally, when someone's regular companion took sick last January. Since I had advertised my interest in the sport, I received a fishing invitation.

"Love to!" I said honestly. "I've been going stir-crazy."

The man nodded. "Look, we start out early. Try to get out on the ice by dawn."

"They bite then, I suppose?"

"Say what?"

"The fish. They bite at dawn?"

He smiled. "Not particularly. But I got to leave the house before the wife and kids wake up."

"I don't have a fishing pole, or —"

"Don't use poles. Just lines. On jig sticks."

"I don't even know what —"

"Don't you worry. I got plenty. You just come — dress *warm,* hear? Bring some lunch. And bring something to drink."

It was fifteen below when I trudged up his driveway; the lake, he assured me, would be colder than that. We set off in his pickup truck as first light pierced the sky and headed for a fishing access twenty miles away. The highway was deserted. As we turned off on a gravel road, my partner cracked a beer and slurped it.

"How far will we have to walk?" I asked, eyeing his matutinal fortification.

"Walk?"

"To reach your shanty."

"Hell with that. We *drive* out."

"On the ice?"

"Sure, we just — hey, you need a beer?"

I guessed that I did, though six A.M. is well before my customary cocktail hour. Soon enough we reached the lake. Half a mile out to sea, as it were, I saw an entire village of brightly painted fishing shanties nestled on the ice. Fifty of them, anyway. Several already had pickup trucks parked alongside them; now our access road turned abruptly out onto the lake.

As I unbuckled my seatbelt, not wishing to go down with the vessel that carried me, we roared across the ice. It was not smooth, but studded with frozen waves and snowdrifts and expansion cracks of alarming size. Sometimes we could feel broad plates of ice shift beneath us, making great peals of eerie thunder. I put my hand on the doorlatch.

"What, you scared?"

I nodded.

"Hell, we won't *hit* nothing. Nothing *to* hit." To emphasize this point, he swung the wheel hard and steered his truck into a wild skid. I clutched my stomach. To a man accustomed to defined roads, on terra firma, lake-driving was utterly unnerving.

"Hey, this ice is eighteen inches thick. You could drive a semi out here."

"*You* could."

"Another beer?"

His shanty door was padlocked; inside, he'd stashed fishing gear and two wooden chairs and — I said a prayer of thanks — an L.P. gas stove. Standing on the bare lake, while he worked to fire up that heater, I experienced the most absolute and enveloping cold I have ever known. Lake Champlain is well over a hundred miles long — in January, a startlingly beautiful, utterly hostile icescape, where nothing stops the wind. Not five layers of clothing, at any rate. Two minutes' stunned appreciation of the view, and I was ready to huddle in the dimly lit hut for the next eight hours.

There are several ways to ice-fish, but the one I learned required simply sitting facing my companion, beer cans and bait board at our knees, each of our four hands manipulating separate nylon lines that trailed down through holes cut in the shanty floor, holes augered through the ice, then down forty feet to near the bottom of the lake. The lines were draped gently, gingerly across the tips of our index fingers — for maximum "feel" — and we raised and lowered our arms in slow, gesticulating rhythms. Smelt was our game, and there must have been thousands milling about directly underneath us. Catching one was less a matter of getting one to take the bait than of managing to stab it with the hook and haul it out before it wriggled free.

The bait for fishing smelt is smelt: either a thin strip sliced off the scaly torso or — better yet — an eye. I cannot believe these offer nourishment to other smelt, but they do attract them to the hook, which is what matters. My companion begged a few smelt from a nearby shanty to get us started, in accord with an established etiquette on the ice. He baited our four hooks, and then we settled down to business. Soon he was pulling up smelt caught by the snout, or the tail, or a gill or fin or by, as he affectionately called it, the touch-hole. I would say he caught one fish per minute for a solid hour, while I struggled to master the technique.

Finally I recognized a strike. It must have been a good one, for there was no subtlety in my chilly fingers. I started yanking up my line — hand over hand, as he had shown me, tossing loops of fishline out across the shanty floor. My loops came recklessly, knotting up my knees and feet. Then a bit of fishline touched the gas stove, melting instantly. Hook, line, and sinker disappeared without a trace into the lake below me.

"Oops," I said.

"Hey, you're too excited. Just calm down." My instructor set new hooks and sinkers onto the bait board, then found and broke the seal on a fifth of peppermint schnapps. "Take a slug of toothpaste," he invited. "Get your nerves settled."

I took his advice — he took his own advice, for that matter — but half a bottle later and without having landed a single smelt yet, I felt my nerves perhaps were getting *too* well settled."

"You can't fish," he told me frankly. "Why don't you try cutting bait?"

This was interesting. This appealed to the butcher in me. There is a correct way to pop a smelt eye from its socket; if one does it incorrectly, soon one's frozen fingertips are smeared with goo. Sclera? Choroid? Vitreous humor? Whatever, when my fishing partner placed a bag of taco chips between us on the bait board, fish eyes unavoidably became the roe — the caviar — of midmorning snack.

"You like blackberry brandy?" asked my fishing partner, opening a flask.

By lunchtime, I knew more than I expected about smelt eyes, and he had filled a two-gallon pail with smelt. We both were roaring drunk. "Lissen, whuzoo bring to drink?" he asked me.

I opened my canvas bag and showed him. "Cognac."

"Whuzahellisconyak?"

"They distill it from champagne."

This sounded good to him; he took a long pull from the bottle. "Jesum crow!" he hollered. "Thassaworse stuff I *ever* tasted!"

Taste did not deter him, though, and half an hour later he announced that we should take the cognac on a little fish survey.

"*Fiss*hurvay?" I gurgled. Soon the two of us were lurching from shanty to shanty, rapping on doors and investigating how our fellow sportsmen were faring. Most seemed to be faring exceedingly drunkenly indeed. And most had overflowing pails of smelt. Thousands of smelt. More than fish, though, we surveyed an unending variety of sickeningly sweet fruit brandies. Retaliating, my host would whip out the cognac bottle from within his jacket.

"Whuzzat say?"

"*Conyak*. Thass *French*. Just go on, try it."

"Good God Almighty!"

"Ain't that the worse stuff?!"

"Hey," I'd whine. "Ish cold out here."

By three P.M. on any given January afternoon, you can see some damn funny driving as fishermen close up their shanties and try to head for land. No enemy of fun, my driver spun his truck through several graceful pirouettes, then stopped to climb out and barf unceremoniously on the frozen lake. With an enormous and mutual effort, though, we managed to adjust from the free choice of routes which ice-driving affords to the seriousness and high purpose which roads represent.

Which is to say, he got me home somehow. Night was falling. Generously, he announced he wanted to divide the day's catch with me. Equally.

"No, I couldn't take that," I protested. "*You* did all the fishing."

But he forced a pail upon me that must have weighed fifteen pounds. "Take it," he insisted. "Hell, you cut the bait. And anyway — you walk in empty-handed, what's your wife going to say?"

My wife does not see me as a restless hunter, braving harsh elements to bring home meat for the table. Good thing, too — because somewhere between my driveway and the front door, two-thirds of the fish he gave me spilled out in the snow. And I never even noticed, not till March came and a thaw revealed several dozen smelt scattered aimlessly across the lawn. My wife claims we *did* eat several smelt for dinner, though, that night. I have some vague recollection: batter-fried, shrimpy little things with all their eyes popped out. "How was your day ice fishing?" she no doubt inquired of me.

"Winter," I no doubt replied, "is one more day shorter."

• Division of Labor

My wife's fighting weight — standing barefoot, tanned, non-pregnant — is a mere ninety-six pounds; a full sack of Portland cement weighs ninety-four pounds, but my wife can lift one off the bed of our pickup truck and carry it across the lawn to my

beloved concrete mixer. All by herself. This is a source of considerable pride for her, and a wonderful convenience for me when I'm
busy mixing up another perfect batch of concrete.

This is the rough equivalent, I reckon, of her sending me to
fetch some beans or broccoli from the freezer while she's bent over
the Cuisinart whipping up a concoction similar to concrete in its
delicate complexity. Salmon mousse, say. Myself, I don't cook
much, and my wife does not make concrete. But we support each
other by serving as willing go-fers. Luckily, most things she makes
me go-fer weigh far less than a sack of cement.

There was a time when I tried to master kitchen skills. In
those days, we made a determined effort to fashion rural lives
such that work would not be portioned out on any sexist basis. I
was younger then, and more politically conscious; words like
"lifestyle" probably peppered my conversation. So I mastered
hamburgers in several arduous cooking sessions and was on the
way to mastering omelettes, too, while my slender wife would
storm the woodlot with our whining chainsaw, felling the odd red
oak and bucking it into fuel wood for our hungry stoves. The point
— if I remember rightly — was that there should be no task we
ought to bar each other from undertaking for any reason, however
sensible. There should be no aspect of our rural lives that either of
us could not in principle accomplish.

Sexism is, of course, a ubiquitous and terribly insidious evil.
Particularly since becoming a parent, I worry daily about the
unconscious messages that children cannot help receiving from
grownups. I also worry, though, about having eight cords of dry,
split firewood under cover right outside the door by November 1,
each autumn. Though I can get the job done in about a week, it
would take my wife three. I don't doubt she has the strength, the
will, or the ability. But *stamina* and *speed* are desirable traits for
loggers, too. Stamina and speed at logging call for someone more
like — well, like me.

A ninety-six-pound woman does not emerge from a day's fun
in the woodlot in a mood eager to cook supper, either. Three weeks
proved much too long to dine exclusively on hamburgers and
omelettes. We have, in short, resigned ourselves to a division of
labor along remarkably sexist lines. It happens to make sense. Our
children, no doubt, will suffer.

The children themselves proved an incontrovertible argument for sexist work roles. Try as I might have, I could not have nursed our babies; although such an observation seems utterly obvious, it is far from trivial. Suddenly my wife had a new, three-hour-a-day chore that exhausted her, that made her need ten hours' sleep instead of eight (though she never got more than two at a time), a chore that made her always tired — a thoroughly disruptive but important chore awarded to her solely on the basis of sex. With this discovery, the last shred of my former idealism vanished.

Our neighbors voice no qualms about such matters and seem utterly at ease with lives that are paradigms of what I used to denigrate as sex-role stereotypes. Farm wives have, for decades, cooked and washed and cleaned, they have managed gardens and preserved food for winter, they have cared for children, done the weekly shopping, and fed the chickens. These women have plenty to fear from "liberation" — they fear it would make them have to do all these tasks *plus* hold down an outside job and clean the barn out, too. One can hardly blame them for being suspicious.

Farm husbands, for their part, seem remarkably content to toil at jobs requiring eight thousand calories of brute strength to be expended daily, so long as they can stomp in from the fields to find dinner ready. There is not a farm chore so disagreeable — not stretching fence, or chasing heifers, or spreading manure — that they would trade it to be "liberated" from this state of affairs. True, these men are apt to take a false and reprehensible pride in feeling they have spared their wives from heavy labor. But at least at day's end, all the work is somehow finished, and neither partner much resents the other's lot in life.

I have known considerable resentment of my wife's lot in life each winter, when one of my chores is keeping our home cozy warm no matter how severe the weather. It takes twenty minutes from my evening cocktail hour just to haul the next day's wood in from the woodpile and arrange it near the stoves so it can thaw a bit. Over the course of an average winter's day, I probably spend an hour fussing with our stoves — loading fuel on, poking coals, adjusting sundry grates and dampers. Thoreau remarked on how appropriate wood heat is for a writer, giving him a little something to do with his hands while thoughts fester in his mind, seeking eloquent expression. He was right, perhaps; I used to have to smoke cigarettes to satisfy this same need.

But when the temperature dives below zero for three or four days straight, managing two wood stoves becomes more than a benign diversion. Heat becomes a round-the-clock obsession. The only way to guarantee no frozen pipes at dawn is to leave a warm bed at two A.M. on a chilly refueling mission. With benefit of a decade's experience, I can now perform this feat without having to actually wake up: automatic pilot. Still, when morning finds the house warm despite −25° F. outside, *I want credit*. The curse of the division of labor that my wife and I now observe is that we take each other's work for granted. Why is this? And why don't I sense it in my neighbors' lives? After all, they fell blindly into the social contract that my wife and I chose with our eyes wide open.

Last March, an awesome thaw and rainstorm cooperated in flooding my lambing barn the week we started lambing out the ewes. Lambs dropped from their mothers' wombs into standing water get a dubious start on life, so I hurried up the road to beg straw from a neighboring dairy farmer. His barn had not flooded, but rain falling on the snowbank under his barn's eaves had frozen the main door solid to the ground. And he *had* to get it open, on account of a downer cow inside. A downer cow is one who can't get up — terminal something or other — but if the farmer can get her into town she may yet be sold for dog food or even bargain hamburger. Frankly, I found my own crisis more grave than his. But I was astonished when his wife appeared carrying an oversized ice spud — the basic digging tool of ice fishermen — and set to work chipping frozen slush from around the doorway.

Here was a farm wife thoroughly out of her natural environment, far from the house/kitchen/laundry/garden area where farm wives are supposed to preside as super-homemakers. But she wielded the tool with a certain innate skill; I asked, "Do they pay you well to do this?"

"It was my idea!"

Ah, I thought, Liberation strikes the frozen north. Cabin fever, doubtless. I asked, "Hired man's day off?"

She shook her head. She laughed, faintly. "Let's just say I'm having fun."

I thought about that while I loaded straw into my truck and glanced back several times at the progress of her labor. Spudding ice is hard work. I wanted to ask her, was she doing this *for credit*?

Certainly her husband could have done it several times as fast. Weren't there dirty clothes to launder, cakes to bake, rugs to vacuum? Suddenly I caught her eye and realized that she was having a ball; this nutty task was giving her the sheerest pleasure. And then I knew why: it was so far removed from her ordinary sphere of responsibility that she could not do it badly. Every chunk of ice she chipped away made her a huge success. I don't think the locally prevailing distinction between women's work and man's work was blurred for one instant in her mind. She was doing man's work — for a change of pace, for fun — and soon she'd go back to the house. Where a farmer's wife belongs.

Life in such a coherent and traditional society can be a little breathtaking after years of choosing values as one chooses clothes. I went home and told my wife: "Look, we tried nonsexist work roles, and they didn't make good sense. Then we tried sexist work roles, but they're bad for the children and dull our appreciation of each other." Or words to that effect. "Wife," I continued, "our barn is flooded. I have backed our truck up to the barnyard fence, and on the truck are twelve eighty-pound bales of straw. Take these bales, toss them up over the fence and spread them in the barn so that our lambs won't be born in muck."

She said: "You've got cabin fever. Doubtless."

"Meantime, I'll whip up a little something for our dinner."

"Suddenly you've learned to cook?"

"I will watch the children, too. I'll play 'tractors' with our son, I'll help our daughter dress up her dolls. I don't ask for Liberation — just a little change of pace."

My wife is most forebearing; she threw on her down jacket and trudged out to the pickup truck. Minutes later she came back. "Eighty-pound bales, my eye! They weigh more than a sack of Portland cement."

"They do?" Eighty, truth be told, was just a round number.

"They must, because I can't lift them."

"Wouldn't you know it." After all these years, I finally put my finger on the pressure relief valve in our neighbor's sexist social contract. We could do things just like them, I thought. Join up. Adopt their ways. And now what put the kibosh on it? Fate — or hazard. Hundred-pound bales of straw. More than my wife weighs, even.

My wife regarded me, unsure what I was thinking. "You

cannot," she said softly, "join a different society by aping it. Even an attractive and traditional society. It has to come from within. And — for you, for me — that may not quite be possible."

"You can't lift those bales of straw?"

"No."

"What a bummer," I said.

To live in a period when social values are in flux has, I suspect, brought great misery to vast numbers of women and men alike — shouts of liberation aside. None more, though, than couples like my wife and me — intellectuals, thoughtful students of social theory plunked down in a place where crucial assumptions are not examined. Our neighbors may be old-fashioned, but they seem to have a good thing going. *Can* one join? Not self-consciously, one can't.

"I've got an idea," my wife said.

"Oh?"

"I couldn't throw those bales up over the barnyard fence. *Up*hill. *Work*. But if you could get the pickup to the north side of the barn — I mean, I could push those bales *down*."

"Too much ice," I said. "And melting snow. Impossible."

"If you hitched the tractor to the truck, and — like the first time they filled the grain bin?"

"You know, you might *have* something."

So we got the tractor running, chained it to the truck, and maneuvered both to a place from which she could push those bales *down*. With the ice and all, they rolled neatly right up to the barn door. Wonderful. "Hey, isn't this fun?" I asked her.

"You know what? We'll never — " she sat down on a bale and caught her breath. "We'll never stop being who we are, of course. But as for becoming Yankees — well, over time I guess one learns a thing or two."

Over time, I guess one certainly does.